An Introduction to the
Theory of Finance

An Introduction to the Theory of Finance

Assetholder Behavior

Under Uncertainty

BASIL J. MOORE

The Free Press, New York
Collier-Macmillan Limited, London

Preface

Money, which represents the prose of life, and which is hardly spoken of in parlours without an apology, is, in its effects and laws, as beautiful as roses.

—Ralph Waldo Emerson

Except for the fact that in the above lines the great poet was almost certainly referring to the quantity theory of money, this book is written in the same spirit and to substantiate a similar sentiment. It is unabashedly concerned with "effects and laws," that is, with economic theory, a concern for which no apologies should be necessary. The economics of money and banking too often has been long on money and banking and short on economics.

Economic theory serves first simply to provide a necessary framework of analysis with which to organize and render intelligible our observations of the world. If a particular analytical system is in addition to be of value as a guide to policy, it must also improve our empirical understanding of the behavior of the economic and social environment. This second task ordinarily can be accomplished only by the piecemeal verification of operational hypotheses, that is, the application of scientific method to refute and quantify explanations of observable behavior.

The present study is directed at the first function of theory outlined above, the development of a conceptual framework with which to analyze reality. For the most part its contribution to the second task, the application of the analysis to empirical problems, had of necessity to be left for another occasion. But while with the exception of the last chapter the orientation is not toward interpretive and substantive exploration of empirical issues, I have at a number of points referred to recent empirical work and engaged in policy discussion. This was done so that the student reader will not receive the impression that abstract analysis is merely formalistic. It does in fact have great potential relevance to real problems. Economic theory is, but is also more than, an intellectual exercise.

The following chapters then are intended as an introduction to the rigorous analysis of financial phenomena in a capitalist economy. This is done by first stating some very general principles of financial behavior under uncertainty, and then applying these principles to the analysis of a variety of financial assets, institutions, and markets. Whatever novelty the conclusions possess follow from the fact that uncertainty, asset stocks and portfolio motivations of wealthowners are consistently and explicitly introduced into the behavioral functions of all private economic units. The attempt has been made throughout to follow the implications of the introduction of uncertainty and portfolio considerations to their logical conclusions, not merely for equilibrium situations but also for the analysis of disequilibrium adjustment processes.

The book as it now appears exhibits only shadows of my own original perceptions, as is surely appropriate for an introductory work. It has been so heavily influenced by a large number of scholars that it is barely possible for me to continue to regard it as my own intellectual creation. If we at times are able to see a little farther than those who have written before us, it is attributable not to our comparative stature, but rather because, though mere pigmies, we are able to stand on their shoulders to scan the world about us. In addition to my general dependence on the literature, there are some intellectual acknowledgments that conscience demands be made explicit.

The basic algebraic and diagrammatic presentation of Chapters 5 and 8 have been adopted from Lloyd Metzler's now classic article, "Wealth, Saving, and Rate of Interest." Instead of following Hicks' IS-LM general equilibrium formulation relating interest rates and the level of real income, the stock of money and wealth remaining constant, it is preferable for financial analysis to follow Metzler in relating interest rates to the quantity and composition of financial assets, holding the level of real income constant. Patinkin's *Money, Interest, and Prices*—in particular his macroeconomic model in Part II which he acknowledges is derived from Metzler—was continually at my side, and its existence served as a beacon illuminating many unrewarding paths, traps, and tangles which would not otherwise have been avoided. Although my assumptions and conclusions are frequently diametrically opposed to his, most centrally with regard to the treatment of uncertainty, of disequilibrium, and of the neutrality of monetary change, the present essay could not have attained its limited success in reaching its goals had not Patinkin's energetic exploration of the territory been available in advance. A third intellectual debt to Jack Gurley and Ed Shaw demands entry in any accounting. Their seminal work, and in particular their book, *Money in a Theory of Finance*, by questioning the sharp traditional distinctions between money and other assets have opened up an entire new perspective on the process of financial intermediation and, in addition, has provided a fruitful set of concepts by which financial behavior can be analyzed and understood. In a significant sense the present essay represents merely a further development of their approach.

A final intellectual godfather must be acknowledged whose influence in many areas has been the most decisive. This is the work of James Tobin. At an early stage in the writing of this book I was referred to an unpublished manuscript of Tobin's in the Cowles Foundation Library at Yale. It would be difficult to overemphasize the extent to which my approach to financial phenomena has been shaped by Tobin's work. The analysis of portfolio behavior under uncertainty, the approach to monetary and financial theory as part of the general theory of asset choice, and the discussion of financial intermediation all lean heavily on Tobin's work. In particular my diagrammatic presentation in Chapters 2, 5 and 8 incorporates Tobin's general asset preference approach, in place of the partial equilibrium focus on the demand for money balances which appears in most post-Keynesian analysis. This makes possible an extremely concise yet elegant formulation of all asset and output markets within a general equilibrium framework.

I have tried persistently not to write a monetary treatise. It is my hope that the present work will prove suitable as supplementary reading for first year graduate courses in money and banking and finance, as well as advanced undergraduate courses. In the interests of readability and brevity—the good if short is doubly good—all but the most essential footnotes and acknowledgments to the literature have been omitted, but recommended readings have been collected at the end of each chapter. The absence of footnotes is not to be taken to imply a claim to originality or priority, and my academic colleagues will be only too acutely aware of the extent to which I have drawn upon the continuing great debate on the theoretical determination of interest and prices which Keynes' _The General Theory of Employment, Interest, and Money_ inaugurated. But it is hoped that the present form will prove instructive and accessible to a somewhat broader public of students and interested laymen, and that the rigor of the argument does not suffer too greatly in consequence for the teacher and scholar.

The book as it now appears has gone through a number of stages and perhaps still bears the impress of difficult labor pains. Its original form was written substantially while I was a Brookings Research Professor at Stanford University in 1962–63, and I am grateful to the Ford Foundation, Brookings Institution and to the Stanford economics department for the privilege of such an opportunity. It has since been completely rewritten, and I would like to express my warm gratitude and affection to Wesleyan University for providing encouraging colleagues as well as financial assistance for my research endeavors. I am indebted to John Arena for providing valuable detailed comment and constructive criticism on an earlier draft. Finally, these acknowledgments would not be complete if I remained silent as to the influence of Professor Fritz Machlup, who through personal example as well as through intellectual criticism and encouragement has deeply influenced my entire approach to the study of economics.

To my wife, Karin, and my children, Jessica and Robin, I am grateful for the domestic enchantments they have provided to offset the at times unaccommodating mysteries of financial theory.

I need hardly add that not one of the above, with the possible exception of my son Robin, is in any way accountable for the imperfections and errors which the following essay contains.

Middletown, Connecticut

BASIL J. MOORE

Contents

An Introduction to the
Theory of Finance

1

An Introduction

to Financial Analysis

There are good reasons to think that the nature of money is not yet rightly understood.

—John Law, 1720

Introduction

Broadly defined, economic goods comprise all things which are scarce and which, at least conceptually, can be bought or sold on a market. Economic behavior was long conceived as the production, exchange, and consumption of economic goods. Some exchange of economic goods takes place *directly*, so that commodities produced or owned by one economic unit are directly exchanged—that is, given or bartered—for commodities produced by other economic units. But the majority of transactions in an economy which has passed beyond the subsistence stage are facilitated by financial instruments. In this case, which may be termed *indirect exchange*, economic units exchange "real" commodities for intangible or financial goods, and financial goods for other financial goods. Financial theory may then be defined

1

most simply as *the analysis of the interrelationships between financial goods and transactions and "real"—i.e., non-financial behavior*, in particular the allocation, distribution, growth, and stability of real output, income, expenditure, and wealth.

The first section of this chapter provides a selective survey of the historical development of systematic thought about the interrelationship between financial and real behavior. Its purpose is to indicate how some important earlier writers have visualized the significance of financial activity. Hopefully this will help to place our contemporary analytical viewpoint in historical perspective.

The economists and philosophers of the seventeenth and eighteenth centuries were chiefly concerned with problems of unemployment, inflation, foreign trade, and economic growth or stagnation. In consequence their policy recommendations centered upon the proper management by the state of the money stock and of bank credit. Their analyses explicitly attempted to wrestle with the dynamic sequence of real economic events propelled by monetary change.

In contrast, most economists of the nineteenth and early twentieth century were concerned with providing a formal analysis of the allocation of economic resources—what exactly determines the price of a cup of tea? To do this they developed a sophisticated static equilibrium model that was formulated in real terms in order to "pierce" a monetary veil which they believed obscured the underlying pricing and productive processes. During the early part of the twentieth century there occurred a revived although specialized concern with the interrelationship between financial and real phenomena in the study of crises and business cycles. The earlier crude quantity theory of money was developed into the equation of exchange and alternative cash-balance equations. The policy recommendations of these economists were directed at central bank influence over the interest rate charged for bank credit to control inflations and recessions.

The view that financial factors may account for the recurrent instability, fluctuations and crises, which overlay and clothe the more fundamental long-run equilibrium relationships determined by real factors, was not displaced until the 1930's and John Maynard Keynes' formulation of the determination of national income. The Keynesian system accorded financial relationships a central role, even though

Keynes himself was highly skeptical of the empirical responsiveness of consumption, savings, and investment decisions to interest rate variations. In response to neoclassical critics, neo-Keynesian theorists were gradually led to introduce real wealth, including both tangible and financial asset stocks, as a variable affecting spending and production behavior. More recently, analysis of economic behavior in the face of uncertainty has led to recognition that the *portfolio composition*, as well as the *total value* of wealth stocks, plays a critical role in influencing assetowner behavior on current account. This realization has finally resolved the bifurcation at the conceptual level between Keynesian and quantity theorists. The areas of disagreement remaining refer to the empirical stability and magnitude of relationships that both groups can accept in general form.

The remaining sections of the chapter provide an introduction to the role of financial assets and financial behavior in economic activity. The chief characteristics, services, and manner of production of tangible and financial assets are described and contrasted. Financial assets and liabilities are shown to originate when the distribution of expenditure among economic units differs from the distribution of income received. Once created, the existence of financial wealth in various forms permits the separation of ownership from administration of tangible wealth in a private property economy. The next chapter then takes up the problem of how, in an uncertain world, economic units distribute their wealth among alternative assets possessing these diverse characteristics.

For interested readers the Appendix supplies a conceptual introduction to the United States National Balance-Sheet and Flow-of-Funds Accounts, which provide the central organizational framework and source of data for the formulation and verification of hypotheses about financial activity.

An Incomplete Sketch of the Development of Financial Thought

By and large, with certain important exceptions, the history of the mainstream of academic economic thought before the Keynesian assault of the thirties had been a history of denial of the lasting importance of any casual relationship between changes in financial and real variables. Classical economists following Adam Smith were primarily concerned to uncover the laws governing the production of wealth and its distribution among various factor shares. After the marginalist revolution, neoclassical economists were concerned particularly to formulate the laws of value governing the relative prices and allocation of commodities and factors of production. Both however were agreed on the necessity of piercing the "veil" in which money and finance envelopes economic relationships, in order to reveal the essential workings of the economic system and, incidentally, to combat the lingering and popular mercantilist association of money with wealth. John Stuart Mill's statement of this conviction is atypical only in the clarity of his formulation:

> The introduction of money does not interfere with the operation of any of the Laws of Value laid down in the preceding chapters. The reasons which make the temporary or market value of things depend on the demand and supply, and their average and permanent values upon their cost of production, are as applicable to a money system as to a system of barter. Things which by barter would exchange for one another, will, if sold for money, sell for an equal amount of it, and so will exchange for one another still, though the process of exchanging them will consist of two operations instead of only one.
>
> There cannot, in short, be intrinsically a more insignificant thing, in the economy of society, than money; except in the character of a contrivance for sparing time and labour. It is a machine for doing quickly and commodiously, what would be done, though less quickly and commodiously, without it: and like many other kinds of machinery, it only exerts a distinct and independent influence of its own when it gets out of order.[1]

This denial of the importance of financial phenomena became formalized by neoclassical economists into what later was termed the neutrality of money doctrine, the proposition that, under the assumptions of perfect certainty, absence of money illusion (so that economic behavior depends on real and not nominal values) and absence of price rigidity, the equilibrium values of all real variables in an economy are necessarily independent of the nominal stock of money.

1. John Stuart Mill, *Principles of Political Economy*, 6th Ed., Book III, Chapter 7. (Longmans, Green and Company, 1900), p. 296.

The quantity theory of money followed logically from the existence of neutrality. In its simplest form it states that, providing no independent changes in preferences, factor supplies, or technology occur, the general price level will move proportionately with changes in the nominal money stock. Thus fortified, the usually cautious Alfred Marshall felt confident to testify categorically, "The total value of an inconvertible paper currency cannot be increased by increasing its quantity."[2]

Nineteenth and early twentieth-century developments of the quantity theory, most importantly the *equation of exchange* of Irving Fisher and the various *Cambridge cash-balance equations*, are well known and will not be recounted here. In developing propositions about money with greater formal precision by the use of comparative-static analysis, the neoclassical economists abstracted from the dynamic transitional sequence which classical and, in particular, preclassical economists had never lost sight of.

It is interesting to note that monetary theory, including what would now be termed monetary dynamics, was initially the most important branch of economic speculation. Its golden age was undoubtedly England in the century preceding Adam Smith's publication of the *Wealth of Nations* in 1776, when, in spite of the absence of agreed principles or concepts and with rudimentary analytical tools, a crude kind of dynamic process analysis was developed. The insights of these preclassical economists have not been fully appreciated.

This was a period in which mercantilist trade policy was subjected to increasing attack, while at the same time the problem of chronic unemployment became a major challenge to eighteenth-century domestic policy.[3] Following the lead of Sir William Petty, "the father of economics," a long school of mercantilists and inflationists recommended a policy of public works, financed at low interest rates by some scheme of public loan banks, in order both to increase employment and to remedy the scarcity of money in circulation. It was in

2. Alfred Marshall, *Money, Credit and Commerce* (Macmillan, 1923), p. 48.

3. "One of the greatest preoccupations of thoughtful men in this age was how to set the poor to work." Sir Thomas Ashton, *An Economic History of England: The Eighteenth Century*, (Menthuen 1955).

criticism of such proposals that the first quantity theory analysis was formulated, in an essay by John Locke published in 1691.[4]

Locke incisively developed the critical distinction between the "value of money" (purchasing power) and the "price of the hire of money" (interest rate). The latter, he held, was determined solely by natural forces in the market for credit and could not permanently be lowered by statute nor by an increase in the supply of money. By comparative-static analysis he then attempted to demonstrate that an increase in money would simply drive up the level of prices, and so concluded:

> The value of money depends only on the plenty or scarcity of money in proportion to the plenty or scarcity of things [commodities].[5]

Writing forty years later, Richard Cantillon, now fondly regarded by many in the profession as "the economists' economist," while accepting Locke's insight insisted upon the mutual interdependence of real and financial activity:

> Mr. Locke has clearly seen that the abundance of money makes everything dear, but he has not considered how it does so. The great difficulty of this question consists in knowing in what way and in what proportion the increase of money raises prices.[6]

Cantillon was the first to show that the effects of an increase in the quantity of money upon employment and real incomes depends upon the *path* by which it is injected into the economy.

Finally, David Hume, whom Keynes asserted "began the practice of stressing the importance of the equilibrium position as compared with the ever-shifting transition towards it,"[7] still exhibited sufficient methodological ambiguity between comparative static and dis-

---

4. John Locke, *Consequences Concerning Raising the Value of Money*, 1691; and *Further Considerations Concerning the Value of Money*, 1696.

5. *Ibid.*

6. Richard Cantillon, *Essay Sur La Nature du Commerce en General*, written between 1730 and 1734, but first published in 1754. (Macmillan, 1931).

7. John Maynard Keynes, *The General Theory of Employment, Interest, and Money* (Macmillan, 1936), p. 343. To be fair, Keynes also remarked in the same passage that, "Hume was still enough of a mercantilist not to overlook the fact that it is in the transition that we actually have our being."

equilibrium process analysis to refute Locke, and to conclude that an increase in the supply of money was generally favorable to trade and employment. Hume's analysis of the dynamics of monetary change, with its implicit assumptions of short-run wage and price inflexibility and elastic supply functions, merits quotation at length. The methodolocical tension is introduced in the form of a paradox that involves the reconciliation of the quantity theory, which Hume accepted logically as the basis for his attack on the mercantilist position, with the historical fact, which he also accepted as a causal relation, of the observed beneficial effects of monetary expansion in western Europe.

It is indeed evident, that money is nothing but the representation of labour and commodities, and serves only as a method of rating or estimating them. Where coin is in greater plenty; as a greater quantity of it is required to represent the same quantity of goods; it can have no effect, either good or bad, taking a nation within itself; any more than it would make an alteration on a merchant's books, if, instead of the *Arabian* method of notation, which requires few characters, he should make use of the *Roman*, which requires a great many. Nay, the greater quantity of money, like the *Roman* characters, is rather inconvenient, and requires greater trouble both to keep and transport it. But notwithstanding this conclusion, which must be allowed just, it is certain, that, since the discovery of the mines in America, industry has encreased in all the nations of Europe, except in the possessors of those mines; and this may justly be ascribed, amongst other reasons, to the encrease of gold and silver. Accordingly we find, that, in every kingdom, into which money begins to flow in greater abundance than formerly, everything takes a new face: labour and industry gain life; the merchant becomes more enterprising, the manufacturer more diligent and skilful, and even the farmer follows his plough with greater alacrity and attention. This is not easily to be accounted for, if we consider only the influence which a greater abundance of coin has in the kingdom itself, by heightening the price of commodities, and obliging every one to pay a greater number of these little yellow or white pieces for every thing he purchases. And as to foreign trade, it appears, that great plenty of money is rather disadvantageous, by raising the price of every kind of labour.

To account, then, for this phenomenon, we must consider, that though the high price of commodities be a necessary consequence of the encrease of gold and silver, yet it follows not immediately upon

that encrease; but some time is required before the money circulates
through the whole state, and makes its effect be felt on all ranks of
people. At first, no alteration is perceived; by degrees the price rises,
first of one commodity, then of another; till the whole at last reaches
a just proportion with the new quantity of specie which is in the kingdom. In my opinion, it is only in this interval or intermediate situation,
between the acquisition of money and rise of prices, that the encreasing quantity of gold and silver is favourable to industry. When
any quantity of money is imported into a nation, it is not at first
dispersed into many hands, but is confined to the coffers of a few
persons, who immediately seek to employ it to advantage. Here are
a set of manufacturers or merchants, we shall suppose, who have
returns of gold and silver for goods which they sent to Cadiz. They
are thereby enabled to employ more workmen than formerly, who
never dream of demanding higher wages, but are glad of employment from such good paymasters. If workmen become scarce, the
manufacturer gives higher wages, but at first requires an encrease
of labour; and this is willingly submitted to by the artisan, who can
now eat and drink better, to compensate for his additional toil and
fatigue. He carries his money to market, where he finds everything
at the same price as formerly, but returns with greater quantity and
of better kinds, for the use of his family. The farmer and gardener,
finding that all their commodities are taken off, apply themselves
with alacrity to raising more; and at the same time can afford to
take better and more cloths from their tradesmen, whose price is the
same as formerly, and their industry only whetted by so much new
gain. It is easy to trace the money in its progress through the whole
commonwealth; where we shall find, that it must first quicken the
diligence of every individual, before it encrease the price of labour.

From the whole of this reasoning we may conclude, that it is of
no matter of consequence, with regard to the domestic happiness of
a state, whether money be in a greater or less quantity. The good
policy of the magistrate consists only in keeping it, if possible, still
encreasing; because, by that means, he keeps alive a spirit of industry in the nation, and encreases the stock of labour, in which
consists all real power and riches.[8]

John Stuart Mill later was to refute this "fallacy" by the simple
expedient of ignoring Hume's assumption of short-run general
equilibrium with less than full capacity utilization.

8. David Hume, *Of Money*, 1752, reprinted in *David Hume, Writings on Economics*. Ed. Eugene Rotwein (Nelson 1955), p. 37–40.

It seems obvious, however, that for every person who thus gains more than usual, there is necessarily some other person who gains less. [This plan] calculates on finding the whole world persisting forever in the belief that more pieces of paper are more riches, and never discovering that, with all their paper, they cannot buy more of everything than they could before . . . An issue of notes is a manifest gain to the issuers—but all holders of currency lose, by the depreciation of its value, the exact equivalent of what the issuer gains.[9]

The above reflects of course Mill's rather unqualified acceptance of Say's Law. Mill argued elsewhere the impossibility that "there should be a deficiency of demand for all commodities for want of the means of payment." Since the means of payment for commodities is simply commodities themselves, a general oversupply of commodities is an impossibility. Further if it is the desire, rather than the means, to consume which falls short of commodities produced: "What do these persons do with their savings? They invest them productively, that is, expend them in employing labour."[10] A commercial crisis was indeed recognized as a temporary general glut of commodities, but it was held to be a consequence not of a general excess of production, but of an excess of speculative purchases, whose proximate cause was a contraction of credit, and whose remedy was simply the restoration of confidence.

The propositions that financial factors may account for instability, business cycles, and temporary crises, "when the machinery gets out of order," but that real factors alone determine the supply and demand for savings, and lead to a unique equilibrium rate of interest unaffected by changes in the stock of nominal money, have generally been regarded as central tenets of classical and neoclassical analysis. In reply to Keynes' challenge in the *General Theory* directed towards another classical theorem, the proposition that, assuming perfect price and wage flexibility, a full-employment general equilibrium is assured, modern defenders of the neoclassical system succeeded in demonstrating that the explicit recognition of wealth in the consumption and savings functions was sufficient at this level of abstraction to restore

9. John Stuart Mill, *op. cit.*, Book III, Chapter 13, pp. 333–4.
10. *Ibid.*, Chapter 14, pp. 338–9 passim.

the automatic tendency of the system towards full-employment equilibrium.[11]

This "wealth effect" follows from inverse changes in the real value of the government's money stock, and hence of real private net worth, as the price level changes. In a system where wages and prices are perfectly flexible downwards, equilibrium at a less than full-employment level of national income can be shown to be impossible. The existence of unemployment and excess capacity causes wages and prices to fall. Concurrently the value in real terms of a constant stock of nominal money balances held by private spending units must necessarily rise. This increase in the real purchasing power of private monetary wealth would shift the consumption function upward at every level of disposable income. There must therefore *always* exist some determinate lower price level where real private wealth has risen just sufficiently to support a level of aggregate demand equal to full-employment aggregate supply. Government spending is assumed to be unaffected by the rise in the real value of government noninterest-bearing debt outstanding, since such debt need never be paid back.

This wealth or real balance effect saved the logical consistency of the classical system from indeterminacy by eliminating the possibility of Keynes' "Liquidity Trap" configuration. Providing all prices are perfectly flexible, the introduction of wealth considerations ensures the existence of a determinate full-employment equilibrium. It was only later realized that substantiation of the full-employment conclusions had been achieved at the cost of destroying the neutrality postulate of the classical model.[12] For example, a higher level of real wealth in equilibrium would reduce planned savings at each level of disposable income, so that the new equilibrium position would be characterized by a higher level of interest rates.

Nominal monetary change alters not only the *total* of real private wealth, but also the *composition* of private wealth among different types of financial and tangible wealth forms. In the situation described in the previous paragraph, the share of money balances in total real wealth will rise. As will be shown in the following chapter, as soon

11. The most complete treatment of this development is to be found in D. Patinkin, *Money, Interest, and Prices* (Chicago, 1965).

12. This was first recognized by L. Metzler, "Wealth, Saving, and the Rate of Interest" *Journal of Political Economy*, Vol. LIX, No. 2 (April, 1951).

as the assumption of perfect certainty is dropped wealthowners may not be regarded as indifferent to the portfolio composition of their assets and debts. Consequently, once wealth is admitted as a factor affecting current economic behavior, portfolio considerations provide an additional reason why financial change can no longer be regarded as leaving the real equilibrium configuration of an economy unaffected.

Some Properties of Tangible and Financial Assets

As will be demonstrated in the following chapter, economic units are not generally indifferent to their balance-sheet position, so that different balance-sheet variables do not have identical implications for current economic behavior, nor need a particular balance-sheet variable have an identical effect on the behavior of different economic units. In order to develop an understanding of the manner in which financial transactions affect economic behavior, it is necessary as a preliminary step to distinguish the most important characteristics of financial and tangible assets.[13]

1. Tangible assets are material things which are highly *specific* in form and use. The annual stream of productive or consumable services they yield are in kind, and must be sold in order to be converted into another form of wealth or income. In contrast, both the principal and services of financial assets are predominantly *generalized* claims against current production. These are usually fixed in nominal money units, but may be tied to some future contingency, or represent pro rata shares in the returns of enterprises.

2. Tangible assets are held primarily for the *physical services* that they yield directly, for example, houses, machines, and consumer durable goods. Financial assets are held primarily as an attractive income-earning *store of purchasing power*, representing an indirect claim to the consumption of or utilization of the physical services of economic goods.[14] The specific services in kind that they yield are

13. The following discussion has greatly benefited from access to an unpublished manuscript kindly made available by James Tobin.

14. This distinction refers to the characteristic motives of assetholders, rather than the characteristics of the assets themselves. The key word above is "primarily." At the margin the distinction becomes quite arbitrary and unclear. Real property can and does serve as a store of value. Land, jewelry, even commodities may be held primarily for speculative purposes, rather than for the physical services they yield.

adaptable by the issuer, and can be tailored with great complexity and sophistication to fit the circumstances and preferences of particular wealthowning groups.

3. Tangible assets are highly *complementary*, and characterized by important externalities in use. With the exception of consumer durables whose services are directly desired per se, tangible goods can be made to yield their services in saleable form only with the cooperation of other productive factors. Financial assets, in contrast, are largely *supplementary*, being much less dependent on the presence of other cooperative factors in order to yield their services. As a result, the prospective yield ordinarily does not vary with the holder as is the case with tangible assets.

4. Tangible assets can be increased only slowly, by net real investment, and are similarly *indurate* in the rate at which their value can be realized. With the exception of inventories, their consumption cannot be hurried markedly if their full value is to be realized. Even though the stream of services from a particular financial asset may be unalterable, financial assets can be created or destroyed virtually *instantaneously* by the act of borrowing or repayment.

5. Tangible assets are less *liquid* than financial assets, where *liquidity* characterizes the *ease of converting an asset into money*. Liquidity is important because in making portfolio decisions asset-holders are concerned, among other things, about their ability to make cash out-payments to meet various future contingencies.

In summary, most of the properties of financial assets are not possessed by the tangible assets to which they ultimately correspond in the balance sheets of their issuers. Many such properties are based on a 'confidence trick,' that is they are essentially extrinsic and, although specified by their issuers, are maintained in large part by the attitudes, credibility, and behavior of their holders. The durability of such characteristics is contingent upon all wealthowners confidentially regarding financial assets as possessing these properties, yet at the same time refraining from simultaneously exploiting them.

The concept of *liquidity* requires special attention. Though one of the most popular terms in financial discussion, it is at the same time one of the most troublesome. In order to comprehend the liquidity concept satisfactorily it is necessary at this point to introduce a number of precise definitions.

The *market value* (or simply the *value*) of an asset may be defined as the maximum amount of money obtainable from the sale of the asset, net of selling costs, after all useful prior preparations for the sale have been made. If the market for a particular asset is imperfect or nonexistent, it may not be possible to determine this market value with exactness.

The *capital certainty* of an asset refers to the predictability with which its expected market value at future dates is anticipated. This may vary over time for the same asset, as well as among assetholders at a moment in time, and so does not permit a unique ordering.

The *marketability* of an asset refers to the proportion of its present market value that can be realized in cash at different time intervals after the decision to sell. Since marketability is governed by the price received net of all costs incurred in effecting the sale relative to the length of notice given, it is a functional relation rather than a single-variate magnitude. Consequently no simple unique ordering of assets by marketability may be possible, as illustrated in Figure 1-1.

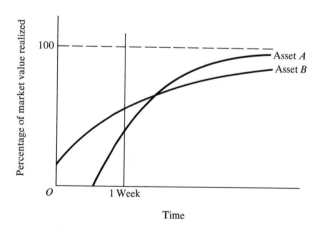

Figure 1-1

To circumvent this difficulty the *realizability* of an asset may be defined as the proportion of its value that can be realized in cash after some (arbitrary) short period of time—e.g., one week. Assets can be ordered uniquely in terms of their realizability.

Finally, the *reversibility* of an asset may be defined as its market value (or for some purposes its realizable value) as a percent of its contemporaneous cost of acquisition.

It is now possible to analyze with some precision what the elusive concept *liquidity* denotes. An asset which can be converted into money quickly, conveniently, and at little cost *combines* the distinct characteristics of high marketability and high capital certainty. Marketability is determined primarily by technical considerations, dependent on the specificity of the asset, the volume of transactions and the organization of the market in which it is traded. Capital certainty is determined to a larger extent by subjective phenomena, the degree of belief in and the dispersion of the probability distribution of expected market value at future dates. The property of marketability (the shape of the curves in Figure 1-1) has logically little or nothing to do with the predictability of an asset's future value (the expected probability distribution of possible future positions of the horizontal 100 per cent line in Figure 1-1).

Since liquidity is not an operationally measurable magnitude, and compounds two quite distinct properties, many economists have concluded that the concept is too imprecise to possess any analytical value. Fortunately or unfortunately, depending on one's point of view, such academic imprecation is unlikely to exorcize the term from popular discussion. Liquidity will continue to be used here simply as a convenient shorthand to indicate the degree to which assets and asset portfolios combine the two properties of marketability and capital certainty. More precisely, due to their greater specificity, heterogeneity, and complementarity, tangible assets are typically less marketable (subject to higher exchange costs) than financial assets. To a lesser extent they are also characterized by lesser capital certainty, although as noted in the previous footnote this relationship may at times be reversed.

There are two further terms which must be thoroughly understood and carefully distinguished as a preliminary to any intelligent discussion of financial phenomena.

The *yield* of an asset comprises all receipts and costs entailed by ownership of the asset over a specified interval of time. The particular services yielded by different types of assets take an indefinitely large variety of forms. It is frequently difficult to assign an exact value to each of these services. In general because of their specificity, complementarity, and low marketability, the yield on tangible assets is more difficult to calculate, and less certain in value, than the yield on financial assets.

The *return* of an asset is the algebraic sum of the value of its yield plus the increment in its market value (capital gain or loss) over a specified period of time. Both yield and return are customarily defined as an annual percentage of initial value.

The Role of Finance in Economic Activity

Economic exchange is conventionally divided for analytical purposes into three subcategories, two or all of which may in practice be comprised in any one transaction:

1. Buying—Selling
2. Taking—Giving
3. Lending—Borrowing

Buying denotes the purchase of economic goods with money and *selling* the sale of economic goods for money (or, as it is sometimes put, the "purchase" of money with goods). *Taking* and *giving* denote the buying and selling of goods at a zero price. *Lending* and *borrowing*, where a market transaction is intended as distinct from personal exchange (lending one's umbrella), are terms used to denote the buying and selling of newly created financial goods.

Financial assets and liabilities *originate only in an act of borrowing*, and are *reduced only in an act of debt repayment or default*. It is important to distinguish the purchase and sale of *newly created* from the purchase and sale of *previously existing* financial assets. The term lending is commonly used to denote the act of purchase of one unit's newly created financial assets by another economic unit. Purchase of its own outstanding securities is termed debt repayment. Borrowing refers only to the act of sale of newly created financial assets which are the liability of the issuing unit. There are no special terms for the purchase and sale of previously existing financial assets, which

effectuate a shift in the composition of individual wealthowner portfolios.

Private economic units in our uncharitable world must operate
subject to some budget constraint, which is determined in addition to
their income by their ability to raise cash, that is, to sell existing assets
and to borrow. Consequently, their current economic behavior is
circumscribed and shaped by their asset, liability, and net-worth
positions, as well as by their income and preferences.

The *net worth* of private economic units is an accounting tautology,
defined as the residual between total assets and total liabilities. It can
be changed only by saving or dissaving out of current earned income,
and by capital gains and losses, i.e., unearned income changes in the
market value of existing assets and liabilities. (For some purposes it is
convenient to define income as the net accretion of economic power
between two points in time, which includes both earned and unearned
income.) In contrast, the aggregate and the composition of total
assets and total liabilities are altered by all types of financial transactions.

It is now possible to outline the role of financial activity in
economic processes. Financial transactions and financial instruments
may be viewed analytically as having two distinct types of effects on
economic behavior, corresponding to flow and stock relationships.
The first, which will be termed *Intermediation Effects*, follow from the
fact that as a result of the above-described properties of financial
assets which tangible assets do not possess, indirect exchange through
the intermediation of financial instruments is technically a more
efficient means of want satisfaction than direct exchange.

On one level, with regard to facilitating the exchange of economic
goods, the intermediation of a financial instrument generally accepted
as a means of payment (money) permits the purchase and sale of
commodities to be decomposed into two distinct acts, which are
separated in time. Consequently, the use of money does not require,
as does barter, a simultaneous dual coincidence of wants if exchange
is to occur.

On another level, with regard to consumption, investment, and
saving behavior, it is convenient to classify economic units as *Surplus
Spenders*, who spend less than current income for current output,
Balance Spenders, and *Deficit Spenders*, who spend more than their

current income for current output.[15] The purchase and sale of financial instruments permits the distribution of current expenditure on commodities among economic units to diverge from the distribution of current income received. The strait jacket of a balanced-budget restraint on individual spending units is thereby loosened. Each spending unit is no longer required to purchase real commodities of an amount exactly equal to its current real income, and the possibility of individual budget deficits or surpluses on current account is introduced. Through the intermediation of financial instruments the current surpluses of some spending units are made available to finance the deficits of other spending units. In consequence the full-employment equilibrium ratio of saving and investment to current income is raised. These consequences will be demonstrated in a later chapter.

In addition to the effects of financial transactions in facilitating, enlarging, and intermediating the flow of economic exchange, financial instruments play a fundamental role in the production, utilization, and ownership of wealth, the creature of economic activity. These stock implications of financial assets, which will be termed *Asset-Transmutation Effects*, follow likewise from the observation that financial goods possess characteristics which tangible goods do not, so that the indirect ownership of real wealth through the holding of financial assets is a technically more efficient means of want satisfaction than the direct ownership of tangible assets.

Given the institution of private property, in the absence of financial instruments all economic units would be required to administer their own real wealth, and their holdings of tangible assets would be tied to their net worth. *A central accomplishment of finance is thus to permit a sharp separation of ownership from administration of wealth.* This function, although frequently pilloried, is of critical importance because given private ownership of property, there is very little in the processes of inheritance, saving, and chance, by which such ownership is determined, to ensure that those who currently own the wealth of a society are those currently most capable and desirous of administering it. Financial assets enable some economic units to own indirectly tangible assets they do not control, and others

15. The terminology is that of J. Gurley and E. Shaw, *Money in a Theory of Finance* (Washington, 1960).

to administer and utilize directly tangible assets they do not own, or of a value greater than their net worth. As will later be demonstrated the consequences are to raise the full-employment equilibrium ratio of tangible capital and wealth to current income.

In a private-property economy national wealth, regarded as some stock of scarce physical assets, is the basis for a complex network of legal claims and obligations among households, business firms, and collectives. The aggregate stock of property rights held by ultimate private wealthowners is not identical in value nor in characteristics with aggregate national wealth viewed as a stock of physical assets. In an important sense the effects of this discrepancy on economic behavior are the central concern of financial analysis. Ideally, a complete theory of finance would be able to specify how different types of indirect exchange and indirect ownership affect the matrix of all real variables of an economy, that is, the set of relative prices, the allocation of resources, the distribution of income and wealth, and the growth of physical output.

National Flow-of-Funds and Balance-Sheet Accounts

Balance-Sheet and Flow-of-Funds Accounts are potentially the chief conceptual tools of financial analysis, in the way that National-Income Accounts have become indispensable to income and expenditure analysis. The failure by economists to make greater use in teaching and research of these important sources of financial information is attributable in part to persisting unfamiliarity with the logical framework underlying construction of the accounts, and in part to certain serious conceptual and statistical limitations in the flow-of-funds system as currently presented. But perhaps the greatest inhibiting factor has been the lack of an accepted theoretical framework, possessing explanatory and predictive value, with which to analyze the interaction of financial and nonfinancial variables. There has been no John Maynard Keynes of flow-of-funds accounting.

National-income and product accounts purportedly embrace all transactions in the creation and distribution of a country's output, yet there is no reference to the financial instruments and transactions that make these exchanges possible. By stripping away the financial veil to focus on the essentials of production and consumption, saving by various sectors is described as the excess of income over consumption, and investment as goods produced but not consumed. What these sectors do with the proceeds of their savings, and how they are made available to another sector to finance its investment, is omitted. The financial dimension of economic activity is totally eclipsed, and production economics are described as though they operated through barter. Flow-of-funds accounts have been designed to supplement national-income and product accounts by documenting changes in the complex of financial instruments with which economic units spend, borrow, and lend.

A sources-and-uses-of-funds statement for an individual economic unit represents a record of changes in its balance-sheet position between two points in time. As shown in Table 1-1, "uses of funds" are simply increases in assets if positive, or decreases in assets if

19

Table 1-1

USES OF FUNDS		SOURCES OF FUNDS
Δ Tangible Assets (investment and disinvestment)		Δ Liabilities (borrowing and debt repayment)
Δ Financial Assets (lending and sale of securities)		Δ Net Worth (saving and dissaving)
ΣΔ Total Assets	≡	ΣΔ Total Liabilities and Net Worth

negative. "Sources of funds" are simply increases in liabilities or net worth (saving) if positive, and repayment of debt or dissaving if negative. Given this accounting framework, the choice of terminology "uses of funds" for "change in assets" and "sources of funds" for "change in liabilities and net worth" is unfortunate. The term "funds" is distressingly metaphysical, since it can neither be defined, nor conceptually identified with, any stock of "funds" that may be added to or diminished. Moreover, to treat dissaving or debt repayment as a "negative source of funds," and reduction in assets as a "negative use of funds," is unnecessarily confusing to the uninitiated, since it requires a mental translation to make it intelligible.

The flow-of-funds matrix for the economy as a whole merely consists of a presentation of all the individual sources-and-uses statements, grouped into sectors and placed side by side. Each financial instrument is by definition someone's asset and someone else's liability (all corporate obligations, whether fixed in money terms or not, being treated as liabilities in economic accounting). Therefore, for the entire economy the total of liabilities must equal the total of financial assets (adjusted for any valuation differences for the same asset by debtors and creditors), although for any one unit or sector its liabilities are not likely to equal its financial assets. The consolidated net worth (wealth) of a closed economy, excluding the foreign sector, is consequently identical to the value of its real assets, an alternative demonstration that, *ex post*, saving must equal investment. In an open economy there can be in addition net claims on the foreign sector.

Saving and investment are the links between the national product and flow-of-funds systems of accounts. Saving in the flow-of-funds accounts are treated as a source of finance to acquire tangible or financial assets, or the means to pay off debt. Saving and borrowing are formally recognized as alternative ways of financing the acquisition of assets. Investment, the acquisition of tangible assets, is treated as a use of the command over resources acquired by saving, borrowing, or the sale of financial assets. Because data on gross flows are not available for most types of financial transactions, it is not possible to trace offsetting or direct flows of funds among sectors, which, together with exchanges within any particular sector, are netted out and unobserved.

Without delving into the technicalities involved in constructing the accounts, it is worth calling attention briefly to some of the problems and limitations of balance-sheet and flow-of-funds accounts for understanding the relationships between financial and "real" behavior.

AGGREGATION

The starting point of classification for analytical purposes must rest upon the principle that balance-sheet variables affecting the behavior of economic units operate via the decision-making processes of these units. The focus of analysis consequently must be on the balance-sheet position as regarded by individual spending units and its role in their calculations.

The consolidation into a combined national balance-sheet for the private sector, by netting out internal claims and liabilities, leaves only the stock of private tangible wealth and the net indebtedness of the government to the private sector. Such an aggregation explains in part the concentration of simple Keynesian macroeconomic analysis on money, insofar as part of currency is government debt, and on government bonds, to the exclusion of internal private financial assets and liabilities. But this cancellation in effect washes out just those variables that are of central concern to any examination of financial behavior. Financial assets and liabilities, while they involve in a sense double-counting and may *formally* be consolidated as a matter of arithmetic, do not cancel out in the decision-making process of economic units. As subsequent chapters will indicate, even for the analysis of aggregate spending decisions a great deal of information and understanding is lost by the assumption that the effects of financial assets and liabilities are exactly offsetting.

It follows that the concern of financial analysis is primarily with changes in the over-all balance-sheet position of individual wealth-owning sectors, rather than movements in combined or consolidated national balance-sheets. Balance-sheet positions must be constructed and analyzed by type of holder rather than by type of asset. If stable behavioral relationships are to be revealed, national balance-sheet data must be disaggregated to reveal the balance-sheet position of those economic subgroups whose balance-sheet position, and whose behavior in response to balance-sheet variables, is relatively homogeneous.

The purpose of sectoring is to assist analysis, and the appropriate extent of disaggregation depends on the questions raised. Sectoring is much more detailed in the flow-of-funds accounts than in the national-income statistics. In addition, sectors are defined institutionally, rather than, as in national-income accounting, functionally. For present purposes it will be sufficient to distinguish, among ultimate wealth-owning units, between households and collectives, such as federal, state, and local governments, and nonprofit institutions. Among nonultimate wealth units, it will be sufficient to distinguish financial and nonfinancial corporations, and noncorporate businesses.

While in principle it would be possible as well as extremely desirable to be able to move easily from one set of accounts to the other, in practice the sectoring is so different as to make it cumbersome or impossible to do so at present. The national-income accounts treat all real investment as a business activity. Neither consumers nor governments, as such, are permitted to invest in the national-income accounts, but rather are treated as split personalities, sometimes belonging to the producing sector. In the flow-of-funds accounts, consumer purchases of durable goods are treated as investment, and depreciation is imputed. There is no imputed rental income, and no imputed rental consumption. Government enterprises are classified in the producing sector in the national-product accounts, but in the government sectors in the flow-of-funds accounts.

In a study of financial phenomena financial institutions cannot be treated as homogeneous with other business enterprises as they are in the national accounts. Similarly nonfinancial corporations, for example corporate and unincorporated enterprises, are distinguished because of differing financial structure, although they are all alike in adding value to the national product.

VALUATION AND MEASUREMENT

From the viewpoint of investigating the relationship between financial change and real economic behavior, the appropriate valuation of balance-sheet items is again that relevant to the decision-making process of assetholders. While the magnitude of some balance-sheet figures is contractually specified, many assets, claims, and obligations have no fixed value, so that a choice exists concerning the basis of valuation.

Current market value is the single valuation principle most relevant for the behavior of intangible assetowners. But for some units it is pragmatically necessary, and in some cases may be preferable, to accept the valuations they themselves put on their assets and liabilities, and rely on book values rather than market judgment as expressed in current recorded prices. A single-valued market price may not exist, or recorded yet marginal market transactions, e.g., for secondhand durables, may not reflect the true valuations of such items as viewed by their possessors. For many intermediaries valuation at market would at times imply negative net worth, even though the institution might be quite profitable on current account.

Acceptance of the methodological principle of relevance to decision making by the possessor implies acceptance of a valuation differential between aggregate national claims and obligations, which will not in general be entered at the same figure in the balance sheets of debtor and creditor units. As a result private domestic claims do not drop out in a consolidated national balance-sheet unless a valuation adjustment is made. With regard to debtor-creditor relationships, obligations are customarily entered in debtor balance-sheets at par value, but in the balance-sheet of creditors nonmarketable claims will be reduced by a bad-debt adjustment. Marketable claims, if long-term, may have a current market price that differs considerably from their face value in the books of debtor units.

With regard to owner-issuer relationships between ultimate and nonultimate wealth units, a quantitatively far more important discrepancy arises. The aggregate value of business tangible assets financed out of retained earnings or new share issue, whether entered at current depreciated replacement cost or market value, ordinarily will be quite different from the market value of such assets regarded as a residual equity interest in the future profits of an operating concern. In the balance-sheets of shareholders corporate stock is valued on a going-concern basis, as represented by the market value of the shares held, a figure which in prosperous periods far exceeds, and in a depression falls short of, the book value of residual equity claims as recorded in corporate balance-sheets.

There are fewer imputations in the flow-of-funds accounts than in the national-product system. Taxes are carried on a cash basis in the flow-of-funds system, whereas some taxes are shown on an accrual basis in national-product accounts. Probably the most important discrepancy between the accounts is the failure of the income and product system to account for, and the flow-of-funds accounts to isolate, capital gains and losses. Since most assets in the flow-of-funds balance sheets are shown at market value, changes in asset levels and in net worth include a composite of savings, defined as the difference between receipts and consumption expenditures on current accounts, plus capital gains and losses. Estimation of capital gains and losses, assignment of them by sectors, and (if possible) distinction between realized and unrealized gains, would enormously increase the usefulness of both accounts for analytical purposes. While economic units tend to think of such gains as nonrecurring, and so may be inclined to save a larger proportion of the proceeds than in the case with current income, their magnitude is such that incentives and current economic behavior cannot but be deeply influenced.

INCLUSION

Flow-of-funds partial balance-sheets presently omit tangible assets and net worth, although the collection of wealth data to complement the existing accounts is currently being explored. There are three important conceptual problems which must be faced with regard to the scope of balance-sheet estimates for financial analysis.

The first concerns the extent of inclusion of nonreproducible real assets. If economic wealth is conceived as a stock of legally enforceable claims, it is appropriate to include only those nonproducible assets which are subject to property rights, primarily land and subsoil assets, and to exclude all other "free" gifts of nature such as climate, water, air, sunshine, etc. Only property rights, as distinct from wealth more broadly conceived, are pieces in the financial game.

A related problem concerns the inclusion of human capital in balance-sheet accounts. Since labor itself cannot be bought or sold, but only labor services, human wealth will not be entered in national balance-sheet accounts regarded as a stock of property claims, although it clearly would have to be considered in any estimate of wealth regarded as all resources which contribute to the production of goods and services over future periods. While national estimates are presently lacking, human capital represents by far the largest single balance-sheet item for most household units. Since it necessarily varies widely over age and occupational distribution within any given income class, it would have to be taken into consideration in any investigation of the effect of balance-sheet variables for household behavior.

A final question concerns the balance-sheet of public economic units. Many public assets have no ascertainable market value, for example, political institutions, social attitudes, tax morality, etc., yet they bear an undeniable relation to the behavior of the public sector. Moreover sovereign governments are much less circumscribed by their balance-sheet position, since the power to levy taxes and issue legal tender loosens the budgetary restraint. As a result the behavior of sovereign public units is less closely related to narrowly defined balance-sheet variables, and requires differential treatment. To the extent that the behavior of private economic units is not influenced by the balance-sheet position of the public sector, aggregate private net worth further exceeds aggregate private tangible assets by the amount of net private claims against the public sector. As a result of this asymmetry, financial transactions to which governments are one party have particular significance for the income and balance-sheet position of private economic units, since total private net worth, in addition to the total and composition of private assets and liabilities, may be altered.

Table 1-2 presents a summary of the National Balance Sheet of the United States at selected dates, as estimated by Raymond Goldsmith. Even a cursory examination reveals the dramatic rise and fall in the ratio of financial to tangible assets over the period. Why have these changes occurred, and what has been the significance for

Table 1-2—National Balance Sheets (Billions of Dollars)

1900

Tangible assets	88.4	Liabilities	44.6
Financial assets	68.4	Equities	112.2
Total	156.8	Total	156.8

1929

Tangible assets	422.5	Liabilities	315.7
Financial assets	550.9	Equities	657.7
Total	973.4	Total	973.4

1933

Tangible assets	318.5	Liabilities	272.2
Financial assets	403.3	Equities	449.6
Total	721.8	Total	721.8

1945

Tangible assets	554.6	Liabilities	778.3
Financial assets	978.2	Equities	754.6
Total	1,532.9	Total	1,532.9

1958

Tangible assets	1,653.0	Liabilities	1,488.4
Financial assets	2,082.3	Equities	2,246.9
Total	3,735.3	Total	3,735.3

Source: Raymond W. Goldsmith and Robert Lipsey, *Studies in the National Balance Sheet of the United States*, Vol. II, Tables 1 and 1a. Reprinted by permission of Princeton University Press © 1963.

the performance of the American economy?

Table 1-3 presents an abbreviated balance-sheet position of each of the three most important private sectors at two moments in time. On what principles is it possible to explain the widely diverse portfolio tastes of different types of economic units? How have the changes

Table 1-3—Sector Balance Sheets (Billions of Dollars)

Nonfarm Households, 1945 & 1958

	1945	1958		1945	1958
Tangible assets			Liabilities		
Structures	130.7	373.1	Consumer debt	5.3	44.8
Land	28.3	92.2	Mortgages	18.4	117.1
Durables	41.1	166.8	Total	30.5	176.3
Total	200.1	632.0	Net worth	592.2	1,425.5
Financial assets					
Currency and					
demand deposits	49.9	61.4			
Claims against					
Financial insti-					
tutions	121.9	333.7			
Bonds and notes	80.8	94.5			
Stock and equity	157.2	449.3			
Total	422.6	969.8	Total liabilities		
Total assets	622.7	1,601.8	and net worth	622.7	1,601.8

Nonfinancial Corporations 1945 & 1958

	1945	1958		1945	1958
Tangible assets			Liabilities		
Structures	62.5	202.1	Trade debt	19.7	68.8
Land	20.0	63.5	Bonds and notes	23.6	69.7
Durables	33.9	145.5	Mortgages	7.8	29.7
Inventory	26.3	78.8	Total	88.2	257.1
Total	142.8	489.9	Net worth	162.8	508.4
Financial assets					
Currency and					
demand deposits	19.7	33.3			
Trade credit	22.7	83.4			
Bonds	21.2	21.8			
Total	108.2	275.6	Total liabilities		
Total assets	251.0	765.5	and net worth	251.0	765.5

Financial Institutions 1945 & 1958

	1945	1958		1945	1958
Tangible assets	2.5	10.3	Liabilities		
Financial assets			Currency and		
Currency and			demand		
demand deposits	77.3	92.6	deposits	185.2	223.2
Mortgages	21.5	135.5	Total	330.6	632.4
Bonds and notes	206.3	281.5	Net worth	21.5	71.1
Stock	7.4	44.5			
Total	349.7	693.2			
Total assets	352.1	703.5		352.1	703.5

Source: *Op. cit.* Table 1.

which have occurred in their portfolio compositions been related to their income and output behavior?

The following chapters represent an attempt to develop a set of behavioral hypotheses possessing explanatory value for just such questions.

RECOMMENDED READING

The new approach to financial activity which is the subject of this book was first presented with great originality in the pioneering study of John Gurley and Edward Shaw, *Money in a Theory of Finance* (Washington, 1960). An earlier brief but provocative treatment may be found in Kenneth Boulding, *A Reconstruction of Economics* (New York, 1950), Chapters 3 and 15.

Joseph Schumpeter's *The History of Economic Doctrine* (New York, 1954) remains the most masterly discussion and reference work of the historical development of financial thought. For a more concise presentation, see Joseph Conard, *An Introduction to the Theory of Interest* (Berkeley, 1959), Parts I and II.

An important early exploration of the role of financial assets and liabilities in economic behavior may be found in James Tobin, "Asset Holdings and Spending Decisions," *American Economic Review* (May, 1952). See also Roland N. McKean, "Liquidity and a National Balance Sheet," reprinted in American Economic Association, *Readings in Monetary Theory* (Illinois, 1951). For a thoughtful discussion of liquidity, which emphasizes the central role of risk, see J. R. Hicks, "Liquidity," *Economic Journal* (December, 1962).

John Powelson, *National Income and Flow-of-Funds Accounts* (New York, 1960) contains an excellent introductory presentation of flow-of-funds accounting. For a more technical discussion of statistical and methodological issues, see *The Flow of Funds Approach to Social Accounting*, National Bureau of Economic Research (New York, 1962). In addition to the *Federal Reserve Bulletin's Quarterly Presentation*, historical series are to be found in *Flow of Funds Savings Accounts, 1946-60* (Supplement 5), Board of Governors of the Federal Reserve System, 1961, and Raymond Goldsmith and Robert Lipsey, *Studies in the National Balance Sheet of the United States*, Volumes I and II (Princeton University Press, 1963). An excellent summary of sources of wealth data and discussion of measurement difficulties may be found in *Measuring the Nation's Wealth*, Joint Economic Committee, December 1964, issued by the National Bureau of Economic Research as *Studies in Income and Wealth*, Vol. 29 (Columbia University Press, 1964).

2

Principles of

Financial Behavior

*That is all very well, but you have no choice; you must place
your bet, you are already committed.*

—B. Pascal,

Pensees

Introduction

How are observed shifts in portfolio composition over time, and
widely diverse portfolio tastes of different economic units at a moment
of time, to be explained? Any examination of financial change necessarily presupposes some hypothesis of assetholder behavior. After a
preliminary discussion of risk and uncertainty the first section of this
chapter develops a general explanation as to how utility-maximizing
economic units, faced with an uncertain future, prefer to diversify
their asset holdings among alternative wealth forms.

All investment opportunities offer uncertain future returns, and
assetholders may be distinguished according to the degree of disutility or utility they receive from bearing risk. Whenever the
expected probability distribution of returns from different assets are

not perfectly intercorrelated, it is demonstrated that the total risk from wealthownership can be reduced for any given level of expected return by diversification of asset holdings. As a result, wealthowners are not indifferent to the *composition* of their portfolios. A diagramatic analysis is developed with the aid of which the optimum portfolio position for any wealthowner may be defined.

The next section develops a two-fold explanation for the wide differences observed in the financial behavior of different economic groups. In terms of the previous discussion this diversity may be related on one side to differences in the set of investment *opportunities* available to economic units from wealthownership. These are in turn related to the differing characteristics, in particular complementarity, among tangible and financial assets. Diverse financial behavior may also be accounted for by differences in the *utility functions* from wealthownership among economic groups. Investors have different preferences for risk bearing, and different accumulation objectives over time. These differences in opportunities and tastes among economic units, which explain differences in financial behavior on capital account, are related to differences in consumption and production behavior on current account as developed in the following chapter.

Asset Management Under Uncertainty

Uncertainty is the *raison d'être* of financial behavior. The very existence of financial assets, institutions, and the system of indirect wealthownership is intelligible only as a response to the fact that few future events can be known with certainty in advance. If all investors possessed the gift of perfect foresight, so that the outcome of every investment decision were known in advance, and if all exchange costs were zero, optimum portfolio policy would simply be to select that asset with the highest rate of return.

In a world characterized by perfect foresight, portfolio diversification would have no purpose. Each assetholder would simply attempt to put his entire wealth into the asset with the highest rate of return. Since all wealth must be held in some portfolio, asset prices would adjust so that each asset yielded an identical return. The rate of interest would be a redundant expression for the rate of return on tangible assets (the marginal productivity of investment). All types of assets in the capital stock would yield the same rate of return, and all wealth would be held directly in the form of tangible assets. Borrowing and lending would not occur, although tangible assets might be rented from their owner. Alternatively expressed, the services of tangible assets, as well as the assets themselves, might be bought and sold on a market.

Even with perfect certainty some diversification would occur as long as asset markets were not perfect, so that exchange costs are nonzero. In this case all assets need not possess perfect liquidity, reversibility, and divisibility. With imperfect asset markets the existence of exchange costs imparts a certain inertia to portfolio selection, which prevents the planned period for holding any asset from being infinitesimally short. Shifting and decision-making costs would lead investors to choose a mixed portfolio according to the timing of their accumulation goals, that is, the anticipated distribution of receipts and expenditures over future periods.

The main ground for asset management and portfolio diversification stems however from the existence of uncertainty. Even if asset markets are perfect, uncertainty about future asset returns will induce cautious investors to diversify, and cause all investors to cease to be indifferent about the composition of their portfolios. For each alternative portfolio mix, a rational wealthowner must attempt to estimate an expected rate of return and the likelihood of alternative outcomes. How does he select an optimum portfolio? The theory of portfolio behavior may be formally defined as the study of the procedure by which information pertaining to particular individual assets and liabilities may be transformed into information about particular portfolios, and of the criteria by which a portfolio may be selected that best meets the objectives and tastes of the assetholding unit.

RISK, UNCERTAINTY, AND BELIEF

Economists have long been conscious of the need to account more adequately for the effects of uncertainty on the consumption and investment decisions of households and firms. Most of the attempts to correct this deficiency have met with limited success. Probably the greatest difficulty in the empirical testing of hypotheses in this area concerns the complex process by which decision-making units on the basis of past experience formulate their expectations of the future on which they base their current behavior. Theory rarely deals with variables that can be observed directly, and nowhere is this operational gap greater than in the measurement of economic unit's anticipations of future events.

In the absence of perfect certainty the information inputs on which portfolio behavior is based are not simply the formal calculation of data on past performance, although these are all that is usually available to the social scientist. The true inputs are the subjective probability beliefs of asset managers with regard to future events, which lean on calculation, but interpret it and go beyond it with intuitive judgment.

Perhaps the first snare to be circled is the distinction between *risk* and *uncertainty*. Both refer to situations in which future outcomes are imperfectly known. The term *risk* commonly denotes only those future events in which the probabilities of alternative possible outcomes are known. *Objective probability* is a measure of the relative frequency of alternative events, and is strictly applicable only to those events which are repetitive in nature, and so possess a frequency distribution from which observations can be drawn and statistical inferences can be made. When a large number of observations are available, the most probable frequency generated by chance closely approximates the objective probability of an event.

Uncertainty refers in contrast to a situation which is unique, so that the frequency distribution of possible outcomes cannot be objectively specified. For many investment decisions no relative frequency distribution is available. Yet even though there may be no objective information about an event's probability density function, the decision maker will ordinarily have beliefs about the likelihood of alternative outcomes. *Subjective probability* may be interpreted as a measure of the degree of ignorance or belief held with regard to the outcomes of particular future events. The less perfectly the conditions of the law of large numbers are satisfied, the more uncertain are subjective probability estimates concerning future possible states of the world. The term *uncertainty* is commonly used to denote the degree of ignorance about the frequency distribution of a future event.

Investor units have no choice but to commit themselves to some decision. *No objective information* about an event's objective probability must not be equated to *no information* about it. Yet a number of eminent writers have opposed treating subjective beliefs in terms of probabilities. In a conflict-of-interests situation, where the outcomes represent the moves of a conscious antagonist rather than an impersonal and impartial outside force (nature or the market), the maxims and strategy of game theory may be more appropriate. For example, the *Minimax* criterion provides a rule which disregards probabilities entirely. Instead, it chooses the alternative which minimizes the worst possible outcome which a future state of the world can inflict. The *Minimax Regret* principle suggests minimizing the difference between actual outcome and the best possible alternative which would have been selected if the state of the world could have been known in advance.

Apart from the games case, in which outcomes are dependent on one's own move, these principles are strictly appropriate only for situations of complete ignorance. Since they take no account of greater or lesser likelihoods, they must at least be compared with the solution arrived at by a heroic estimate of probabilities. Ignorance is ordinarily "perfect" only within some range of possible values. Subjective probabilities must be incorporated into a theory of behavior because in effect they characterize a degree of likelihood *whose magnitude investors ordinarily cannot avoid estimating for the purpose of making rational decisions.*

The question how to incorporate subjective probability into a model of decision making is more difficult. The suggestion that subjective probability beliefs may be treated as a single-valued estimate by adding a certainty-equivalent discount of some sort, to compensate for the use of less reliable information, must be rejected. No one has yet suggested how an operational measure of this degree of certainty adjustment for different circumstances might be independently devised. In the following discussion decisions under uncertainty will be treated as if they were a case of risk. Putting the thorny problem of operational difficulties of measurement to one side, subjective probability beliefs may for present purposes simply be regarded as some imperfectly foreseen frequency distribution of alternative outcomes.

It must be emphasized that the degree of confidence or belief in subjective probability estimates is a function of the information at the investor's disposal, and his ability to interpret it. Both will differ among investors, and both ordinarily may be varied at a cost. Policy and strategy represent the premeditation of decisions, and flourish best where decisions can be anticipated. For example, decisions made under pressure typically favor intuition as against analysis. Confidence also depends on the personal makeup of the individual decision maker. It may be noted in passing that in business life there is a strong commitment to action—"heroic" man versus "economic" man. "It is to this love of taking a chance that we owe most of mankind's greatest progress."[1]

EXPECTED UTILITY

The classical solution of revising a certainty model to incorporate risk was to make *expected* return, or rather its discounted value, the object to be maximized by a rational decision maker. In the long run the expected value becomes the "certain" value, in the sense that a sample mean, drawn repeatedly and independently from the same population, will asymptotically approach its population counterpart.

The expected return rule has considerable intuitive appeal, and is a defensible strategy for many decisions. Yet, in the case of extreme outcomes, it leads to results which contradict observed behavior. The classic demonstration of this limitation is Daniel Bernoulli's St. Petersburg paradox.[2] Less exotically, the maximization of expected

1. Emile Borel, quoted in Paul Masse, *Optimal Investment Decisions* (New Jersey, 1963), p. 394. Chapter Five of this book presents an excellent introduction to uncertainty concepts.
2. A person buys a chance to flip a fair coin until a head appears. Should it appear on the first throw, he receives $2. Should it appear on the second, third, or nth throw, he receives $4, $8, 2^n, respectively. How much should he rationally pay for a chance to play the game? The expected value ($\bar{V}$) can be computed as follows:

$$\bar{V} = (\tfrac{1}{2}) 2 + (\tfrac{1}{2})^2 4 + (\tfrac{1}{2})^3 8 + \cdots + (\tfrac{1}{2})^n 2^n + \cdots$$
$$= 1 \quad + 1 \quad + 1 \quad + \cdots + 1 \quad + \cdots$$
$$= \sum_{n=1}^{\infty} (\tfrac{1}{2})^n 2^n = \infty$$

The expected value of the game is infinite. Yet few people are willing to pay more than ten or twenty dollars for a chance to play. Why?

return criterion is also incompatible with portfolio diversification behavior.

To meet these objections, maximization of expected return was replaced by maximization of *expected utility* as a more general principle of rational behavior under uncertainty. Investors are not ordinarily symmetrically indifferent between extreme values equidistant from an expected value. In general, "a full purse is not as good as an empty one is bad."[3] Not only may satisfaction not vary in proportion to income, but subjective probabilities may be biased so that, for example, very small probabilities may be systematically undervalued, as the St. Petersburg paradox suggests.

For heuristic purposes each decision-making unit may be described as possessing a utility schedule that permits him to determine the subjective value of every outcome. He may then be regarded as selecting the alternative with the highest expectation of utility. No hedonistic interpretation of behavior is imputed. The decision maker merely attaches numbers—"utility"—to chance outcomes. The optimum portfolio is then simply that particular asset combination (or combinations) within the economic unit's external budget constraint that promises the highest expected total utility.

The next problem lies in specifying the form of the utility function from wealthownership and in identifying the variables that must be included. As described in the previous chapter, assets yield a great many heterogeneous services, all of which may be expected to enter into the utility function, and about most of which economists as economists have very little to say. In traditional demand theory such factors are subsumed under the label tastes or preferences, the *ceteris paribus* assumption is invoked, and the analysis focuses upon the more or less objective variables of income and prices.

Expected utility from ownership of different assets may be a function of, for example, social approval, social prohibition, the will to create, the fun of gambling, etc., in addition to the subjective probability expectation of gain or loss. Otherwise expressed, rational choice depends not merely on subjective probability beliefs of outcomes, but on how they are generated, since utility is attached to the "game" itself as well as to the receipt of a sum. Since the means by

3. Jacob Marschak, *Three Lectures on Probability in the Social Sciences*, Cowles Commission for Research in Economics, No. 82 (1954).

which the distribution of outcomes are generated will frequently be significant, an assetholder may with perfect consistency have an aversion to risk on some assets and a taste for risk on others. A related question concerns the extent to which it is legitimate to attribute collective utility functions to a firm. Institutions account for a large proportion of tangible and financial investment. Business managers typically are constrained in asset choice to conform to those socially-defined behavior patterns considered appropriate for their institution. The manner in which institutional preferences arise and influence institutional behavior will be considered in Chapter 3.

For each portfolio available to him, a portfolio manager may be imagined to estimate a subjective probability distribution of alternative outcomes. How will the investor rank these portfolios? Other things being equal, assuming expected gain to be good, he will prefer greater expected return to smaller. Since future prospects of gain are uncertain, and most investor units are not neutral about risk, the expected utility attached to any subjective probability distribution of outcomes will also be related to the uncertainty of exceptional gain or loss. In order to explain choices involving risk, the utility function must have certain properties. To make possible comparisons of differences in risk the utility scale must be cardinal. More precisely, an interval scale, with an arbitrary zero point and an undefined but constant unit of measurement, is implied since intensity of preferences among alternatives, rather than mere ordinal ranking, is revealed by the act of selection among uncertain outcomes.

In Figure 2-1 three different types of utility schedules are depicted graphically. Utility Schedule I is a straight line, implying constant marginal utility of return throughout. Utility Schedule II shows diminishing marginal utility of return, and Utility Schedule III shows increasing marginal utility of return. For convenience of comparison the utility attached to zero return has been set arbitrarily at equal utility U_2 for each schedule.

Figure 2-1 illustrates that except for investors whose utility function is linear (Utility Schedule I), preferences among portfolios on the basis of expected utility will be determined by other properties of the subjective probability distribution of outcomes *in addition to* expected return. In particular the likelihood of exceptional loss and exceptional gain must be considered. Putting to one side temporarily the question of how risk is to be measured, Figure 2-2 depicts the indifference map implied by the three utility functions illustrated in Figure 2-1. Each indifference curve relates the various combinations of return and risk to which the decision maker is indifferent.

The indifference curves of individuals with linear utility functions (Schedule I), who rank portfolios solely in terms of expected return, are a family of horizontal straight lines as shown in Figure 2-2I. Such individuals may be termed *risk neutral*.[4] Investors with diminishing marginal utility of return (Utility Schedule II) will, among portfolios with identical expected return, prefer those with a smaller chance of exceptional loss. Such decision makers will be termed *risk averters*. The indifference curves of risk averters are convex from below, as shown in Figure 2-2II. Such investors can be induced to increase the risk they will bear only if it is accompanied by a compensatory rise in expected return. Investors with increasing marginal

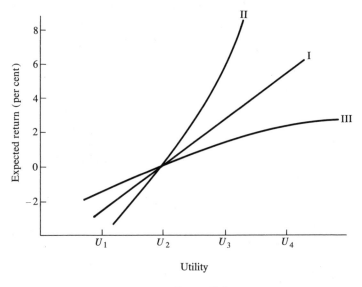

Figure 2-1

4. These terms and much of the discussion follow that of James Tobin, "The Theory of Portfolio Selection," in F. Hahn and F. Brechling (eds.), *The Theory of Interest Rates*, (Proceedings of a Conference held by the International Economic Association), (London, New York, 1965).

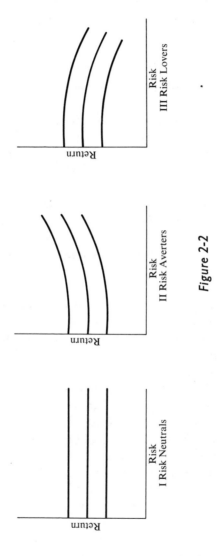

Figure 2-2

utility of return (Utility Schedule III) will, among portfolios with
the same expected return, prefer those with a greater chance of
exceptional gain. Such assetholders will be termed *risk lovers*. The
indifference curves of risk lovers are concave from below, as shown
in Figure 2-2III.

The foregoing discussion indicates that, for all except risk-neutral
investors, the optimum portfolio defines some trade-off between
expected return and risk of return. In order to rank alternative portfolios asset managers must, explicitly or implicitly, focus upon some
measure of the central tendency of their subjective probability
distribution, and some measure of the likelihood of exceptional loss
or gain.

The specification of particular focus measures to summarize the
relevant characteristics of subjective probability distributions remains
at present largely a matter of analytical and operational convenience.
This rather unsatisfactory situation is due to our imperfect understanding of the psychological process of decision making under
uncertainty.

With regard to expected return, a number of alternative measures
of the central tendency of a probability distribution are available—
mean (average), median (midpoint), and mode (most frequent). The
mean or *mathematical expectation* of return from a particular portfolio
is the weighted average of all possible outcomes, using as weights the
probabilities of these outcomes. It represents the mathematically
"fair" value, in the sense it indicates the average return if the investor
were to hold the portfolio in an indefinitely large number of situations.
The mean is more sensitive to changes in extreme values and, arith-
metically, the relation between portfolio and asset means is more
convenient to handle than median or mode, so that it is widely taken
as the most appropriate measure of central tendency. This is not to
suggest that for very skewed one-tailed distributions, for example
the log-normal, another measure such as the mode (most likely return)
may be the more relevant statistic of central tendency on which asset
managers actually focus their expectations.

With regard to risk, the choice of an appropriate measure is
considerably more difficult. The spread or dispersion of a probability

distribution may be measured by the range, standard deviation, variance, or higher moments about the mean. The *variance* is the average of the squared deviations of all observations from their mean, and the *standard deviation* is the square root of the variance. The standard deviation is directly comparable to the mean, and is the most convenient and general measure of variability in that, independent of the unit of measurement, most outcomes for most distributions may be expected to fall within two standard deviations on either side of the mean. The variance on the other hand is mathematically more convenient to work with than is the standard deviation in deriving relationships between the probability distribution of assets and portfolios. As a measure of risk, the two are not the same thing. For example, if one asset has twice the standard deviation of another, it will have four times the variance.

A more basic limitation with the above measures is that dispersion *per se* is not the property of the probability distribution of outcomes relevant to the utility function of wealthowners. Risk averters are not deterred by the chance of above-average gains, but only by the likelihood of loss or unsatisfactory return. Similarly risk lovers are not attracted by the possibility of exceptional loss, but attach positive utility only to the chance of exceptional gain. The probability of exceptional loss and exceptional gain must therefore be distinguished, while variance and standard deviation treat high and low returns as equally undesirable. Only if subjective probability distributions are symmetrical will the above measures of dispersion also provide a measure of these likelihoods.

A measure which meets this objection is the *semivariance*, which is defined as the average of the squared deviation of all undesirable outcomes, below some specified minimum return.[5] Its disadvantages are primarily technical. It is both less familiar and less convenient to handle mathematically than the standard deviation or variance. Other measures, for example, probability of loss, expected value of loss, or "focus" loss may be constructed, but are again operationally awkward

5. $$S_b = \frac{1}{N} \sum_t (r_t - b)^2,$$

where this sum is confined to $r_t < b$, S_b is the semivariance around b, and N is the number of outcomes r_t.

or impossible to deal with mathematically, and frequently imply objectionally shaped utility functions.

Instead of restricting the subjective probability distributions of expected outcomes to particular two-parameter families of curves, indifference curves with the properties shown in Figures 2-2II and 2-2III may be derived from the assumption that assetholder utility functions are quadratic over the relevant range. In this case only the mean and standard deviation of the probability distribution are relevant.

INVESTMENT OPPORTUNITIES

All that now remains is to consider the opportunity sets available to wealthowners. The subjective probability distribution of gain and loss attached to the ownership of particular tangible assets will vary widely among different wealthowners, in proportion to the information at their disposal and their ability to convert implicit services-in-kind into income. For financial assets with an income yield the explicit return is invariant to the particular holder, although the anticipated return may vary among investors, and services-in-kind may have different values.

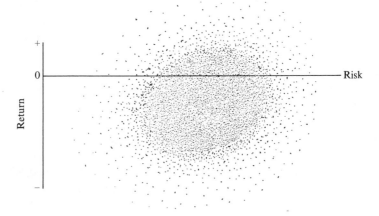

Figure 2-3

The estimated return and risk combinations, from each individual asset considered by a particular wealthowning unit, constitute its field of available investment opportunities. These are represented by points in the density set of investment opportunities shown in Figure 2-3. Although the total number of investment opportunities is indefinitely large, for any individual wealthowner most assets have negative expected returns and so are ordinarily excluded from consideration for wealth portfolios.

THE EFFECTS OF DIVERSIFICATION

It is now necessary to consider the relationship between the return-risk combinations expected from holding individual assets, and the return-risk combinations expected from holding wealth in portfolios made up of a collection of different assets.

Whenever the anticipated return distributions from individual assets are to some degree independent of one another, by holding a portfolio diversified among different assets it is possible to reduce the uncertainty of the collective return *below* the weighted average of the separate risks associated with the individual assets comprising the portfolio. This follows, providing always that the individual outcomes are not perfectly positively correlated, because unusually low returns on some assets are likely to be more or less offset on balance by unusually high returns from other assets. These risk-reducing effects of diversification, better known as the principle of not keeping all your eggs in one basket, may be demonstrated more rigorously.

The covariance between two random variables is defined as the expected value of the product of their deviations from their respective means. As such, it is a measure of the extent to which the two variables move together. If two random variables are independent, their covariance will be zero. An elementary theorem of probability states that the variance of the sum of N random variables is equal to the sum of their variances plus twice the sum of all their individual covariances. It follows that if the variables are uncorrelated, the variance of the sum is identical to the sum of the variances. Given N uncorrelated random variables, each having the same mean and variance, the average of the sum of these variables is equal to the average expected value of each variable. But the variance of the average of the sum is equal to $1/N$ times the variance of each variable.

The above reasoning suggests that, if asset returns were uncorrelated, the variance of the expected average return on diversified portfolios would approach zero as N, the number of assets held, increases. It is because of this relationship that diversification leads in general to a risk much smaller than the weighted average of the separate risks.

Since most asset returns are in fact positively correlated with one another, the covariance between individual asset returns are not zero. Diversification is as shown above an extremely powerful technique to reduce the risk involved in holding wealth when outcomes possess substantial independence, or are negatively correlated. It is much less effective in reducing risk when outcomes are highly positively correlated. In this case, the variance of the portfolio return, as the number of assets held increases, rapidly approaches not zero, but the value of the average of all the distinct covariances.

This reveals that rational asset managers, instead of looking at the return-risk combination of an asset in isolation, must consider its covariance with their entire portfolio. Total portfolio risk can be reduced by diversification extended to include an asset of greater individual risk, providing its covariance with assets already held in the portfolio is low or negative. An asset which reduces the total risk of one portfolio may be inappropriate and may increase the total risk of another portfolio. While the disutility attached to uncertainty can be shown to lead rationally to the diversification of investments, it should be remembered the act of diversification always implies some sacrifice of chance for gain. This principle is applicable to business mergers into different ventures as well as to financial asset management.

PORTFOLIO OPPORTUNITIES

These effects of diversification in establishing the feasibility frontier of the opportunity set from holding wealth portfolios may also be depicted graphically. A portfolio will be defined as *efficient* if it is impossible to obtain a higher expected return with no greater risk, or to obtain greater certainty of return with no less expectation of return.

For presentational simplicity consider a two-asset portfolio selected from the positive quadrant of the density set of investment opportunities in Figure 2-3. Point A in Figure 2-4 represents the return-risk combination anticipated from holding asset A and point B

the return-risk combination associated with asset B. If the expected outcomes from each asset were perfectly positively correlated, the opportunity frontier from holding all portfolio combinations of A and B would simply be the straight line AB. But providing some outcomes are independent or negatively related, collective portfolio risk will be *smaller* than average individual risk, so that the portfolio opportunity frontier becomes the curve ACB. Only the portion CB of this frontier is efficient since all investors are assumed to prefer a higher expected return at identical risk. If A and B were perfectly negatively correlated (a sufficiently negative covariance), it would be possible to eliminate risk entirely, and the opportunity frontier would be the curve ADB, with DB being efficient.

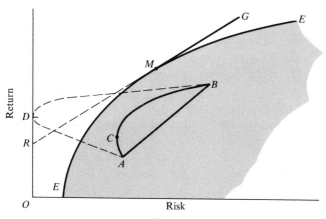

Figure 2-4

When more than two assets exist the set of portfolio return-risk combinations is no longer a single curve but becomes an area (shaded in the diagram). The calculation and delineation of the efficient frontier EE' becomes more complicated. Nevertheless it will always be convex from above as long as the outcomes of different portfolios are not perfectly correlated, and the maximum risk portfolio will always be undiversified.

The possibility of borrowing, which enables economic units to hold assets in excess of their own net-worth position, may easily be introduced into the above presentation. Borrowing raises the opportunity frontier from wealthownership by permitting debtor units to move to a higher return-risk combination on their wealth portfolios than they could attain with their own resources. For any portfolio combination of assets, e.g., M, the act of borrowing can be shown to extend the return-risk combination rightward along some straight line, e.g., MG. The slope of the extension MG will depend on the interest cost of debt, relative to the expected return on that asset combination M. The length of the extension MG is a function of the degree of leverage, that is, size of the loan relative to the borrower's net-worth position. As long as the obligation to pay interest on debt can be regarded as *certain*, MG is a straight line, and the borrowing rate OR may be measured on the y-axis as in Figure 2-4. Strictly speaking, in the real world no claims or obligations are of absolutely known and certain value.

This shows that, for any given interest cost of borrowing, ordinarily only *one* tangency-point combination of risky assets M will be financed by the issue of debt, *irrespective* of the degree of leverage undertaken. Other combinations will lie below MG unless the amount borrowed is limited.

The above argument assumes that the return on investment opportunities is independent of the amount of investment undertaken in any asset, otherwise MG would also be convex from above. If OR were to represent a risk-free lending rate, the efficiency frontier would be extended along MR. The implications of this analysis for the determination of financial asset prices are developed in Chapter 5.

PORTFOLIO BALANCE

It is finally possible to formulate a general theory of portfolio behavior. Each investor may be regarded as moving along his "efficient" opportunity curve, representing various portfolio combinations, until he reaches that position where his expected total utility from wealthownership is maximized. This may be illustrated by combining Figures 2-2 and 2-4. In Figure 2-5 the preferred diversified portfolio position for a risk averter is represented by the point P_E, where the efficient opportunity frontier EE' is tangent to the highest indifference curve. The slope of the indifference curve U_1 at P_E represents the marginal rate of substitution of return for risk, and may be regarded as an index of the assetholder's aversion to risk.

The preferred portfolio mix ordinarily would include some debt, issued until the marginal cost of borrowing bears a relationship to the expected marginal return on assets held which is specified by the degree of risk aversion.

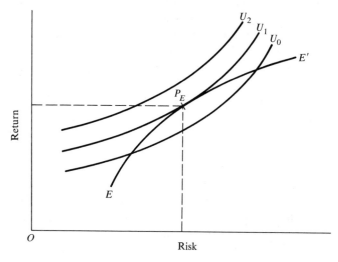

Figure 2-5

Some assetholders, for example risk neutrals and risk lovers, would choose the portfolio represented at E'. Such maximum risk portfolios will ordinarily include debt, and need not be undiversified in the sense of consisting of only one asset. The different assets held ordinarily will be complementary, as is the case with capital goods. More precisely, the expected return on most assets held in such port-folios are perfectly positively correlated with one another. Such asset combinations may be treated as a single asset for portfolio purposes.

The optimum portfolio composition will in general differ among various investors. It will depend both on their tastes and preferences that determine their expected utility from return and risk, and on the shape and position of the efficient opportunity frontier available to them.

The subsequent chapters are devoted to developing the implica-tions of financial change and financial control. In terms of Figure 2-5 such disturbances and controls operate by shifting the efficiency frontier from wealthholding EE' perceived by some or all investor units.

The particular portfolio composition that is optimum for each wealthowner will, as indicated, vary with the returns anticipated on alternative assets. An increase in the expected return on a particular asset, its risk remaining unchanged, will rotate the opportunity curve upward and, providing the "substitution" effect dominates the "income" effect, increase the proportion of that asset desired in the optimum portfolio.[6] This may be shown by rotating the efficiency frontier in Figure 2-5. The efficiency frontier EE' becomes flatter (steeper) as the expected return differential between assets decreases (increases). As indicated by the shape of the indifference curves of a risk averter in Figure 2-5, providing tastes and relative risk remain unchanged, the preferred diversification mix will shift to the left as the efficiency frontier between return and risk becomes flatter, and to the right as the efficiency frontier becomes steeper. If one asset is an inferior good, the income effect of a change in expected return could conceivably swamp this substitution effect. For a risk neutral or a risk lover the preferred portfolio may remain unchanged.

It is important to notice that the effects of a change in the current price of an asset on portfolio composition can be decomposed into the substitution and income effects of traditional demand theory *only* if current and expected future prices may be assumed independent. If elasticities of expectation are not zero, which for example is clearly the case with corporate equities, a change in current prices will affect expected future prices and so the expected return and utility from holding that asset. A rise in an asset's current price need not then reduce its expected return. If the portfolio frontier were defined in terms of *current* rather than *expected* return and risk, changes in expectations would then have to be incorporated into investors' utility functions, so that tastes or preferences could not be assumed independent.

6. For a detailed examination see W. Brainard and J. Tobin, *Financial Intermediaries and the Effectiveness of Monetary Controls*, Cowles Foundation Discussion Paper. No. 63 Revised 1962.

An abridged version has been published in the *American Economic Review*, Vol. LIII, No. 2 (May 1963).

These effects may be seen more clearly in the alternative presentation of Figure 2-6. Given two distinct assets with different return-risk probability outcomes, let a and b represent their respective anticipated mean returns, so that $b - a$ represents the anticipated return differential. In Figure 2-6 the horizontal distance OO represents an investor's total asset portfolio. The share of total assets held in asset A is measured from the left ordinate rightward, and the share of total assets held in asset B is measured from the right ordinate leftward.[7] The point P_1 indicates the optimum portfolio mix for a particular combination of anticipated returns a_1 and b_1, and represents an

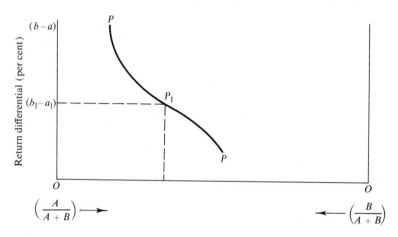

Figure 2-6

alternative presentation of the point P_E in Figure 2-5. As the return differential $b - a$ increases (decreases), relative risk remaining unchanged, a greater (smaller) proportion of total wealth is invested in holdings of asset B, and a relatively smaller (larger) proportion in asset A. The curve PP, which traces out for any individual investor his preferred diversification mix, will be termed the *portfolio-balance* relationship.

Providing that portfolio tastes and the distribution of wealth-

7. If the horizontal axis were defined in terms of absolute quantities of A and B, rather than their percentage share in total assets, the vertical axes must be regarded as spreading apart or together when total wealth changes.

ownership may be assumed to remain unchanged as asset prices and returns vary, it is possible simply to aggregate the preferences of all wealthowners, so as to derive a *portfolio-balance* relationship similar to that shown in Figure 2-6 for the entire economy.

The locus of preferred or equilibrium portfolio composition as asset prices and returns vary is represented by points along *PP* in Figure 2-6. If wealthowners when faced by a set of asset return-risk combinations are indifferent between some range of portfolio composition, the *PP* relationship must be visualized as a broad band rather than a line of equilibrium positions.

A change in asset market prices and returns will initially push wealthowners out of portfolio balance. From the previous analysis it is not possible to state *a priori* the rate at which various wealthholders will attempt to adjust their actual asset stocks to eliminate portfolio disequilibrium. They may restore portfolio balance rapidly by trading existing asset holdings, so as to maintain a preferred position on *PP*. Alternatively they may be content to move toward portfolio equilibrium more slowly, for example by adjusting only their new asset purchases out of current savings and funds from maturing issues. In general the rate of adjustment will vary both among wealthowners and among assets. The speed of adjustment to portfolio imbalance will be shown to play a critical role in the theory of the determination of asset market prices and returns and the analysis of monetary disturbance as developed in Chapters 5 and 8.

Heterogeneous Financial Behavior

As stated in Chapter 1, economic units may conveniently be classified as deficit spenders, balanced spenders and surplus spenders on current account, depending on whether their current expenditure on goods and services exceeds, equals, or is less than their current earned income. Similarly, economic units may be classified as debtor wealthowners, balanced wealthowners, or creditor wealthowners on balance-sheet account, depending on whether their holdings of non-financial assets exceed, equal, or are less than their total net worth, or, alternatively expressed, on whether their financial liabilities exceed, equal, or fall short of their financial asset holdings. These observed differences in financial behavior on income and wealth account may now be interpreted with the assistance of the analysis of the previous section.

Given any set of relative prices and distribution of income and wealth, the preferred portfolio composition of households, nonfinancial business units, and financial business units differs dramatically, even though each may be regarded as attempting to maximize expected utility from wealthownership. There are two distinct explanations for such heterogeneous behavior.

The first stems from differences in the set of investment opportunities (as illustrated in Figures 2-3 and 2-4) available to economic units from asset ownership, even in the face of the same set of relative asset prices. As developed in the previous chapter tangible assets differ widely from financial assets, particularly with regard to their degree of specificity, complementarity, and absence of an explicit income yield. The expected return from most tangible assets consequently varies widely with the holder, since their services are yielded only in cooperation with other factors. In general, the realization of their full potential income return requires as a prerequisite that existing stock of assets, experience, and expertise associated with a going business concern. This is itself sufficient to exclude households from holding most producer's goods. It is reinforced by the indivisibility of many tangible assets, and by the large scale of production required for efficient utilization that is beyond the net worth of even the wealthiest individual household wealthowners. As a result, business units rather than households are induced to hold tangible assets, since only they are equipped to combine the specific services of such assets to yield an attractive income return.

Aside from residential structures, land, and consumer durables, which for the most part yield services-in-kind that are directly utility-producing and supplementary, households choose to hold the overwhelming bulk of their wealth in the form of financial assets. The explicit services of most individual financial assets are largely supplementary, so that the anticipated return which ownership entails is less variable among holders than is the case with tangible assets. Nevertheless there are important diversification and scale economies that affect the opportunity curve from a large class of financial asset portfolios. This leads to specialization in the ownership of certain financial assets by financial business units, the implications of which will be examined in Chapters 4 and 5.

The second general explanation for differential financial behavior stems from differences in the utility function from income and wealthownership, in particular different tastes for risk and different preferences regarding the time path of future income. Economic units less adverse to bearing risk can satisfy these preferences by holding more risky assets and, by issuing debt, can hold total assets of an amount greater than their own net-worth position. Conversely greater risk averters can hold a larger part of their net worth in the form of those financial assets whose future capital and income values are relatively certain.

This diverse behavior on wealth account is related to diverse behavior on income account. Risk averters who have a greater-than-average taste for risk, risk neutrals, and risk lovers will typically be deficit-spending units out of current income, whereas risk avoiders, with a lower-than-average taste for risk, will choose a surplus-spending position. Households as a group are in all countries and under most circumstances on balance surplus spenders on income account, and creditors on wealth account. Business units in contrast are on balance characteristically deficit spenders on income account, and debtors on wealth account.

Although wide differences in behavior and in utility functions exist within the household and business sector, there is strong empirical and theoretical evidence to suggest that business units are typically characterized by a lower aversion to risk than household units. Virtually all economic behavior is consistent with the hypothesis that households are subject to decreasing marginal utility of income over most of their utility function. Insurance or diversification has no rationale for a decision maker whose utility function is linear in the outcome, and who wishes to maximize expected utility. The indifference curves of a "representative" business unit may therefore plausibly be expected to be less steeply upward-sloping than those of a "representative" household.

Conservative or risk-avoiding investor and business practices are after all rationally adopted precisely because capital resources are limited. Household and business asset behavior may be regarded as a particular strategy undertaken in a "game" against an opponent of vastly superior resources. This suggests that the larger net worth and possibilities of diversification of business units, and *a fortiori* of government units, is in itself sufficient to reduce their aversion to uncertainty in individual ventures below that of households.

It must immediately be acknowledged that within both household and business sectors there exist risk-neutral and risk-loving wealth-owners, whose behavior is consistent with the hypothesis that they anticipate, at least over some range, constant and even increasing marginal utility of income. Discontinuities in diminishing-utility functions may be sufficient to induce over-all risk avoiders to "take a long shot" with a small proportion of their wealth. A large part of such behavior may alternatively be explained in terms of the psychic return derived from the suspense of taking a chance, or simply by a basic striving to innovate, create, or succeed. The risk-lover concept may prove of interest for the analysis of innovational and entrepreneurial behavior. But it is likely to be descriptive of the portfolio preferences of only a small minority of economic units.

The imputation of a marginal utility of income schedule to a business corporation seems at first glance somewhat artificial, even when stripped of all hedonistic overtones. Yet most business behavior can be made plausible by regarding corporate managers as placing an evaluation or utility on different possible profit outcomes, and then attempting to maximize such a function, rather than attempting to maximize expected profits themselves. The relation of expected utility to expected business profits will vary with the type of institution, with socially and legally defined behavioral patterns, and with the structure of the markets within which it operates. The manner in which institutional preferences are formed, and how they shape institutional behavior, are considered in the following chapter.

Wealthowner preferences differ not only with regard to their attitude to the uncertain prospect of adverse returns or exceptional gains. Their utility functions from asset holding are also related to their preferred distribution of income through time. In a world where uncertainty and exchange costs exist the ranking of asset portfolios will be influenced by the time-shape of investors' accumulation objectives. For investors with distant objectives of wealth accumulation, the relevant choices may well include portfolio sequences over time in addition to an existing portfolio composition. Future events will add to the investor's information about the more distant future, and may change his preferences for risk, consumption, and accumulation. In the future, tastes as well as opportunities must be regarded as uncertain.

The ranking of assets and portfolios by expected riskiness is thus dependent on the timing of the future accumulation objectives of the assetholder. Since investors are not characterized by identical target dates for wealth accumulation, the distribution of wealth among economic units of different accumulation time preferences is an important determinant of the relative demand for assets of different maturities. If this distribution is weighted toward wealthowners with near (distant) objectives, the prices of short-term (long-term) financial assets will be relatively higher. The related implications of financial intermediation for the maturity structure of financial-asset yields will be examined in Chapter 4.

RECOMMENDED READING

In addition to the Paul Massé chapter previously referred to, a valuable summary of the at times mathematically formidable literature on decision making under uncertainty may be found in Kenneth Arrow, "Alternative Approaches to the Theory of Choice in Risk-Taking Situations," *Econometrica*, Vol. 19 (October, 1951).

The most thorough presentation of the effects of diversification, although developed for normative rather than explanatory purposes, is Harry M. Markowitz, *Portfolio Selection: Efficient Diversification of Investments* (New York, 1959). Part of James Tobin's work in this area has been published as "The Theory of Portfolio Selection" in F. H. Hahn and F. P. Brechling (eds.), *The Theory of Interest Rates* (London, 1965). See also his "Liquidity Preference as Behavior Towards Risk," *The Review of Economic Studies*, XXV (February, 1958). An excellent introduction to asset management under uncertainty may be found in Donald Farrar, *The Investment Decision Under Uncertainty* (New Jersey, 1962), Chapter 1.

William F. Sharpe has shown how the tendency of asset prices and returns to move together simplifies the process of investment choice in, "A Simplified Model for Portfolio Analysis," *Management Science*, Vol. 9, No. 2, (January, 1963). John Lintner has distinguished two types of portfolio decisions, the proportion of risky assets in a portfolio, and the composition of risky assets, for which standard deviation and variance respectively are the relevant measures of risk. "Security Prices, Risk, and Maximal Gains from Diversification," *The Journal of Finance*, Vol. XX, No. 4 (December, 1965).

For an alternative formulation of the problem of portfolio choice, see A. D. Roy, "Safety First and the Holding of Assets," *Econometrica*, Vol. 20 (1952).

3

The Interrelation of Financial
and Real Economic Behavior

*Though the high price of commodities be a necessary consequence
of the increase of gold and silver, yet it follows not immediately
upon that increase: . . . It is only in this interval or intermediate situation, . . . that the increasing quantity of gold and
silver is favourable to industry.*

—David Hume
Of Money, 1752

Introduction

The theory of asset management under uncertainty developed in
the last chapter was carried out at a high level of abstraction. In order
to give substantive content to the relationship between portfolio configurations and current expenditure of different decision makers it is
necessary to specify considerably more about the particular objectives,
institutions, and conventions that shape real and financial behavior.
This chapter examines the behavior of the two most important types
of private economic units: households and business firms. These
microeconomic models of individual decision units will form the build-
ing blocks for the hypotheses of aggregate behavior developed in
subsequent chapters.

The first part of this chapter introduces a number of elementary concepts that recur at various points throughout the book. Perhaps the most critical distinction is that between stock and flow dimensions, and how they affect the definition of equilibrium in asset markets. The second part examines the relationship between household capital and income accounts. Household consumption, saving, and investment decisions are interpreted as part of a life plan. It is shown that assets, and not saving, are what households desire. The rate of asset accumulation may be viewed as dependent upon the relationship between actual and desired asset stocks. A number of separate motives for asset holding are considered, which suggest an interpretation of the observed composition of household portfolios.

The third part considers the relationship between business behavior on capital and income account. Several types of business firms are distinguished. Business investment decisions are interpreted within a stock-adjustment framework. A dynamic model of investment behavior is developed which emphasizes the interdependence of financial, pricing, and growth policies in product, factor and financial markets.

The chapter concludes with a summary of the chief difficulties in formulating the cost of corporate capital. The effects of varying the leverage ratio, the retention rate, and the rate of growth of expected earnings on the cost of capital are examined consecutively.

Concepts and Definitions

The basic private decision units of an economy are households and business firms. The guiding principle of private economic behavior will be assumed to be expected utility maximization in the face of uncertainty.

Households attempt to estimate the likelihood of future events because they are concerned with maximizing utility not merely in the present, but over their entire anticipated lifetime. Household total utility is some function of the quantity of each type of good or service they are able to consume in the present, and the expected quantity, together with its likelihood, of different goods and services they will be able to command over their future horizon.

Households in a capitalist economy are the ultimate owners of business firms. As a result it is possible to regard the utility functions of firms as *derived* from the preferences of their owners with respect to present and future return and risk. The properties of such derived functions are dependent on the ability of owners to communicate and enforce their collective preferences on the business managers who actually administer their property. This ability, and resulting firm behavior, may be expected to vary among business units depending on firm size, the quality and degree of management control, conventional and legal standards of behavior for particular industries, and the structure of the markets in which the firm operates.

The reconciliation of stocks and flows has proven to be one of the most difficult problems in modern economics. *Stocks* represent the anount of an economic good outstanding at a moment in time. *Flows* denote the quantity of economic goods produced, consumed, exchanged, or received over some period of time. Unlike stocks, flows must always possess a time dimension. For example, the quantity of *money* outstanding is a stock, while the amount of *credit* or new loans extended over any period is a flow.

The change in a stock between two points in time equals the netflow acquisition over the period, minus the using up of the stock over the same time. For financial assets, which do not depreciate, the change in the stock outstanding is simply equal to the net flow, plus any capital gain or loss due to changes in asset valuation.

In national-income accounts the difference between current income and current consumption is defined as *saving*. Its magnitude will obviously depend on how income and consumption are defined and measured. Since *investment* is defined as all goods and services that are produced but not consumed, national saving and investment are identical by definition. Both are flow concepts. The stock of reproducible wealth represents the accumulation of past savings plus cumulative capital gains or losses.

As stated in Chapter 1 conventional national-income analysis ignores the financial side of the saving-investment process, the accompanying balance-sheet changes in asset stocks and liabilities.

For an individual economic unit net saving represents a positive addition to net worth. It is divided between net additions to existing stocks of financial and tangible assets, and reduction of debt. An increase in portfolio holdings of particular assets need not imply net saving, since it may also result from a portfolio exchange of previously existing assets, and from new borrowing.

The behavior of all decision units may thus be recorded on two related accounts, an *income* account and a *capital* account. The income account comprises *flows* over a period of time. The capital account records *stocks* of assets, liabilities, and net worth at a moment of time. By an elementary accounting identity, the increase in net worth of an economic unit over a period must equal its net saving over the period, plus any capital gain, or minus any capital loss.

The *behavioral* as distinct from the *accounting* connection between income and capital accounts follows from the fact that, in the presence of uncertainty, economic units as has been shown are not indifferent to the size and composition of their stocks of assets and liabilities. As a result, current-account activities depend in part on the structure of the capital account. Given their preferences, resources, opportunities, and expectations, economic units desire to hold particular quantities of different assets and liabilities at present and future dates. They adjust their actual holdings toward these desired holdings by regulating the net flow over some transitional adjustment period.

For any particular economic good, an *equilibrium price* refers to a situation of equality between supply and demand in the market period, so that there is no tendency for the price to change. For full equilibrium in asset markets two sets of equilibrium conditions must be fulfilled. The price must be such as to equate at a moment in time the portfolio demand for the asset with the existing stock of the asset. This may be termed *stock equilibrium*. The price must also be such as to equate the supply of the asset over some market period (the increment to outstanding stocks) with incremental (flow) demand for the asset over the same period. This may be termed *flow equilibrium.*

As will be shown in Chapter 5, when using the concepts of equilibrium and disequilibrium with reference to asset markets it is important so specify the type of equilibrium referred to, since the time period of adjustment may be very different. There may be no tendency for prices to change in the short run if one set of relationships is satisfied, yet a considerable change may be required over a longer run to satisfy another set of equilibrium relationships.

The speed at which actual asset stocks are adjusted to desired asset holdings will vary among assets according to asset characteristics and the conditions of the market on which they are traded, and among decision units depending on their utility functions, exchange and decision costs, and opportunities and expectations. In empirical estimation it is frequently convenient to assume that the speed of response is directly proportional to the difference between actual and desired quantities, so that the period of adjustment is constant.

Analysis which considers only initial and final equilibrium positions resulting from a change in the data is termed *comparative static* analysis. *Dynamic* analysis deals with the equilibrium or disequilibrium behavior of the variables in which one is interested over some noninstantaneous time period. Comparative static analysis may be regarded as a special case of dynamic analysis in which the events of the adjustment path do not affect the convergence to a unique and stable equilibrium, so that the conclusions of both analyses correspond.

General equilibrium analysis attempts to recognize explicitly the mutually interdependent character of all economic variables. *Partial equilibrium* analysis focuses on certain variables and certain markets, and assumes away the effects of others. Partial analysis typically represents an attempt to render intelligible the complexity of economic processes by characterizing them in cause-and-effect terms. In a fully interrelated system the notion of causality becomes obscure because of the difficulty or impossibility of establishing the unidirectional nature of simultaneous interrelationships. To reduce this complexity to manageable proportions, without using the methodology implied by cause-and-effect notations, it is convenient for many purposes to break the circle of interdependence by distinguishing *dependent variables* and *exogeneous variables*, which are determined outside the system. *Policy instruments* represent one type of exogeneous variable over which public authorities exert control.

Household Saving and Investment Decisions

In national-income accounting, saving is defined as the difference between income and consumption. From *defining* saving as a residual it was but a short step to regard saving *behavior* as residually determined. It was John Maynard Keynes who initially hypothesized, as "a fundamental psychological law," that consumption expenditures are a highly stable and dependable function of current income. After the decision on the proportion of income to be saved, Keynes argued that individuals must then decide on the form in which they wanted to hold their savings.

In a world of perfect certainty and perfect markets only the first decision would be necessary. Yet even under such circumstances the decision to save cannot be divorced from portfolio considerations. *Most fundamentally this is because it is assets, and not saving, that households desire.* The desired amount of asset accumulation is in general no more "residually" determined than any other household outlay.

Once saving is viewed as the demand to accumulate assets, purchases of consumer durables and investment in education become of the nature of capital expenditures. Consumption ideally should then be defined as expenditure on nondurable goods and services, plus the depreciation and carrying costs of direct-service-yielding capital goods. Income ideally should be defined to include the total flow of services from asset stocks. In practice it is extremely difficult to measure the value of stocks of consumer durable goods and the imputed current services which they yield. Investment in human capital likewise presents formidable measurement problems. This wide divergence between theoretical constructs and observed magnitudes occurs in most areas of economic behavior. Ordinarily it necessitates more restrictive assumptions about behavior in order to generate operational hypothesis for empirical research. Unless otherwise noted investment expenditure will henceforth be used to refer to the accumulation of all forms of capital assets.

LIFE-CYCLE THEORIES OF SAVING

As an alternative to Keynes' misleading and somewhat mysterious "law," it will prove instructive to review briefly the pure theory of consumer's choice. Consider first the case of perfect certainty. Each individual is assumed to attempt to maximize total utility, which is derived from present and future consumption and from net worth to be bequeathed. The condition for utility maximization is that the individual must so allocate his expenditures that the expected marginal utility from the last dollar spent on each commodity purchased is identical.

The allocation of income and wealth between present and future consumption may be illustrated for a two-period model with conventional indifference-curve analysis. In Figure 3-1 present consumption C_P is measured on the horizontal axis, and future consumption of the next period C_F on the vertical axis. Bequests must be considered future consumption. The slope of the indifference curves indicate the rate at which the individual is willing to substitute future for present consumption. The individual's present income is Y_P and his future income is Y_F. If r is the rate at which future income is discounted

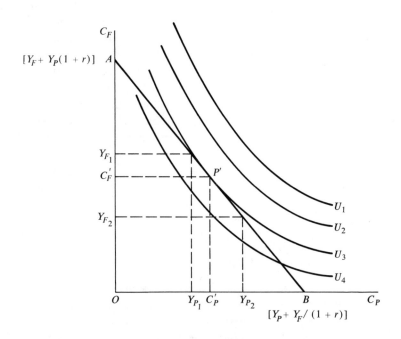

Figure 3-1

over the period, his present wealth is $Y_{F/(1+r)}$, and his future wealth, if he spent nothing in the present, would be $Y_P (1 + r)$. This defines his budget restraint line AB, and represents his consumption possibilities over the two years. The slope of AB is equal to $(1 + r)$.

The optimum allocation is the point at which the budget line is tangent to the highest indifference curve, the point P' in Figure 3-1. Present consumption is C'_P and future consumption C'_F. The amount currently saved will ordinarily be positively related to the interest rate, but may be negatively related if the "income effect" dominates the "substitution effect." In a two-dimensional diagram multiperiod future income and consumption must somehow be represented by the single and composite quantities Y_F and C_F.

This extremely elementary and general presentation already reveals that there need not be any close and regular relation between consumption and income over any short period. This may be demonstrated in Figure 3-1 by varying the relative size of Y_P and Y_F along the constant total present and future consumption possibilities line AB, eg. $Y_{P_1} Y_{F_1}$ and $Y_{P_2} Y_{F_2}$, so that present and future consumption remain unchanged. The amount of current consumption is part of a plan which extends over an individual's lifetime, and may be expected to be adjusted to what he regards as his "normal" or "permanent" income, rather than his current receipts. As can be visualized from Figure 3-1, saving may occur at zero and even negative rates of interest if, e.g., present income is substantially greater than future income.

It follows that with perfect certainty and perfect markets there would be only two motives for saving, that is, for accumulating the single asset with the highest perfectly foreseen return. The first is to adjust the time-shape of prospective lifetime receipts to the pattern of preferred consumption over the individual's life horizon. The need to maintain some level of consumption after retirement is of paramount importance in this objective. The second is the simple desire to add to future net worth, presumably for the benefit of one's heirs.

The introduction of uncertainty and asset exchange costs present insuperable complications for the above diagrammatic presentation. Since neither future tastes, future incomes, nor future interest rates can be forecast perfectly, the sharp separation shown in Figure 3-1 between tastes and opportunities is destroyed. The utility attached to any outcome therefore no longer depends solely on its expected value, which could be represented along AB in the diagram. As shown in the previous chapter the degree of uncertainty which characterizes the subjective probability distribution of outcomes now enters as an

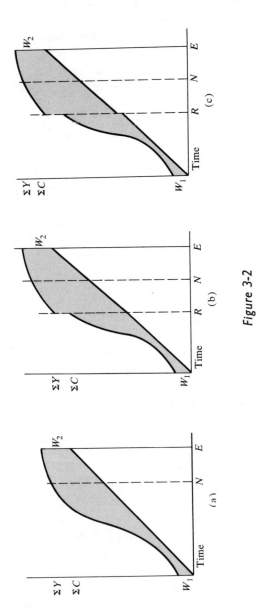

Figure 3-2

argument in household utility functions. In consequence a change in prices, return, or expectations will in general shift the position of the indifference map portrayed in Figure 3-1. The quarry must now be pursued on foot.

Even in the presence of imperfect foresight, planned consumption expenditures may plausibly be regarded as related to the individual's normal or permanent income anticipated over his decision horizon. This suggests that a change in current income will affect an individual's current consumption primarily through its effect on his expected normal income.

The marginal propensity to save out of short-run changes in current income is extremely unstable. The quantitative magnitude of windfall income and capital gains or losses on current consumption expenditure is an empirical issue which has not yet been completely resolved. The effect of changes in capital values on current consumption will clearly depend in part on whether such changes are regarded as temporary or permanent. The marginal propensity to save is also likely to increase with the relative size of the windfall. Some alternative possibilities are presented in Figure 3-2[1].

Cumulative current income and consumption are measured on the vertical axis and time is measured on the horizontal axis. Households accumulate assets and plan their consumption to maximize utility over some expected lifespan E. In Figure 3-2a it is assumed that planned consumption is equal each year. Expected working life is represented by N, inherited wealth equals W_1, and W_2 represents the positive target bequest. Net worth at any time equals the shaded vertical difference between cumulative current income and current consumption.

Imagine that an unanticipated once-and-for-all capital gain occurs at time R. The evidence to date suggests that household consumption and saving response is more closely approximated by Figure 3-2b, depicting a substantially lower but still positive short-run propensity to consume out of transitory income. Figure 3-2c represents a situation in which capital gains are fully incorporated into normal income in the period in which they occur.

There is considerable evidence that many individuals behave as

1. The diagram has been adapted from J. Arena, "The Wealth Effect on Consumption: A Statistical Inquiry," *Yale Economic Essays* (Fall, 1963).

if they have a "life-cycle" savings plan as illustrated in Figure 3-2. The proportion of income saved rises and then falls with age. It is also positively associated with the degree of instability associated with current income, as occurs in certain occupations and as evidenced by farmers and businessmen. The hypothesis that the ratio of normal consumption to normal income is independent of total resources has not yet been empirically established.

The "life-cycle" hypothesis states that net worth is built up over an individual's working life for dissaving after retirement. As a result, aggregate saving will be positively related to the rate of growth of the population, since the more rapidly-growing the population the smaller the proportion of dissavers. Similarly, aggregate saving may be expected to be positively related to the rate of growth of per capital real income, since a higher growth rate implies a relatively smaller level of normal income and consumption for dissavers than for savers.

The presence of uncertainty and asset exchange costs give rise to at least three additional motives for acquiring assets. Households in an uncertain world will desire to accumulate assets as a *precautionary* reserve against unforeseen contingencies. Certain assets are particularly suited to serve as a buffer of liquid purchasing power against unexpectedly low receipts or high consumption needs. They also serve to be held for *speculative* purposes. As a result many assets provide satisfaction not merely because they represent command over future consumption, but because in addition they reduce the uncertainty that unanticipiated future needs and opportunities may not be satisfied.

As developed in the previous chapter, in the face of uncertainty assets are desired on the grounds of portfolio *diversification* to reduce the total risk associated with wealthownership. The type of assets demanded for this purpose are not necessarily low-risk assets, but assets whose expected returns are independent of, or negatively correlated with, the return expected on other assets in the portfolio.

Finally, uncertainty combined with imperfect markets limit an individual's ability to incur debt beyond a certain proportion of his total assets. Asset exchange costs ordinarily drive a wedge between his borrowing and lending rates, and raise the cost of renting many services that assets yield. This provides an additional motive for asset accumulation. It is frequently *cheaper* to buy an equity in rather than to rent "lumpy" tangible assets if it is desired to receive services from them.

THE BEHAVIORAL RELATIONSHIP BETWEEN HOUSEHOLD INCOME AND CAPITAL ACCOUNTS

Upon the basic hypothesis that consumers possess a utility function based upon the flow of economic goods consumed over their entire life cycle, and so derive utility from the stock of assets held at any point in time, a model may be developed to explain the manner in which consumers allocate their resources between current consumption and asset accumulation. The hypothesis implies that with a constant real income there is a limit to the quantity of assets that will be accumulated. Otherwise expressed there is, at least over a wide range of consumers, some level of wealth that will induce zero and even negative saving out of current income.

Given current and expected future income, and the stage in the life cycle, there exists some desired or equilibrium ratio of net worth, and of individual assets and liabilities, to consumption. Although an individual asset may be demanded for more than one motive, different asset forms typically have a comparative advantage in satisfying specific needs. It follows that the amount of current income saved will be dependent upon the relationships between desired and actual stocks of different assets and liabilities. In general the change in each stock will be negatively related to the initial level of the stock in question, but positively related to the initial level of other stocks.

This may be shown more rigorously. The *desired* stock of any particular asset or debt A_t^* at the end of the tth period may be expected to be a function of consumer tastes, normal income, the stage in the life cycle, total nonhuman wealth, and relative asset prices and returns. For simplicity all variables except normal income Y_t will be ignored. The linear approximation may then be written

$$A_t^* = a + b(Y_t) \tag{1}$$

where $b > 0$. Let A_{t-1} be the *actual* stock of the asset existing at the end of the $t - 1$ period. Saving or asset accumulation may then be described as some adjustment of actual to desired asset stocks:

$$A_t - A_{t-1} = c_t(A_t^* - A_{t-1}) \qquad (2)$$

where $(0 \leqslant c_t \leqslant 1)$. The constant c_t varies between zero and one, and measures the fraction of the adjustment households make toward equating their actual and desired asset stocks during the period t. It is likely to vary for different assets, different stages in the life cycle and different households. When $c_t = 1$, the adjustment is completed during the period of observation t.

Equation (2) provides a simple and commonly used model to describe the adjustment process. Substituting Equation (1) into Equation (2), asset and debt accumulation may be seen to be positively related to income, and negatively related to the existing stock of the asset.

$$(A_t - A_{t-1}) = c_t a + c_t b(Y_t) - c_t(A_{t-1}) \qquad (3)$$

or

$$A_t = (1 + c_t) A_{t-1} + c_t a + c_t b(Y_t) \qquad (4)$$

Empirical estimation of stock-adjustment models similar to Equations (3) or (4) for a variety of financial assets generally yield low values of $c_t(0.1-0.2)$ over a period t of three months. This suggests slow rates of adjustment to portfolio imbalance. Too much confidence cannot yet be placed in these results, since it may be shown that ordinary least-squares estimates of c_t are seriously biased downward in the presence of certain changes in tastes, or serial correlation in the data, such as occur in virtually all economic time series.

THE COMPOSITION OF HOUSEHOLD CAPITAL ACCOUNTS

Observed household portfolio composition in the aggregate is relatively stable in the short run. Moreover changes in relative asset prices alone appear to explain only a small proportion of observed variation in asset holdings. There are a number of explanations for inelastic household portfolio preferences among broad asset categories. Although an asset may be held for a number of purposes, different assets are not equally efficient substitutes for each objective. Variations in the importance of different wealth objectives among different individuals, and over various points in the life cycle for the same individual, are reflected in wide differences in the composition of individual household balance sheets.

Households with lower net worth, and households in the early stages of family formation, put a larger proportion of their wealth and saving into consumer durables and houses. They ordinarily find it necessary or desirable to incur debt to finance the purchase of such assets. Very high rates of return may be anticipated from the acquisition of most durable goods in comparison with the costs of acquiring similar services in the market place.[2] This in turn provides a rational basis for borrowing.

For households already owning a particular durable, the return on investment in another asset of the same kind drops rapidly. Households are therefore likely to have large positive or negative margins between their yield on investment and their cost of borrowing. As a result variations in consumer loan interest rates, and moderate variations in the relative price of durable goods, are not likely markedly to alter the volume of consumer investment in durables.

Consumer durables are held primarily for the specific services they supply, which for the most part are not close substitutes for other asset services. With the exception of some observed association with liquid assets (negative) and debt (positive) household acquisition of durables does not appear to be related closely to considerations of overall portfolio composition. Households do not appear to regard their stock of durables primarily as potential command over resources, but rather in terms of the services they yield. Home ownership represents the largest single commitment of wealth for most households. It appears to have an important impact on portfolio composition between real and financial assets and debt. The proportion of con·sumer durables and real estate in household asset portfolios falls sharply as wealth and income levels increase.

The speculative and precautionary motive for holding wealth is best satisfied by liquid assets: cash, demand deposits, and savings deposits in financial institutions. The effect of stocks of liquid assets on consumption is difficult to evaluate empirically. A higher ratio of liquid asset holdings to income may reflect greater thriftiness and risk

2. Depending most importantly on the number of children, the annual return on an automatic washer and dryer have been estimated to range between 1 and 27 per cent, and on a television set from negative to 77 per cent. J. Poapst and W. Waters, "Rates of Return on Consumer Durables," *Journal of Finance*, Vol. XIX, No. 4 (December, 1964).

aversion (differences in taste), or larger reserves against contingencies. A large majority of all financial assetholders hold only liquid assets, which suggests that they either lack the financial sophistication and information to take advantage of investments bearing a higher yield, or do not regard nonliquid assets as being sufficiently marketable.

The ratio of liquid-asset holdings to income is positively related to the age of consumer units, suggesting that the need for precautionary reserves increases with age. As previously stated it is negatively related to family size and stocks of durable goods. Consumers who expect higher future incomes hold a lower proportion of liquid assets, and have lower current saving. As wealth and income levels increase, the ratio of liquid assets to income first declines, and then rises again at the highest income ranges.

Asset accumulation for retirement income is satisfied for a large proportion of households by contractual saving in public and private pension funds, life insurance premiums, and annuity or mortgage payments. Conventional saving rules-of-thumb are not obviously irrational for households with stable incomes, even though such arrangements ordinarily reduce the short-run variability of the saving ratio over the life cycle. Households typically have little ability to alter their net worth held in these reserves in response to changes in the return and price of other assets, or in the level of income.

Asset accumulation for intergeneration transfers of wealth is best served by equity in corporate and noncorporate businesses, which offer protection *par excellence* against long-term erosion in the purchasing power of money. Equity ownership as a proportion of total assets is strongly positively related to income and wealth level, so that the distribution of stock ownership is highly skewed.[3]

For this reason capital gains and losses on corporate equities, even if completely foreseen, affect the capital accounts and so the behavior of only a very small proportion of household units. The very large experienced capital gains in the postwar period have had no dis-

3. In the United States in 1962 the top five per cent of all consumer units received twenty per cent of total personal income, but owned ninety per cent of total corporate stock held by the household sector. Among stockholders, the upper seven per cent, which made up less than one per cent of all consumer units, possessed seventy per cent of all corporate stock. "Survey of Financial Characteristics of Consumers," *Federal Reserve Bulletin* (March, 1964).

cernable impact on aggregate consumption expenditures. Otherwise expressed, if household disposable income were defined to include capital gains or losses, shifts in disposable income resulting from stock market fluctuations cause virtually identical movements in household saving. As will be developed in Chapter 10, a large part of capital gains on equities in a growing economy may be regarded as *involuntary* household saving, undertaken by tangible wealth administrators in the form of corporate depreciation and retained earnings for the ultimate owners of business enterprises.

The transfer of assets to succeeding generations are in part deliberate (bequests and gifts), and in part an unused residual of assets intended for consumption. Questionnaire surveys indicate that liquid assets and real estate are the most favored form of assets for bequest purposes. This is not surprising when it is remembered that the vast majority of wealthholders do not own corporate equities. It does underline the fact that there is not always a close correspondence between motives for asset accumulation and the characteristics of particular wealth forms.

As increasingly important proportion of capital transfers now takes the form of human investment in the education of the younger generation. This suggests that in order to comprehend the behavioral relation between household income and capital accounts it would be desirable to record expenditures for education as an investment rather than a consumption good, and to include estimates of human as well as nonhuman capital in household portfolios. Investment in education clearly competes with the holding of tangible and financial assets and debts as well as with consumption outlays, and may be more closely related to the former.

To recapitulate: in the face of uncertainty there is both theoretical and empirical evidence that households attempt to maintain some balanced portfolio position, depending on their tastes, occupation, age, information, and opportunities. Each form of asset appears to have a desired normal level. The recognition of saving as a demand for assets underlines the perhaps obvious fact that, with regard to the goal of economic development and growth, the crucial relationship is not simply the magnitude of the *ratio* of saving to income, but the *form* that saving takes. The diversion of current income to the accumulation of land, cathedrals, precious metals, or inventories will not in itself generate a rise in future productive capacity. It is the particular set of assets that are accumulated, the investment rather than the saving process, which is critical.

As will be developed in the following chapter, financial assets play an important role in the growth process by facilitating the transfer of purchasing power from surplus- to deficit-spending units to finance real capital formation. A partial balance sheet, showing household financial asset and debt holdings in the United States, is presented in Table 3-1.

Table 3-1—Household Financial Assets and Liabilities,
Dec. 31, 1965 (Billions of Dollars)

ASSETS		LIABILITIES	
Liquid Assets	370		
Demand Deposits and Currency	93	Mortgages	217
Time and Saving Accounts at		Consumer Credit	86
Commercial Banks	106	Other Loans	34
Time and Saving Accounts at			
Saving Institutions	171		
Credit Market Instruments	802		
U.S. Government Securities	79		
State and Local Obligations	40		
Corporate Stock	669		
Life Insurance Reserves	105		
Pension Fund Reserves	152		
Total Financial Assets	£1,447	Total Liabilities	£342

Source: Table 5, Flow of Funds Accounts, *Federal Reserve Bulletin*, May, 1966,

Business Saving and Investment Decisions

The principle object of the business sector is the earning of profit from combining tangible assets and labor in the production of goods and services. Business units may be viewed as providing the intermediary function of administering the stock of real productive assets for their ultimate household owners. Income earned by firms is distributed either directly, or if retained indirectly in the form of capital gains, to household owners of claims against the business sector. Part of household voluntary saving is used to acquire additional claims against business units, and so to finance business tangible asset accumulation.

THE UTILITY FUNCTION OF BUSINESS FIRMS

As previously suggested the utility function of business units with regard to present and future return and risk may be regarded as *derived* from the preferences of their owners. The nature of this derivation, and the resulting institutional preference map, may be shown to depend importantly on the internal structure of the firm.

In the case of small owner-managed firms the utility function of owner and firm may be regarded as identical. Each firm can legitimately be treated as a single person, with a unified and integrated set of preferences. The traditional theory of the firm is here most applicable. For large business corporations, where ownership and management are separated, there need not be a one-to-one correspondence of the preferences of managers and owners in all situations, It is further possible to distinguish fiduciarily-owned firms, such as mutual companies, whose managers are similar to trustees and have no significant ownership claims themselves. There are also nonownership 'firms,' such as nonprofit organizations, where no legal ownership right to receive earnings even exists. Different principles of behavior may be appropriate to explain the behavior of these different types of firms. The objective of profit maximization is not universally applicable. It is clearly inappropriate for nonownership firms, and may be replaced by the more general formulation of utility maximization.

Pursuit of self-interest is a characteristic of human persons, not organizations. It follows that in those types of firms where the functions of ownership and management are carried out by separate groups of people, individuals in each group may reasonably be regarded as motivated by their own self-interest.

Corporate shareowners typically possess only very limited *ex post* information about a firm's situation. The fact that the rights of ownership can be transferred inexpensively and easily produces a relatively impersonal relationship between the modern corporation and its owners. Stockholders are typically apathetic in exercising their voting rights. Most stockholders would rather switch than fight. Under such circumstances owners may be pushed to being "*satisficers*" rather than *maximizers.* Equity holders are likely to approve of a firm's management providing only that some minimal criteria of performance based on comparisons with competitors is realized. What then are these criteria?

Stockholders are interested in the return on their own investment. The earning of a large absolute *level* of profits on the historical value of capital invested in the firm is not ordinarily sufficient to ensure management a quiet life. Stockholders will be concerned that future earnings do not *fall.* But current owners may have bought in when the equity price level already reflected this high current yield on investment. In any case their own current rate of return will be much lower, as determined by the stock market. This reveals that stockholders benefit not from a high *level* of profits *per se,* but rather from *increases* in the level of profits. They will particularly be concerned that earnings and dividends for a firm *grow* over time, so as to produce a higher yield on the historical value of their own investment. In addition in an expanding economy growth is essential merely to maintain a firm's competitive market position *vis-à-vis* its competitors. For both of these reasons stockholders are concerned fundamentally about the *growth prospects* of their corporation, rather than with static profit maximization.

The valuation of an individual firm's shares by the stock market does of course ensure that its rate of profit on invested capital will be compared to the rates earned by other firms. Stockholders benefit from an *increase* in profits from whatever source. This serves *ex post* to punish inefficient and unprofitable management. The threat of potential shareholder rebellion may create for top management an asymmetry in the punishments for exceptional misfortune and the rewards for outstanding success, leading to high risk aversion. Recognizing that capital market discipline over management is weakened by investor ignorance and apathy, and by the ability of many firms to obtain capital internally and so to avoid any direct capital market test, *investors are likely to be chiefly concerned with the dynamic performance of profits over time.*

Corporate managers may similarly be presumed to act to maximize their own individual utility functions, which include expected lifetime salary, bonuses, power, prestige, leisure, and prospect of failure. A number of eminent writers have argued that the divorce of ownership from control, and the bureaucratic structure of large corporations, cause manager and owner preferences to deviate systematically. Sheer size both compels owners to delegate authority, and at the same time makes it impossible for owners to control fully management behavior. The extent of this conflict is difficult to test operationally, apart from questions such as management salaries and expenses.

The most important characteristics of manager utility functions for present purposes concern the variables that they are led to maximize and the constraints that apply with regard to investment and financial behavior. In general, firm investment and saving decisions will be subject to the underlying constraint that expected outcomes be consistent with a satisfactory environment for present management. Some growth in the level of profits is ordinarily necessary to keep the shareholders from baying at the door. This ensures an investment in research and development directed towards technical innovation in production and consumption. "Successful firms both forsee events and make events."[4] In addition, for any firm possessing some market power in product markets there is ordinarily a tradeoff between the profit markup over costs at which it sells its products, and the rate at which it can expect to expand its future sales and future earnings. At the same time lower current profits reduce the funds available to finance expansion. Similarly increased earnings-retention increases the funds available for investment, but at the expense of current dividend income.

The decision rule for such alternatives that is in the current shareowners best interest is, "Maximize the market value of the shares held by the current owners of the firm." The implications of this criterion will be explored in the discussion of the cost of corporate capital in the subsequent section. It must be emphasized that this is a normative rather than a descriptive rule of management behavior. What deviations from this rule are likely to occur in actuality due to the location of ownership and control in different groups?

There is unfortunately no general consensus as yet as to what firms actually do attempt to maximize. Maximization of individual share price is identical to maximization of the total value of all shares outstanding only for the case in which the number of shares is held con-

---

4. R. J. Ball, *Inflation and the Theory of Money* (Chicago, 1964), p. 92.

stant. Which is applicable? Questions of control apart, the psychic and possibly disclosure costs to financial managers of floating new share issues in themselves appear to lead management to be predisposed to favor internal generation as a source of new funds. Neither of the above maximization targets is equivalent to maximization of the total market value of the firm, including debt and equity securities. Each rule leads to different decisions, each may be an appropriate nomative rule for different wealthowner groups, and none may be descriptive of actual management behavior. The relationships of managerial indifference maps to those of ultimate owners remains a difficult problem for the theory of collective choice.

Stock options are a widely used means to reduce divergence between owner and manager self-interest. Both managers and owners may then be less likely to finance rapid expansion out of new stock offerings, due to concern for the dilution of their own interest, even if this conflicts with maximization of share prices. It is widely believed that an increase in the supply of a corporation's stock will temporarily depress its value. The existence of stock options reinforces management preferences for internal generation, and in general leads to divergence of interest with regard to retention policy. Since the holder of a stock option is not entitled to dividends during the period when he possesses only the option, the dividend payout optional for an option holder will always be lower than the level optional for a stockholder.

As suggested in the previous chapter, a firm may fruitfully be viewed as a portfolio of tangible and financial assets, whose over-all composition is by no means completely specified by technological factors. Due to the difficulty of integrating information, control, and responsibility within a bureaucratic hierarchy, top-level managers may be unable, and lower-level managers unwilling, to operate on the firm's opportunity frontier. As a result the firm remains within the feasible opportunity set. The recognition that the utility functions of both owners and managers include security ensures that firms will not be neutral with regard to risk, i.e., that return-risk indifference curves will not be horizontal.

Shareowner risk aversion is reflected in the price at which the stock market capitalizes the corporation's future earnings stream. Top management will avoid highly risky ventures or policies, such as a highly levered financial structure, if the detrimental effect of the possibility of lower future earnings on share prices, or manager discomfort, more than offsets their higher expected value. Restrictions on competition, at least to the extent permitted by law, must be viewed as a means of reducing risk as well as of increasing return. Diversification, both by product innovation and by merger that does not involve horizontal or vertical integration, represents an attractive and legally permitted means of reducing risk for corporate tangible asset managers as well as for managers of financial asset portfolios. Such firms will have lower average profit rates, but less variability of earnings growth, than if expected profit maximization alone were the criterion. Managers may in addition be expected to avoid policies, such as dependance on external sources of finance, whose adverse possible outcomes are likely to punish, embarass, or reduce the control of present management, even if on balance such policies may be expected to maximize share prices.

BUSINESS SAVING AND INVESTMENT UNDER PERFECT CERTAINTY

Under the assumptions of perfect certainty and perfect markets the saving and investment behavior of business firms may be simply stated. Due to the presence of diminishing returns and diminishing marginal utility the marginal efficiency of investment schedule for the individual firm slopes downward. As the classical model dictates, the firm will maximize profits providing it continues to invest until the marginal efficiency of investment equals the marginal cost of raising capital. Under perfect certainty, irrespective of the size of a corporation's profits, the cost of capital schedule is a perfectly elastic function at the single market rate of interest. This represents the opportunity cost of borrowing or lending purchasing power. This situation is illustrated in Figure 3-3.

Under such circumstances financial policy disappears. For any given (known) level of investment and future earnings, the finance mix selected cannot affect the total value of the firm. The retention ratio, and the division between internal and external finance, is irrelevant. Dividend policy serves merely to determine the division of stockholders' return between current cash receipts and capital appreciation. Retained earnings always yield identical capital gains. They are equivalent to full dividend pay-out, simultaneously accompanied by a

fully-subscribed preemptive issue of common stock. The division
between equity and debt external finance is also irrelevant. The return
on equity and on debt is identically equal to the return on tangible
assets. The total value of a firm's securities would always equal the

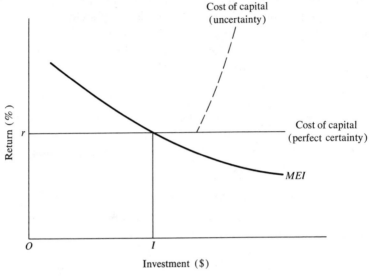

Figure 3-3

book value of its assets. In fact, as developed in the previous chapter,
under perfect certainty financial assets and financial behavior would
be nonexistent.

Under real-world conditions there exists a bewildering variety of
securities and anticipated yields, each with different kinds of claims to
a portion of the uncertain future earnings of the firm. It is no longer
obvious which yield or combination of yields is the relevant cost of
capital for rational investment decisions. The supply schedule of
capital is no longer perfectly elastic, but as shown in Figure 3-3 is
sharply upward-sloping in the short run. Variables measuring the
availability of funds—depreciation, retained earnings, liquid assets,
debt—play an important role in the explanation of investment behavior. The relevance of financial policy emerges because alternative
sources of raising capital have different costs.

A STOCK-ADJUSTMENT VIEW OF INVESTMENT BEHAVIOR

The elasticity of the cost of capital curve has important implications for investment behavior. Business firms like other assetholders may be regarded as having some desired stock of tangible assets for a given level of sales and income. The desired stocks of different tangible assets are usually regarded as determined jointly by technological considerations, market and risk considerations, and relative factor prices.

Let *desired* holdings of tangible assets at the end of the tth period be represented by K_t^*. Ignoring all variables except current income Y_t, the linear approximation may be written:

$$K_t^* = a + b(Y_t) \tag{1}$$

where $b > 0$. Let K_{t-1} represent the *actual* stock of tangible assets owned by business units at the end of the $t - 1$ period. Business investment expenditures in the tth period I_t may then be regarded as the adjustment of actual tangible asset holdings to desired levels:

$$K_t - K_{t-1} = I_t = d_t(K_t^* - K_{t-1}) \tag{2}$$

where $(0 \leqslant d_t \leqslant 1)$.

Substituting (1),

$$I_t = e + f(Y_t) - d_t(K_{t-1}) \tag{3}$$

The constant d_t represents the speed-of-adjustment coefficient. It measures the proportion of the adjustment completed during the period t, and is affected by existing stocks of debt outstanding, the elasticity of the cost of capital schedule, and the elasticity of supply of capital goods.

In the polar case of rapid stock adjustment, $d_t = 1$, so that the actual capital stock at the end of each period equals the desired stock. Equation 3 may then be rewritten::

$$I_t = e + b(Y_t - Y_{t-1}) \tag{4}$$

This states that the level of investment is some function of the *change* in the level of output, as implied by *accelerator* and sales theories of investment behavior.

In the opposite polar case of slow stock adjustment, $d_t = 0$. Equation (3) may then be rewritten:

$$I_t = e + f(Y_t). \tag{5}$$

This states that the level of investment expenditure is some function of the *level* of output and income, as implied by retained earnings and *capital availability* theories of investment.

In the real world corporations are faced with inelastic cost of capital schedules. Investment is backlogged in periods when investment opportunities are very favorable. Most evidence suggests that the rate of adjustment of actual to desired tangible stocks is very slow, and only completed over a period t as long as several years.

Business saving and investment behavior on income account is in this manner dependent on corporate capital account variables, in particular the imbalance between desired and actual tangible asset stocks relative to the cost and availability of corporate capital.

In addition to physical assets, nonfinancial business firms hold financial assets for transaction and precautionary balances. Their desired holdings of liquid assets will be related to taste for risk, the level and variability of sales, the expected return differential on existing investment opportunities, and the variance of their expected net earnings flow so as to meet interest obligations and maintain a steady dividend flow.

Quantitatively the most important financial asset held and owed by business firms in the aggregate is trade credit. This is a financial instrument that reduces the reliance on credit and the need for means of payment for the business sector as a whole. Trade credit permits a permanent rise in business total assets, financed by short-term credit payable.

Business firms similarly have some preferred ratio of debt to total assets. New debt issue may be viewed as the adjustment of actual to desired levels of debt outstanding. Business firms in the aggregate have maintained over the long run a relatively stable ratio of debt to total assets, even though the leverage of individual firms, even within the same industry, varies widely.

BUSINESS SAVING AND INVESTMENT UNDER UNCERTAINTY

It is finally possible to formulate a dynamic theory of corporate saving and investment behavior. In a world of uncertainty, technological change and imperfect markets, the saving and investment behavior of modern business corporations cannot be adequately comprehended in terms of static maximizing assumptions. Prices, profits, and the supply of capital for growing firms are intrinsically interrelated. A great deal of traditional static analysis of the firm is normative rather than positive. While it offers criteria for *judging* existing market behavior, it provides few predictions or testable hypotheses offering an explanation of how firms *actually* behave.

For firms possessing market power, pricing policy is related to the long-run growth of the firm as well as its short-run profitability. Administered prices unlike competitive prices are relatively insensitive in the short run to changes in demand. Full-cost pricing reflects a longer-run policy to earn a certain target rate of return on total assets or total equity. The difficulty with the full-cost approach is that in itself it offers no adequate explanation for the particular level of, and differences in, profit targets among firms.

One way out of this impasse is to recognize the interrelation between price and investment policy when viewed within the context of dynamic analysis and growth. As previously developed, and as has been suggested by a number of writers, in a dynamic analysis the *rate of growth* of output and profits is the prime concern of the firm, rather than the *level* of these variables.[5]

As previously argued the "managerial civil service" must regard growth as a central objective in order to keep equity holders satisfied. In an economy with growing markets and rapidly changing technology, new investment is ordinarily an essential ingredient of successful competition. Failure to grow is likely to mean failure to survive. Yet at the same time the faster the firm attempts to grow, the larger are its current capital requirements, and so the greater the necessity for retained earnings. For this reason managers must be concerned with current profit rates, even if profit maximization *per se* is not the primary goal.

5. For a provocative discussion see R. J. Ball, *Inflation and the Theory of Money, op. cit.* Ch. 6. See also W. Baumol, "The Theory of Expansion of the Firm", *American Economic Review*, Vol. 11, No. 5 (December, 1962).

As a simple extension of static demand theory, a firm's future market share, and hence the future *growth* of its expected sales, will in general be negatively related to the price it charges. A lower pricing policy implies a lower rate of profits on total capital invested. At the same time the average short-run cost of capital is positively related to the volume of capital requirements relative to current earnings. As will be shown in the next section it is also positively related to the expected future rate of growth of earnings.

The above sketched interdependence between the rate of return earned on tangible assets and the growth rate in *factor and product markets*, and the interdependence of the investment rate, the rate at which future earnings are discounted and the expected rate of growth of earnings in *financial markets*, may be illustrated in a two-dimensional diagram, with the help of some heroic assumptions.

In Figure 3-4 the current rate of profit r earned on total assets is measured on the vertical axis. The expected rate of growth of earnings g, over some investor horizon, is measured on the horizontal axis. It is functionally related to the proportion b of total profits invested. As b rises the proportion of external financing ordinarily increases, and must increase when $b > 1$. The curve *II* represents the firm's expected dynamic investment opportunities set. It shows the extent to which it must tradeoff a lower current earnings yield r in order to achieve greater future growth g. The extent to which *II* slopes downward will vary widely among firms, depending on their growth prospects. Reflection suggests that it will be concave to the origin.

The various *PP*-curves represent equal-price curves for the corporation's stock. They represent, for firms of a particular risk class, the increase in the growth rate of expected earnings required by the capital market to compensate for a lower current earnings yield so as to maintain a constant share price. As will be developed in the following section, these equal-price curves will be convex to the origin. For any given expected growth rate, a higher profit rate results in a higher price per share. Conversely for any given profit rate higher expected growth increases share prices.

Assuming that corporate managers attempt to maximize share prices, they will choose that attainable combination of profit rate and growth rate tangent to the highest equal-price curve. Firms with greater growth prospects in terms of sacrifice of current earnings (a less rapidly falling *II* schedule) will choose a higher investment ratio *b*, a lower current profit margin *r*, and a more rapid expansion path *g*. Investor preferences between present income and future growth are represented by the shape of the equal-price curves. The more highly growth is valued relative to present return (the steeper the *PP* relationships), the higher will be the growth rate *g* selected by corporate management, and the greater will be the reliance on external finance *b*.

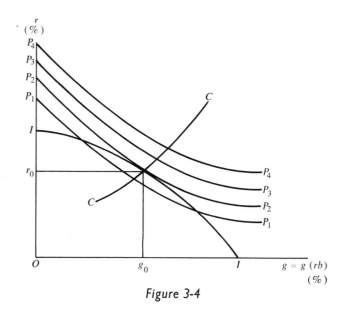

Figure 3-4

The interdependence of pricing, financial, and growth policies in determining a corporation's cost of capital may be alternatively formulated on the same diagram. As a corporation grows more rapidly, its demand for funds and its average cost of capital will rise. This is represented by the average cost of capital curve *CC* in Figure 3-4. Share-price-maximizing corporate managers will select that mix of investment, pricing, and financing policies where the cost of capital schedule *CC* intersects the investment opportunity schedule *II*. This determines simultaneously the profit rate r_0.

The Cost of Corporate Capital

The cost of corporate capital may be defined as the minimum prospective yield a proposed investment must offer to be just a worthwhile undertaking from the standpoint of the current owners (or managers) of the firm. This cost of capital is some weighted average of the cost of depreciation, retained earnings, debt, and external equity finance.

Financial policy is concerned with specifying that finance mix which minimizes the average cost schedule of raising funds at each alternative level of investment. One class of problems concerns the effects of *varying* the mix of debt, or varying the reliance on internal versus external sources of funds, on the average cost of corporate capital. Another concerns the appropriate definition and measure of the average cost of capital of a *given* financial mix.

The traditional view in financial literature has long held that debt funds are initially cheaper than equity funds, so that over some range increasing leverage will lower the average cost of capital. This will continue until, as some conventional but unspecified debt limit is reached, stock and bond yields rise substantially because of increasing risk. At this point the average cost of capital begins to rise. The significance of changing the mix of debt for lowering the average cost of capital has recently been sharply challenged in the literature.

Consider first the case of perfect capital markets, zero exchange costs, and zero taxes. Providing that risk aversion, information, and the supply curve of borrowed funds is the same for individuals as for firms, the total market value of all securities depends *only* on a firm's future earnings, and will be independent of the firm's financial structure. If total shares of unlevered firms of a particular risk class were "undervalued," investors could "roll their own" leverage by borrowing on personal account to buy these shares. The apparent gain in terms of a lower average cost of capital in using a higher proportion of 'cheaper' debt finance under such circumstances is completely offset by a correspondingly higher cost of equity finance as the leverage ratio, and hence the riskiness of levered shares, rises.

Relaxation of any of the assumptions necessary for this perfect "arbitrage" operation implies that the total market value of all the securities of a firm is not independent of its financial policy. In a world of imperfect markets and limited liability, personal leverage will be only a *partial* substitute for corporate leverage. In particular once the assumption of zero taxes is dropped, interest payments which are deductible from corporate income tax liability in effect result in the government paying a subsidy to firms using debt finance. With zero shifting, the present value of this future stream of tax-deductible payments is simply the corporate tax rate times the market value of the debt. This suggests that the average cost of capital declines as leverage increases. To the extent corporate income taxes are shifted, the value of the tax subsidy on interest is correspondingly reduced.

Corporate managers, depending on their attitude to risk, have some preferred ratio of debt to total financing. The amount of debt desired will ordinarily be positively related to the differential between the rate of return earned on tangible capital, and the interest cost of borrowing. To the extent the government tax subsidy on debt finance is effective, the preferred debt burden shifts upward.

Lending is rationed by a collateral requirement, which defines the degree of risk, as well as by an interest charge. The *effective* corporate debt limit may thus be determined from the demand side, by the maximum degree of leverage acceptable to the risk-aversion preferences of lenders. In the United States the proportion of debt finance in total financing has remained extremely stable, at about 30 per cent, for all nonfinancial corporations over a considerable period. At the same time the ratio of total external to internal finance has fallen.

In a world of uncertainty and imperfections the question of optimum dividend policy, and the relation between internal and external equity finance to the average cost of capital, is also extremely complicated. In the presence of the present tax subsidy on capital gains income it may be shown that new stock issues are a significantly more expensive source of equity finance than retained earnings. Corporate earnings paid out as dividends are immediately subject to personal income tax. Retained earnings avoid this immediate tax liability entirely. In the United States approximately one-half of this tax liability is recaptured in the form of capital gains tax, providing the investor chooses to realize his gains. If capital gains are nonrealized until death they escape taxation altogether.

There are a number of additional considerations that raise the relative cost of external versus internal equity finance to stockholders. The transaction costs involved in floating a new stock issue are avoided when funds are raised by retention. In addition to underwriting costs, which may vary from 3 to more than 33 per cent of net proceeds, authority regulations impose costs in time and information in providing "full and fair disclosure." New equity capital cannot be drawn from the market as a tap issue, while retained earnings flow continually and predictably. With new issues a firm may be forced to seek new purchasers of its securities who, because of imperfect information and differing tastes, had not previously bought into the company. These purchasers will now buy its shares only at a discount from the previous price, or after large selling expenses.

All of the above reasons raise the optimum retention ratio for a given corporation that maximizes the price of its stock. It may be concluded that the cost of capital schedule exhibits a sharp upward discontinuity at the point where external equity finance is initiated. On the basis of the low proportion of new equity issues in total sources of funds (currently less than 1 per cent for all manufacturing corporations), the overwhelming majority of corporate managements, with the exception of the regulated utility industries, appear to favor strongly internal generation. The chief exceptions to this rule appear to be occasional bulges in the need for funds by rapidly growing firms that cannot be deferred, but yet all other sources of funds have been exhausted.

Assume that an optimum financial mix between retained earnings and new debt issue has been determined. Perhaps the greatest difficulty still lies ahead. How ought the cost of equity capital to be defined and measured, so as to calculate the average cost of corporate capital from all sources? Since one opportunity cost of investment funds always available to a corporation is the repurchase of its own shares, it is sometimes argued that the return on equities itself is the appropriate floor cost of capital.

The rate that the market discounts future per share earnings will depend on investor estimates of the riskiness and the rate of growth of the future income stream from share ownership. How can this rate of discount be determined from the market valuation of a corporation's stock?

The current earnings-price ratio is an appropriate measure of the cost of equity capital only for nongrowing income streams. For growing income streams the rate of discount must always be higher than the current earnings-price ratio. This may be shown as follows. Suppose that a firm has an opportunity to invest some constant proportion b of its present and future after-tax earnings in investment opportunities which yield an average tax-adjusted rate of return r, in excess of some assumed constant rate r_E at which the market discounts future dividends. This implies that earnings will grow at a constant rate of $g = rb$ per year. Let E_0 represent current per share earnings, If the period over which the growth rate rb is anticipated is infinite. the current price of a share P_0 may be formulated precisely. It is simply the present value of a future stream of earnings E_0 growing at the rate rb and discounted at the rate r_E. This may be expressed:

$$P_0 = \frac{E_0}{r_E - (rb)} \qquad (1)$$

Rearranging (1),

$$r_E = \left(\frac{E_0}{P_0}\right) + (rb). \qquad (2)$$

The marginal cost of equity capital, defined as the rate of return required if a new investment is not to lower the price of the stock, necessarily *exceeds* the current earnings-price ratio for growing companies. The extent that it is greater than the current earnings yield on the corporation's stock depends on the expected future rate of growth of the corporation (rb), and the degree of uncertainty with which these expectations are held.

Equation (1) implies that b must be less than unity, and the expected growth rate rb must always be less than the rate of discount r_E. If these conditions are not satisfied the price per share, and the price-earnings ratio, will rise through infinity.

In the real world corporations whose past growth has been extremely rapid $(rb > r_E)$ do not sell at infinite prices. This suggests that investors do not believe that such corporations can maintain these above-average growth rates indefinitely, but only over some finite period. Alternatively expressed, the marginal rate at which projected future earnings are discounted is not constant, but increases over time, by an amount depending in part on the growth rate, since the uncertainty with which such expectations are held increases as earnings recede into the future.

The above conclusions apply to firms in a given risk class. Irrespective of the rate of growth, the cost of capital will be greater the greater the variance of expected future profits, and the greater the variance of the expected ratio of future stock market prices to future earnings.

As a corporation's *ex post* and expected future growth rate increases, the price-earnings ratio will rise, as implied by Equation (1). Yet higher price-earnings ratios are associated with substantially greater risk of capital loss to investors should the future growth rate decelerate, or should investors generally become more pessimistic about future prospects. For this reason rapidly growing firms selling at high price-earnings ratios represent a higher risk to equity owners, and have a correspondingly higher cost of equity capital. The cutoff rate of return required on investment projects for such corporations consequently is higher than for companies growing at lower rates, if new investment projects are not to lower the price of the company's stock. For example a glamour growth company, whose shares have been bid up to 50 times current earnings, does not have a cost of capital of 2 per cent. Were its earnings widely expected to grow indefinitely at, for example, 15 per cent per year, from Equation (1) its actual current cost of capital would be 17 per cent. This is at the same time consistent with the same market determining a cost of capital (earnings-price ratio) of, for example, 10 per cent, for a nongrowth company whose earnings stream is characterized by comparable degree of *nonfinancial* risk.

RECOMMENDED READING

The theories of household saving outlined in this chapter were first developed independently by Milton Friedman, *A Theory of the Consumption Function* (Princeton, New Jersey, 1957), and Franco Modigliani and Richard Brumberg, "Utility Analysis and the Consumption Function: An interpretation of Cross-Section Data" in K. Kurihara, (Editor) *Post-Keynesian Economics* (Rutgers, New Jersey, 1954). For a concise summary see M. Farrell, "The New Theories of the Consumption Function," *The Economic Journal*, Vol. LXIX, (December, 1959).

James Tobin has directed a number of studies of household portfolio composition. See particularly, Harold Watts and James Tobin, "Consumer Expenditures and the Capital Account," Cowles Foundation Paper No. 165 (New Haven, 1961). James Duesenberry has provided a lucid descriptive examination of diverse sectoral portfolio behavior in the post-war period in, "The Portfolio Approach to the Demand for Money and Other Assets," *Review of Economics and Statistics*, Vol. XLV, No. 1, Pt. 2, Supplement (February, 1963).

There has developed relatively recently an extensive literature on business investment behavior and the cost of corporate capital under uncertainty. For an attempt to distinguish types of business firms, see R. J. Monsen, Jr. and Anthony Downs, "A Theory of Large Managerial Firms," *The Journal of Political Economy*, Vol. LXXIII, No. 3 (June, 1965). The traditional view of corporate financial policy has been challenged most forcefully by Merton Miller and Franco Modigliani. Their most recent article, which contains a bibliography of the controversy, is, "Some Estimates of the Cost of Capital to the Electric Utility Industry, 1954–57," *American Economic Review*, Vol. LVI, No. 3 (June, 1966). For an alternative approach see Myron Gordon, *The Investment, Financing and Valuation of the Corporation* (Illinois, 1962). Also important is John Linter, "Optimal Dividends and Corporate Growth Under Uncertainty," *Quarterly Journal of Economics*, Vol. 78, (February, 1964).

In addition to J. R. Ball's book previously mentioned, an attempt to integrate corporate financial, investment, and pricing behavior in a manner similar to that developed above may be found in Eugene Lerner and Willard Carleton, *A Theory of Financial Analysis*, (New York, 1966).

4

Innovation in Financial Assets
and Financial Markets

*Interest is the barometer of the state, and its lowness is a sign
almost infallible of the flourishing condition of a people.*

—David Hume

Of Interest, 1752

Introduction

This chapter examines the implications of new forms of financial
assets on selected real profiles of an economy. Section one demon-
strates how innovations in financial technology satisfy simultaneously
the diverse asset preferences of debtor and creditor groups. One consequence, termed "Intermediation Effects," is to increase the full-
employment equilibrium ratio of savings and investment to current
income, given the real factors of time- and risk-preference and technology. Another, termed "Asset Transmutation Effects," is to raise
the full-employment equilibrium ratio of real wealth to current
income for any given level of technology and time- and risk-preference.

Up to this point the analysis has proceeded as if financial activity
was confined to primary securities, that is claims issued by deficit-
spending economic units to finance a level of expenditure on current

output in excess of their current income. Part two introduces financial institutions and secondary securities into the analysis. What are the causes and consequences of financial intermediation in capitalist economies? Most centrally financial specialization is shown to occur because of the existence of economies of scale in lending and borrowing, which make it profitable as an econony develops for some business units to intermediate between borrowers and lenders. Financial intermediaries in effect *transmute* the primary securities of debtor units into other forms of financial wealth that possess properties more attractive to assetholders. As a result they are able to earn a higher rate of return on their primary security portfolios than the rate that they must pay wealthowners to hold their own secondary securities.

Part three considers the significance of the behavior of financial markets and financial institutions for some important real contours of an economy's performance. The necessary conditions for static allocational efficiency are first defined. It is then shown that the growth of an economy is critically circumscribed by the ability of the institutional stage of financial technology attained to *reconcile* the full-employment supply of and demand for financial assets by nonfinancial deficit and surplus spending units. Finally, some general causal relationships are explored between the volume and composition of financial assets and debts outstanding and the cyclical stability of an economy's aggregate output.

The effects of financial innovation are demonstrated rather more rigorously in the Appendix with the aid of the diagrammatic analysis developed in Chapter 2.

Primary Financial Assets

The capital market in private property economies fulfills two basic economic functions, which correspond to the *Intermediation* and *Asset Transmutation Effects* of financial activity introduced in Chapter 1. The first is the allocation of the flow of an economy's current saving among users and uses. This is important because, due to differences of preferences and opportunities among spending units, saving is to a large extent separated from real investment. Surplus spending units, primarily households, account for a large proportion of net saving, while a substantial proportion of net real investment by business requires deficit financing. The second is the facilitation of transfers in, and the transformation of, ownership and control of the stock of existing assets, both tangible and financial, among individual wealth-holding economic units. It is instructive to look briefly at the significance of innovations in primary financial technology from this framework.

Let us consider first a rudimentary economy in which only one type of financial asset exists—commodity money, for example gold and silver coins generally accepted as a means of payment. Economic units thereby avoid the inefficiency and inconvenience of barter, and need not seek those other units with a precisely inverse coincidence of wants and commodities in order for exchange to occur. But with such a primitive financial technology no economic unit can persistently spend more than its current income. Deficit spending is limited to the decumulation of existing money balances or existing tangible asset stocks. Enterprise is restrained, since those economic units with higher opportunity curves from tangible asset ownership, and willing to bear greater risk, are unable to expand their holdings of real assets beyond the limit of their own net worth. Accumulation is also restricted, since economic units desirous to hold their net worth in assets of relatively stable value with negligible risk of default can apply their savings only to the accumulation of money or durable tangible assets.

As economic growth proceeds the divergence between the distribution of wealthownership and the distribution of ability and desire to administer tangible assets directly becomes more marked. The reverse side of this development is that it becomes more profitable to attempt to bridge them. The innovation of interest-bearing private debt, such as bonds, mortgages, and loans, breaks the tie between the distribution of expenditure for current output and the distribution of income received. Financial assets that represent claims against those spending units whose principle economic activity is to buy and sell productive factors and current output may be termed *primary securities*.[1]

The possibility of borrowing permits economic units with lower aversion to risk and/or higher opportunity curves from wealthowner-

1. The term is that of J. Gurley and E. Shaw, *Money in a Theory of Finance* (Washington, 1960).

ship to hold tangible assets in excess of their net worth. At the same time risk avoiders are enabled to exchange money and physical asset holdings for contractual securities that provide greater liquidity and lower risk of income and principal. For both groups the possibility of borrowing in future contingencies reduces the need to hold money balances in the present for precautionary purposes, as well as providing an alternative low-risk wealth form as a store of purchasing power. Physical assets acquired by debtor units are in effect represented by lower-risk securities in the portfolios of creditor units, so that both greater and lesser risk-averting wealthowners are enabled to move to a preferred portfolio position (Asset Transmutation Effects).

Business units are led to issue interest-bearing obligations in order to finance the holding of tangible assets in excess of their net worth position. Business investment expenditures grow as firms are now able to spend more than their current income for current output. Simultaneously households now have the attractive new alternative of holding their past and present saving in an income-yielding asset of low risk. As a result they are led to spend less of their current income for current consumption, and to increase their current saving (Intermediation Effects).

In an economy in which money and various forms of debt securities are the sole types of financial assets, all business units must be ultimate wealth entities. In developed capitalist economies the ownership and administration of business wealth is very largely in the hands of different groups. While business units control and operate most of the real capital stock, private wealth is owned ultimately by individuals who compose the household sector. This separation is achieved as a result of the innovation of a new form of business organization and a new type of primary security—equities. Owners of business units find it advantageous to organize in corporate form. The transformation is carried out by the issue of corporate equities. Each individual share of stock represents a limited liability *pro rata* ownership equity in the enterprise. Equities may be defined as a marketable property right entitling the owner to any dividends declared by the managers of a corporation, and a vote in determining the selection of corporate management.

As was the case with debt, the introduction of equities and a market on which they may be traded similarly permits an important further relaxation in the budget restraint of private economic units (Intermediation Effects). Corporations may now finance additional accumulation of tangible assets by attracting the savings of a large number of individuals without incurring additional debt, so that their ability to deficit-spend in order to accumulate tangible assets beyond their current income is increased. Household units may now accumulate nonfixed-income-earning financial assets that, while representing the ownership of tangible assets, possess none of the administrative responsibilities and disadvantages of such ownership. Household incentive to save is considerably increased, since they can now effectively protect their savings against upward movements in the price level, and in addition participate in the future growth of income payments to capital administrators.

Simultaneously, the innovation of corporate equities enables diverse asset preferences of different groups to be further satisfied (Asset Transmutation Effects). Ownership of business units is no longer confined to a single or a small group of individuals. Owners of business units, who previously were forced to hold and administer tangible assets directly, are now able to sell some equity in their own business and purchase shares in other businesses.[2] Wealthowners may diversify their portfolios more effectively than before equity instruments existed. In addition ultimate wealthowners now benefit from the limited liability that equity ownership confers, relative to the unlimited liability of individual business proprietorship. The result is to lower total portfolio risk. Household wealthowners not possessing the skill, knowledge, and risk inclinations required for direct business ownership are thus enabled to participate in the fruits of business enterprise. The anticipated return from holding wealth, for any given degree of technology, uncertainty and time preference, is consequently increased for all assetholders, shifting their wealth opportunity curves upwards. By increasing the attractiveness of wealth holding *vis-à-vis* current consumption, the reservation price of wealthownership is reduced.

2. "It is as though a farmer, having tapped his barometer after breakfast, could decide to remove his capital from the farming business between 10 and 11 in the morning, and reconsider whether he should return it later in the week." J. M. Keynes, *The General Theory of Employment, Interest, and Money*, p. 151.

To recapitulate: financial innovation simultaneously permits both spending and asset preferences of household and business units to be satisfied to a greater degree. The results are twofold. By making borrowing and lending more attractive, the full-employment saving and investment ratio, and so the potential rate of growth of real capital and income, are increased over that which existed prior to the financial innovation (Intermediation Effects). By making asset holding more attractive, the reservation return that must be paid to ultimate wealthowners, and so the marginal return that must be earned in full employment on tangible capital goods, is lowered (Asset Transmutation Effects). These results follow even though all "real" factors, resources, tastes (including time and risk preference), and non-financial technology, remain constant.

It should now be clear that *Intermediation Effects* and *Asset Transmutation Effects* represent simply the flow and stock dimensions of financial change. As will be shown in the following chapters the strength of these two effects differs for different types of financial assets, and their impact will be distributed over different time periods.

Financial Intermediation and Secondary Financial Assets

Financial assets that represent claims against those spending units whose principal economic activity is to buy and sell productive factors and current output have been termed *primary securities*. The previous section described how the issue of primary debt and equities by business corporations makes possible the indirect ownership of tangible wealth by ultimate wealthowners. This permits specialization in the direct ownership and administration of tangible assets by non-financial business units, which perform the role of *real wealth intermediaries*. In a similar fashion certain financial business units specialize in the direct ownership and administration of financial assets, and so perform the role of *financial wealth intermediaries*. The result is to make possible the indirect ownership of primary securities by ultimate wealthowners.

Claims against financial institutions or financial intermediaries (the two terms will henceforth be used synonymously), those business units whose principal economic activity is the purchase and sale of financial assets, have been termed *secondary securities*.[3] The central operations of financial institutions comprise the acquisition of primary securities issued by nonfinancial borrowers, and the provision of their own secondary securities to the portfolios of nonfinancial lenders. The revenues of all financial intermediaries are composed primarily of income received from primary security holdings. Their costs comprise the expenses they incur in providing explicit and implicit returns to holders of their own secondary securities, and the costs of acquiring and administering the primary securities in their portfolios.

Since many economic units combine both nonfinancial and financial activity, borderline cases occur where the distinction between primary and secondary securities is somewhat ambiguous and arbitrary. Equity issues of financial institutions are best regarded as primary securities, reflecting the 'current output' aspect of financial transactions. Certain operations of governments and government agencies (including the central bank) are particularly difficult to classify. For example money or bonds issued to finance government purchases of current output or tangible assets are primary securities as defined above. But identical monetary instruments issued in the act of purchasing financial assets, for example through open-market security operations of the central bank, must be classified as secondary securities. It is useful for some purposes to distinguish *tertiary* financial institutions, enterprises that interpose themselves between financial intermediaries and nonfinancial lenders or borrowers.

As developed in part one, the existence of primary financial assets permits the distribution of spending for current output to diverge from the distribution of earned income from current production. The transfer of generalized claims against current output from surplus to deficit spending units is effectuated in all economies partly through direct finance, in which case primary securities of ultimate borrowers are sold directly to ultimate lenders. But as capitalist economies mature indirect finance gradually predominates, in which case ultimate borrowers sell primary securities increasingly to financial intermediaries, and ultimate lenders in turn enlarge their purchase of a wide variety of secondary securities. Because of important differences in their effects it is convenient to distinguish monetary and non-monetary financial intermediaries, according to whether their second-

3. J. Gurley and E. Shaw, *ibid*.

ary securities are or are not directly acceptable as means of payment. Following the previous discussion all innovations in financial intermediation may be analysed in terms of Intermediation (flow) and Asset Transmutation (stock) effects. The introduction of monetary intermediation further relaxes the budget restraint between income and expenditure, and so raises the full-employment equilibrium ratio of savings and investment to current income. Saving allocated to the accumulation of bank deposits is transformed into incremental demand for those primary securities that banks purchase. Lending to a bank represents no sacrifice of liquidity (convenience lending), so that both creditor and debtor units choose to hold part of their asset acquisitions in the form of deposit balances. Demand for currency is sharply reduced.

The asset-transmutation consequences of monetary intermediation are equally striking. Banks are able to transmute primary securities, which are characterized by uncertain capital value and liquidity, into bank deposits of high liquidity, convenience, certain redemption value, checking privileges, general acceptability as a means of payment, and certain income yield. The result is a reduction in the risk and inconvenience of indirect wealthownership, so that if asset preferences remain unchanged ultimate wealthowners are willing to yield up to wealth administrators' claims against current output for a lower return. Alternatively expressed, for any given expected return on tangible assets, the full-employment equilibrium ratios of tangible capital and wealth to income rises in response to the lower reservation price of indirect wealthownership.

Similarly, the innovation of nonmonetary intermediation may be analyzed in terms of intermediation and asset transmutation effects, which again raise the full-employment equilibrium ratios of saving, investment, tangible assets, and wealth to income. The cost of external finance to borrowers is similarly reduced, while the marginal utility of saving relative to current consumption is increased. Nonmonetary intermediation effectuates an alchemist transmutation of primary securities into a wide variety of wealth forms particularly attractive to nonfinancial lenders yet ill-adapted to provision by nonfinancial borrowers. Since intermediary secondary securities are characterized by lower capital and income risk and greater convenience and reversibility than the primary securities that they acquire, and are endowed with a maturity and a variety of other services specially tailored to assetholder preferences, ultimate wealthowners are willing to yield up to wealth administrators claims against current output at a lower income return. Alternatively stated, wealthowners desire to hold a greater amount of wealth in real terms at each rate of return on tangible assets and level of real income. The effects of monetary and nonmonetary intermediation will be examined in detail in Chapters 6 and 7.

Why is it that some business enterprises find it *profitable* to interpose themselves between ultimate borrowers and lenders, to acquire the primary securities of borrowers and provide their own secondary securities for the portfolios of lenders? In the case of real wealth intermediation through direct finance, the higher return-risk opportunity curve from tangible assets available to nonfinancial business corporations in comparison with household units, plus a lower aversion to bearing risk, was sufficient to explain the specialization in tangible asset investment and ownership by the business sector, and in financial asset acquisition and ownership by the household sector. But as previously described financial assets are much less complimentary in use than tangible assets. The explicit income return on individual financial assets, unlike the case of tangible assets, is typically independent of the holder and of the amount of other assets owned. What then are the advantages of financial intermediation that make indirect ownership of primary financial assets both profitable for financial institutions and desirable for households?

Most generally, these advantages follow from the ability of financial intermediaries to exploit economies of scale in lending and borrowing operations. The most important scale economies that enable financial intermediaries to command a higher rate of return on their primary security portfolios than the lending rate they must pay on their own secondary securities may be briefly summarized:

Market Imperfection. The fixed cost element of trading in financial assets implies that exchange costs vary inversely as a percentage of the money value of financial transactions. Consequently financial institutions with large total assets and continuous operations possess a trading advantage of lower per unit exchange costs over individual nonfinancial wealth units. By spreading fixed costs over a larger volume of transactions, financial intermediaries can afford to break down their own secondary obligations into smaller units more attractive to household portfolios.

Diversification. As a result of exchange costs primary securities are imperfectly divisible. Optimum diversification of financial assets consequently is generally possible only with much larger financial portfolios than most individual household wealthowners command. The very magnitude of financial intermediary portfolios permits a significant reduction in total risk through diversification not available to individual household lenders.

Specialization. Individual households do not in general have the expertize, time, nor possibly the desire to manage their financial asset portfolios so as to attain the efficient set of return-risk opportunities from wealthownership. The task of asset selection and portfolio management consequently is delegated to professional specialists, in effect by granting a power of attorney over asset portfolios. If total assets of the individual wealthowner are sufficiently large he may pay for financial advice and management directly, without necessarily granting power of attorney, as in the case of trust companies. The specialization of intermediary operations permits administrative economy and expertize in the negotiation, appraisal, service, accounting and collection of assets and liabilities that, due to the large fixed costs involved, cannot be matched by nonfinancial surplus units. It is because economies of scale in lending and borrowing are so important that the assets and particularly the liabilities of financial intermediaries are highly specialized.

Liquidity. Fluctuations in individual spending unit wealth portfolios are to a greater or lesser degree offsetting. As a result movements in an aggregate of particular financial asset claims show a much higher degree of stability than movements in the component accounts. Financial institutions are able to take advantage of this statistical property of large aggregates to increase the liquidity of their secondary debt over that of the corresponding primary securities held in their own portfolios.

Certainty. The pooling of independent risks to form a predictable distribution, and the scheduling of maturities to match anticipated outflows, permit financial institutions to offer a reduction in uncertainty to individual wealthholders. The irregular time-shape of future individual claims for repayment is transformed into a more predictable time distribution of aggregate cash inflows and outflows. This reduces uncertainty below that faced by nonfinancial borrowing units. Intermediaries are thus able to take advantage of the law of large numbers to sell certainty as well as liquidity.

Miscellaneous Services. Financial institutions, in seeking to attract purchasers for their own indirect securities, provide additional services not related directly to the process of intermediation. Specialization permits intermediaries to tailor such services much more closely to the demands of specific lending groups than is generally feasible for individual nonfinancial borrowers. The liabilities of financial institutions are characterized not only by smaller default risk, greater predictability of future capital and income value, shorter maturity, and lower exchange costs, but in addition by a miscellany of nonincome services directly attractive to ultimate wealth-owners.

These scale advantages of financial intermediaries achieve a reduction in the subjective uncertainty and inconvenience of holding wealth in the form of financial assets at every expected rate of return. This upward shift in the opportunity curve to ultimate wealth-owners is then the *raison d'être* for indirect ownership of financial assets. While all financial institutions interpose themselves between nonfinancial borrowers and lenders, they perform the intermediation and asset-transmutation functions to various degrees.

A variety of criteria exist by which intermediaries may be classified, the most important for analytical purposes being balance-sheet characteristics that reflect the markets within which an institution operates. Due to regulation and highly developed product differentiation, most intermediaries issue only a very limited variety of indirect debt—demand, short- and long-term deposits, shares, equities, and insurance policies being the most important. Consequently intermediary types are conveniently classified by their liabilities. The range of primary securities purchased by most individual intermediaries is typically broader, even though considerable specialization is evident in the type of assets purchased: marketable versus nonmarketable securities, government, business and household obligations. Finally, with regard to ownership, both private and public intermediaries coexist, and privately owned institutions are further divided into stock, mutual, and cooperative form.

Financial Markets and Economic Performance

What are the implications for general economic behavior of the use of financial markets and institutions to reallocate purchasing power between lenders and borrowers? It is convenient to distinguish criteria for the adequacy of financial performance with regard to their effect on the allocation, growth, stability, and distribution of an economy's real output.

ALLOCATION

Under certain restrictive assumptions it can be shown that perfectly competitive financial markets result in an optimum allocation of resources at a point in time, *given the level of financial technology*, in the limited sense that no economic units could improve their present or future position without at the same time worsening the position of other economic units. The conditions necessary if competitive markets are to ensure an optimum allocation may be briefly noted:

1. Market information widely distributed to all participants.
2. Known preferences and maximizing behavior on the part of borrowers and lenders.
3. Absence of externalities, i.e., discrepancies between private and social marginal costs and benefits.

If all participants acted rationally to maximize expected utility, and if all financial assets were homogeneous with respect to risk and maturity, then perfectly competitive markets would generate a uniform 'pure' yield on all financial assets that exactly equates incremental supply and demand in all financial markets. Under such circumstances any observed yield differentials would provide a simple measure of the degree of market imperfection, that is monopoly power and exchange costs, in different financial markets. In the real world yield differentials among assets arise most importantly from differences in risk, maturity, and costs of intermediation and information. Moreover, not all participants act rationally in the above sense, while aversion to and evaluation of risk differs. Consequently in practice it becomes extremely difficult to determine empirically the extent to which observed return differentials are attributable to market imperfection and risk respectively.

The operating efficiency of financial institutions can be judged by standards similar to those applied to other industries—performance, behavior, and structure. Performance may be judged unsatisfactory if firms persistently earn larger than normal profits, if operations are "backward looking" and highly traditional, if innovation or risk-taking is absent, or if unjustifiable lags appear in taking advantage of technological progress. Behavior may be judged by observing the presence or absence of competitive practices, restrictive agreements, and price inflexibility. Absence of active competition in pricing, services, and other lending terms, while not a proof of inefficiency, suggests that competition alone cannot be relied on to ensure efficient performance. Efficiency may be inferred from structure by examining the relationship between market concentration, size, cost schedules, and profit margins of financial enterprises. If it can be shown that there are many firms which are too small or a few firms too large for maximum efficiency, or that significant entry barriers exist, it may be inferred that competitive pressure is not forcing financial institutions towards cost minimization and optimum output.

GROWTH

With regard to the significance of financial market performance for economic growth, it is frequently assumed that the criteria for static optimum allocation of funds by financial markets also assure an allocation of resources between current uses and output-creating activity consistent with private, though not necessarily social, preferences between present and future income. Public policy to alter the composition of output to increase the rate of growth—which must be distinguished from policy directed at the maximization of potential full-employment output at a point in time—is attributed frequently to externalities and to lack of correspondence between individual and collective time and risk preferences. Such a view implicitly presupposes a *given* financial technology. From a long-term perspective a strong case can be made that market imperfections producing divergences from the static efficient allocation optimum are probably less significant for growth than the discontinous and lagged response of financial innovation to changing economic conditions.

Where ownership and administration of real wealth diverge, efficient private capital formation implies a distribution of investment expenditure among economic units widely different from the distribution of current saving. Given a target rate of real output growth consistent with factor availability and efficiency, an optimal program of private capital formation produces as a by-product incremental supply of primary securities. For financial balance these must not be in excess of the amounts the financial system can either absorb directly, or transmute into secondary securities that satisfy incremental demand for financial assets by surplus units. Assume that the locational divergence between wealthownership and wealth administration, and between planned saving and investment, is given. The inability of a primitive financial technology to accommodate, at the required level of capital formation and saving, the incremental demand function for financial assets by household savers, and the incremental supply function of primary debt issue by business investors, leads to financial inbalance, which in turn prevents the realization of the target rate of growth.

In underdeveloped countries savers typically prefer to accumulate tangible assets, for example real estate, precious metals, inventories, jewelry, and foreign exchange, in place of domestic primary and secondary financial assets. This reflects in part traditional experience with inflation, expropriation and default, and in part prejudice, uncertainty and the absence of information. But most importantly it reflects a primitive financial technology. Such wealth forms represent "low-priority" investment for purposes of growth, yet investors in "high-priority" capital projects may be unable to issue primary debt to finance their deficits on terms acceptable to such savers.

A rudimentary financial system, unable to reconcile incremental demand and supply of financial assets at the socially desired growth rate, forces three types of readjustment towards financial balance. In the absence of government intervention, balance may be achieved with a lower and less efficient program of capital formation, and a consequent reduced rate of growth of real output and primary securities. In this case economic units with promising investment opportunities, but lacking outside finance, are compelled to forego deficit expenditures. Other economic units spend their saving on low-priority projects. The distribution of expenditure is forced back toward the distribution of current income, resulting both in a lower level of capital formation and saving, and in a less efficient ordering of investment expenditures.

Alternatively, the government may attempt to induce the development of financial assets and institutions. The predominant financial intermediary in all underdeveloped countries is the monetary system, but its obligations, whether currency or deposits, generally do not possess the properties necessary to attract a volume of real saving sufficient to finance the desired rate of capital formation. Given the level of financial technology, the spread between borrowing rates that must be offered to savers and lending rates chargeable to borrowers may not, on the basis of private calculation of risk and costs, provide a profitable anticipated return to private intermediation. Nevertheless government intervention may be justified due to its lower risk-aversion, or to the presence of externalities in the process of financial intermediation. Private financial intermediation, both monetary and nonmonetary, may be better able to bridge the gap between the financial terms on which borrowers can issue direct debt, and the asset properties required to attract savings from surplus units, with the aid of government intervention directed at reducing private subjective risk. This may occur through government guarantees of primary securities issued by high-priority investors, government insurance of the indirect debt of private financial institutions, and the establishment of government-operated lending and borrowing institutions.

Finally, in the absence of induced financial innovation, capital formation nearer the target rate may be achieved by reducing the divergence between ownership and administration of real wealth. This may occur either through government action, or through centralization within the private sector itself. Central direction of spending and saving decisions by state enterprises reduces the amount of primary debt created at every rate of development, since a greater proportion of investment is financed internally. Consolidation of private enterprises similarly reduces the divergence between an efficient distribution of investment spending and the distribution of saving.

Any process that reduces the number of wealth-owning units, or combines wealthownership and wealth administration, reduces the degree of indirect ownership of tangible wealth compatible with a target rate of capital formation. Failure of financial innovation to produce indirect debt forms acceptable to private wealthowners at an income return below the marginal return on productive tangible assets may persuade some governments to expropriate private property in certain industries and administer it directly, in an attempt to reduce the supply price of wealth accumulation. In a socialist economy in which all means of production are publicly owned, no reward must be paid private wealthowners to induce them to accept financial assets and to yield up administration and control of their wealth for productive uses. An extremely primitive financial system consequently suffices.

STABILITY

Finally, it is interesting to consider the implications of financial behavior for economic stability. Given the matrix of financial asset prices at which wealthowners are willing to hold existing asset stocks, at a full-employment level of output and income incremental supply of primary securities by deficit-spending units, in the absence of perfect price flexibility in all markets, may diverge from incremental demand for financial assets by surplus-spending units. Fluctuations in aggregate demand occur whenever planned expenditure on current output in excess of current income by deficit-spending units exceeds or falls short of the planned excess of current income over expenditure by surplus-spending units. The greater is the sensitivity of incremental supply of and demand for financial assets to price and yield changes, the greater will be the stability of aggregate demand for current output in the face of autonomous shifts in investment and consumption plans.

As will be shown in Chapter 8, it is only to the extent that planned deficits and surpluses are sensitive to financial asset stocks, composition, yield, or other credit terms that monetary control can be successful in stabilizing cyclical fluctuations in aggregate demand. If borrowers and/or lenders do not respond to changes in asset returns, induced moderate movements in financial asset prices will not operate as an allocator of funds. The very large induced movements in relative prices then necessary to equate full-employment supply and demand for each type of financial asset are likely to be unacceptable on distributional grounds.

It is possible to formulate some general causal relationships between movements in financial variables and cyclical fluctuations in the level of economic activity. If all private real capital formation were externally financed, and no private debts were incurred for pure consumption purposes, the ratio of primary securities (and primary debt) to real wealth would approximately equal unity. Similarly if all private financing were indirect, the ratio of secondary securities to primary securities would equal unity. Although its particular value at any time is sensitive to historical, technological, institutional, and price-level changes, the ratio of total private financial assets to total real wealth may thus be expected *a priori* to have an upper limit in the vicinity of two.

The recognition of government financial activity raises the probable ceiling ratio of total financial to tangible assets, since central government issue of primary securities, particularly during periods of war or Keynesian unemployment, is much less likely than private debt issue to be associated with the finance of real capital formation.[4]

Assume for simplicity that the stock of human and nonhuman capital and the rate of growth of real output increase *pari passu*, so that tangible assets may be regarded as a surrogate for real wealth. A short-run rise (fall) in the ratio of financial to tangible assets not caused by price level movements reflects an increase (decrease) in the rate of deficit expenditure by some units, and is ordinarily associated with an expansion (contraction) in the level of aggregate demand for current output.

4. Goldsmith has calculated the ratio of financial assets to real (nonhuman) tangible assets for several countries. This "Financial Interrelations Ratio" has been seldom below 0.5 for most developed countries, and ratios in excess of 1.5 are found only with large "dead-weight" government debt. For the United States Goldsmith made the following estimates of the FIR ratio:

1850— .45	1900— .80	1939—1.21	1952—1.08
1880— .50	1929—1.24	1945—1.70	

The U.K. has been characterized by much higher FIR ratios:

1913— .95	1932/4—1.45	1947/9—2.6

Germany in contrast has experienced extremely low FIR ratios:

1913— .95	1925— .35 (reform)	1929— .65	1938— .80
	1948— .22 (reform)	1951— .40	

Raymond Goldsmith, "Financial Structure and Economic Growth in Advanced Countries" in *Capital Formation and Economic Growth*, National Bureau of Economic Research, (Princeton, 1955).

In macroeconomic models it has been customary to assume that the effects of private financial assets and debt offset one another, so that private debt may be netted out. The above discussion in contrast suggests that it is possible to hypothesize some "normal" ratio of private financial assets to real wealth, appropriate to a particular institutional setting and level and rate of growth of income and output. What is the significance if any of an actual ratio below or above this normal level? What is the mechanism by which "subnormal" or "supernormal" financial ratios are corrected? The net effects of the particular *level* of the ratio of financial to tangible assets, which must be distinguished carefully from the effects of a *change* in the ratio, may be examined by conceptually dichotomizing spending units so as to consider them separately in their role as assetholder and as borrower.

Higher levels of financial-asset ratios imply larger aggregate total assets of all economic units at any given income level. This operates through the asset or wealth effect to raise aggregate planned expenditure of spending units in their role as assetholder at each level of aggregate income. This rise in spending propensities is reinforced to the extent that the parameter of the asset effect on expenditure is higher for debtor units, whose relative ownership share of total assets will increase as financial ratios rise.

The expansionary impact on aggregate demand of a higher financial-assets-income ratio is however increasingly dampened by the accompanying change in total portfolio composition. The return on financial assets relative to tangible assets required for portfolio balance must increase as the ratio of financial assets to tangible assets rises. This depresses planned investment expenditure to accumulate tangible assets. Consequently the expansionary impact on aggregate demand from spending units in their role as assetholder may be expected to be positively related to the ratio of financial asset to tangible assets, but by a *decreasing* function, since the return on financial assets rises relative to the return from holding tangible wealth.

Consider now the behavior of spending units in their role as debtor. Low debt ratios encourage deficit spending by debtor units. A rise in the ratio of primary debt to tangible assets exerts an increasingly depressing effect on additional expenditure for current output, as interest expenses on outstanding debt increase relative to current income. The strength of this effect may be expected to be positively related to the debt-asset ratio, but by an *increasing* function.

This follows from the recognition of optimum and ceiling debt-asset ratios, which are determined for each type of borrower by the conventional collateral requirements and preferences of lenders. As debt-asset ratios approach some critical level, additional external financing is regarded as accompanied by sharply increasing lenders' risk. This both reduces the availability of external finance, and increases its cost. The argument applies to corporate bond and equity financing through the concept of an optimum leverage ratio and to consumer debt through increased default risk. Debtor units consequently are increasingly deterred from further deficit expenditure. As the debt ratio rises, more and more debtors will attempt to lower their debt ratio by internal financing of capital expenditure and by debt repayment.

A ceiling debt-asset or debt-income ratio may similarly be postulated for state and local governments and self-financing government corporations. The concept is much less appropriate to central government behavior, whose budgetary inbalance is determined primarily by stabilization and political objectives, and much less by the constraint of future interest burden and public credit considerations.

Upon combining these two effects, it may tentatively be concluded that relatively low or "subnormal" ratios of private financial assets to tangible assets and income exert on balance an *expansionary* influence on aggregate demand, and may in addition be expected to shift the composition of final demand toward investment goods. Subnormal ratios tend to correct themselves by stimulating deficit-spending on the part of those economic units who desire to hold tangible assets in excess of their net worth but have not reached a limiting debt ratio. Conversely relatively high or "supernormal" ratios of financial assets to tangible assets and income exert on balance a *deflationary* pressure on aggregate demand, and shift the composition of demand toward consumption goods. They also tend to correct themselves by depressing debt issue and deficit spending for current output by debtor units.

Since central governments do not ordinarily alter their expenditure plans out of consideration for their role as debtor, the concept of an equilibrium debt-income ratio does not appear to be applicable to public debt. Central government outside debt consequently exerts only a net expansionary influence on private aggregate demand, which is positively related to the amount of such debt outstanding. The effect of public debt-income ratios on the composition of private demand between consumption and investment depends on the distribution of public debt ownership relative to tax liabilities.

In addition to increasing the net worth and the total financial assets of the private sector, government debt provides the liquidity and collateral to support a larger superstructure of private debt at every level of real income and real wealth. While the *issue* of public debt preempts private savings, and so ordinarily displaces new issues of private debt, the *existence* of public debt may at times increase the ease of private debt issue by satisfying the liquidity requirements of lenders and the collateral needs of borrowers.

The financial system as has been shown transmutes some proportion of the incremental supply of primary securities into secondary securities that possess properties, most importantly realizability of capital value and certainty of income return, more attractive to ultimate wealthowners. The terms on which primary debt can be issued, for any given ratio of financial assets to tangible assets and income, have been seen to depend importantly on the level of financial technology attained by the financial system. The degree of asset transmutation accomplished by financial intermediaries affects the magnitude of the asset or wealth effect, to the extent the composition and liquidity of financial asset portfolios affects spending decisions.

The monetary system plays a paramount role in this process. If the incremental supply of monetary assets falls behind the growth of primary securities, the result is to erode the total liquidity of financial asset portfolios, increase the cost of external finance, and reduce the net expansionary effect of any given ratio of financial assets to real wealth and income. Conversely, a rise in the proportion of monetary to primary securities may be expected to increase the net expansionary effect associated with a given stock of financial assets.

Given the degree of divergence between the administration and ultimate ownership of real wealth, and the resultant degree of specialization in investment and saving activity, the incremental supply of primary debt and hence the ratio of financial assets to real wealth and income are an *increasing* function of the rate of capital formation and the growth in real income. A more rapid rate of economic growth, by increasing incremental supply of primary financial assets, raises the ratio of financial assets to real wealth, and necessitates a higher return on financial assets relative to real wealth for portfolio balance. These changes operate to depress the rise of aggregate demand. This effect is accentuated if the growth of primary debt outruns the ability of financial institutions to issue secondary securities, so that the liquidity of financial asset portfolios declines.

Conversely a reduction in the rate of economic growth propels a fall in financial assets ratios, and in the return on financial assets relative to real wealth, tending to provide an expansionary support to aggregate demand. As a result of such relationships, it is possible to define a required "financial" growth rate, as that rate of growth of real income that satisfies portfolio balance considerations with no change in the return on financial assets.

Since many financial assets are fixed in money terms, changes in the price level of current output, factor prices, and existing tangible assets alter the ratio of real primary debt to total real wealth and income. A rise in the price level of current output reduces the real value of financial assets and debt in wealth portfolios. Debtor units find their financial position improved as their debt-income and debt-tangible assets ratios fall, encouraging them to deficit-spend, while creditor units find the real value of their assets reduced. The distribution of wealthownership is shifted towards economic units whose desire to administer real wealth exceeds their net worth. The foregoing analysis, that the consequences of a change in private financial asset ratios on debtor and creditor units are not symmetrically offsetting, but bear more heavily on debtor behavior, suggests that a rise in the general price level, contrary to widely accepted conclusions derived from a model in which private assets and debt are netted out, is likely to have a net *expansionary* effect on aggregate demand. This appears particularly probable in the later stages of a boom in which financial asset ratios already exceed their "normal" levels.

Conversely a fall in the general price level increases the real value of financial assets, and so the ratio of private financial assets to real wealth and income. The net effect on aggregate demand again depends on the initial relation of financial asset ratios to their equilibrium values. Were private debt ratios previously near their critical levels, as is more probably after a sustained boom, a significant fall in the price of current output could induce, at least initially, cumulative debt deflation, as debtor units find themselves forced to liquidate their tangible asset holdings.

Finally, the structure of relative prices also shapes the response of economic units to movements in financial variables. The relation between the price of previously existing and currently produced capital goods is of particular significance. While the price of existing reproducable tangible assets rarely exceeds their current cost of production, if the price of currently produced capital goods is inflexible downward a reduction in investment demand may cause a curtailment in production in the capital goods sector, and a fall in the market value of existing tangible assets and in the equity-market price of existing firms below the supply price of new capital assets. Under such circumstances deflation-induced declines in the debt ratios of business units, reductions in the cost of debt finance, and even increases in the money stock will not eliminate excess capacity in the capital goods sector until the price of commodities and existing tangible assets has risen relative to the supply price of currently produced capital goods.

Similarly if wages are more inflexible downward than commodity prices, the market rate that must be paid to labor at the lower commodity price level may exceed labor's marginal revenue product, causing a fall in profit rates. Again, unemployment of labor may not be substantially reduced until the price of current output has risen relative to money wage rates.

APPENDIX TO CHAPTER 4

Innovations in Financial Technology

To recapitulate the argument of parts one and two, financial markets and instruments fulfill two basic economic functions, corresponding to what have been termed *Intermediation* and *Asset Transmutation Effects* of financial activity.

In modern private property economies saving (the excess of current income over current consumption expenditures) is to a large extent separated from investment (expenditures for new construction, equipment and inventories). This specialization and decentralization of saving and investment decisions among economic units is achieved by means of the sale and purchase of newly issued and previously existing financial assets. The dependence of the distribution of expenditures for current output on the distribution of current incomes received is thereby relaxed, and deficit-spending household, business and government units are enabled to borrow funds from surplus-spending units to realize planned expenditures in excess of their current income.

At the same time outstanding stocks of financial assets and the possibility of transactions in existing assets permit the separation of ownership and administration of national wealth, while the properties that financial assets possess raise the opportunity curves from wealth-ownership. The existence of primary securities issued by nonfinancial business, government and household units permits the indirect ownership of real wealth by ultimate wealthowners in the household sector. The existence of secondary securities issued by financial institutions effectuates the indirect ownership of primary financial assets by ultimate wealthowners. Assetholders may diversify their portfolios more efficiently, and participate in the fruits of tangible asset administration without possessing the skill, knowledge, and risk inclinations required for direct ownership and operation.

Given the underlying "real" factors of thrift (including risk aversion as well as time preference), technology, and wealth distribution, *Intermediation Effects* raise the equilibrium ratio of saving and investment to current income, and *Asset Transmutation Effects* raise the equilibrium ratio of tangible assets and wealth to current income.

These effects of financial innovation can be demonstrated somewhat more rigorously with the aid of the diagrammatic analysis developed in Chapter 2.[5] Consider the case of the introduction of bonds into a money economy. In Figure 4-1, total wealth is represented by the distance OO' on the horizontal axis, and the return on tangible assets r is measured on the vertical axis. Aggregate portfolio preferences to hold real money balances M/p and tangible assets K are represented by the Portfolio Balance curve PP. The actual proportion

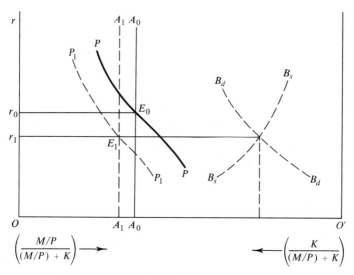

Figure 4-1

of money balances and tangible capital in total assets is represented by $A_0 A_0$. In equilibrium, given the prevailing marginal return on tangible assets r and the implicit return on money balances, the amount of real money balances and tangible capital demanded in wealthowner portfolios must exactly equal the existing stocks of these assets outstanding. The initial equilibrium position before the innovation of bonds and debt is shown at E_0.

5. This figure has been adapted with kind permission from a manuscript of James Tobin.

As previously described the effect of the innovation of fixed-interest-bearing bonds and debt is to increase the demand for tangible assets and to reduce the demand for money balances. As a result the Portfolio Balance relationship PP shifts downward and to the left. The extent of the shift will depend upon the diverse asset preferences and opportunities of potential borrowing and lending groups, and the resulting interest rate of bonds. The equilibrium interest rate on bonds must be such as to clear the bond market. For a particular interest rate on bonds, the dashed curve P_1P_1 now represents the total amount of money balances and tangible assets demanded by assetholders at different marginal rates of return on tangible assets.

Bonds and debt may now be introduced into the figure. The horizontal distance between A_0A_0 and the dashed line B_dB_d represents the amount of bonds demanded by lenders, at a particular interest rate on securities. The amount of bonds demanded increases as the expected return on tangible assets falls. The horizontal distance between A_0A_0 and the dashed line B_sB_s represents the amount of securities offered by borrowers at this same given rate of interest. The amount of bonds supplied increases as the return on tangible assets rises. An increase in the interest rate on bonds would shift B_dB_d rightward and B_sB_s leftward, and conversely with a fall in bond yields. The extent of the shift in bond supply and demand schedules would depend on the interest elasticity of incremental demand and supply of bonds. Whether P_1P_1 would shift leftward or rightward in response to a change in bond yields cannot be stated *a priori*. It would depend on which of money or tangible assets was a closer substitute for bonds in wealth portfolios.

The final full equilibrium position is reached at that rate of interest on securities that satisfies simultaneously total portfolio balance of *both* debtors and creditors. The amount of money balances, bonds, and tangible assets demanded must exactly equal the stock of money, bonds, and real capital in existence. In this new equilibrium the amount of tangible assets yielded up by ultimate wealthowners in exchange for securities exactly equals the amount of tangible assets demanded by wealth administrators in return for the issue of debt.

The extent that the real money stock must be reduced to satisfy the conditions of the new equilibrium position depends on the extent of the leftward shift of the PP relationship, and the degree the marginal return on tangible assets declines. Assuming the demand for real money balances falls, if the nominal money stock remains constant the price level must rise throughout the adjustment process, shifting the AA relation leftward. Increases in the stock of tangible assets also shift the AA line to the left.

The new equilibrium position is shown in Figure 4-1 as E_1. In this configuration as a result of capital accumulation the real return on physical capital has fallen to r_1. The new ratio of real money balances to capital stock is represented by A_1A_1. At this return on tangible assets r_1 the amount of bonds demanded equals the amount of bonds supplied (B_dB_d intersects B_sB_s) at some determinate interest rate. This interest rate is not shown in the figure. Depending on investor preferences, it will lie somewhere within the boundaries set by the return received from holding tangible assets r_1, and the implicit return received from holding money balances.

RECOMMENDED READING

Very little work has been done on the process of financial innovation *per se*, although a great deal has been written about financial markets and institutions. The outstanding exception is J. Gurley and E. Shaw's, *Money in a Theory of Finance*.

Roland J. Robinson's, *Money and Capital Markets* (New York, 1964) is an excellent introductory presentation of financial markets in the United States. Raymond Goldsmith has almost single-handedly provided most of our empirical knowledge in this area. See his *Financial Institutions in the American Economy Since 1900* (Princeton, 1958), and *The Flow of Capital Funds in the Postwar Economy* (New York, 1965). A wealth of Information is contained in the studies prepared for the Commission on Money and Credit. See especially, *Private Financial Institutions* (Englewood Cliffs, N. J., 1964) and *Private Capital Markets* (Englewood Cliffs, N. J., 1964). In the latter book Hyman Minsky attempts to develop a theory of financial instability, "Financial Crisis, Financial Systems, and the Performance of the Economy."

The Canadian and English financial systems as allocators of savings are comprehensively examined in *The Report of the Canadian Royal Commission on Banking and Finance* (Ottawa, 1964), and *Report of the Committee on the Working of the Monetary System* (London, 1959). (The "Radcliffe Report").

5

The Determination of Financial
Asset Prices and Yields

.

> *The rate of interest, though ultimately and permanently*
> *governed by the rate of profit, is, however, subject to temporary*
> *variations from other causes.*
>
> —David Ricardo
> *Principles of Political Economy and Taxation,* 1817

Introduction

It is now possible to attempt a general explanation of the forces determining the price and yield of individual financial assets under uncertainty. The first parts build on the theory of asset management and behavior developed in Chapters 2 and 3. Using the concept of portfolio balance to define a stock-adjustment model, the conventional dichotomy of stock versus flow explanations of interest rate determination is shown to be invalid. Both flow and stock demand and supply relations must be considered. The relative importance of stock and flow relations is shown to depend critically on the *speed of adjustment* to portfolio disequilibrium on the part of assetholders and assetissuers. Two types of equilibrium situations are distinguished.

Section two outlines the forces determining financial asset prices in the short run, a period in which the stocks of assets in existence are given and must all be held in wealthowner portfolios. In section three the long-run determination of financial asset prices is formulated. Flow supply and demand relations are shown to play a dominant role in determining long-run equilibirum.

The fourth part considers the forces affecting the relative structure of financial asset prices and returns, particularly with regard to maturity and risk differentials. For interested readers the chapter closes with a brief review of the literature on the theory of interest, with particular reference to its relationship to the portfolio approach to the determination of asset prices.

A General Equilibrium Theory of Financial Asset Prices

Interest rates refer to the effective annual yield of a financial asset, where *yield* is calculated as that discount rate which equates the present value of a stream of expect future receipts of interest and principal to the current market price. Interest yields as conventionally calculated consider only those receipts to which an explicit monetary value may be attached, even though as previously noted a diverse bundle of services is typically associated with ownership of any particular wealth form. The *return*, as distinct from the yield, of a financial asset is defined as its yield plus or minus any capital gain or loss created by a change in market price, the latter calculated as an annual percentage of initial market value.

It is important to recognise that because asset services, as separate from assets themselves, are not exchanged in capital markets (unless assets are rented), it is asset *prices* rather than asset yields that are directly market-determined and observed. Asset yields are a derived mathematical relationship, which may be calculated from *estimated* future receipts once the present market price of an asset is known. Prices are the exchange ratios between assets. Strictly speaking what is directly determined in capital markets is not a family of interest rates, but the price of particular property rights, each representing a claim to an expected series of future services. Only in the case of perfect foresight, when future values of all receipts and costs are certain, does the market price of a property right uniquely determine the "pure" rate of interest on an investment.

Financial asset prices, like all other prices, are determined in equilibrium where the quantity demanded equals the quantity supplied. The problem lies in identifying the appropriate variables that must be included in the supply and demand functions, and in specifying the nature of the market-clearing process. Contemporary explanations of interest rate determination are conventionally dichotomized into loanable funds versus liquidity preference theories. According to the first, equilibrium rates of interest are those rates that equate the supply of and demand for loanable funds, i.e., the demand for and supply of newly issued securities over some period of time. According to the second, equilibrium interest rates are those rates that equate the demand for and supply of the stock of money balances and securities existing at some moment of time. The central controversy concerns whether the relevant quantities in the supply and demand relationships are to be expressed in flow or stock dimensions.

The reconciliation of stock and flow relationships is of the greatest importance and difficulty for financial analysis. Supply and demand relations may formally be stated in both stock and flow dimensions, resulting in four supply and demand equations to determine a single price. Are stock relations dominant in some markets, flow relations dominant in others, and some combination of the two appropriate in still other markets? In so far as the difference between stock and flow specification is merely terminological, no difference in the general formulation of the two hypotheses need be implied. This is because a flow concept can mechanically be translated into a stock concept, and vice versa, simply by noting that net flow is the difference between stocks at the beginning and end of the period.

Substantive differences do exist with regard to the explanatory value of the two hypotheses, depending on whether the underlying behavior of market participants is pursued in terms of stock or flow objectives. Do wealthowners define their financial goals in terms of desired flows over some period of time, or do they formulate their goals in terms of desired asset stocks at some moment in time? Or do their goals comprise both stock and flow magnitudes? Otherwise expressed, can the observed variation in security prices more satisfactorily be explained by the flow supply of new issues coming on the market over a particular period in relation to the flow demand from current saving and credit creation over the same period, or by the stock of securities in existence relative to portfolio demand to hold assets by wealthowners, or by some combination of the two? Thus formulated this is ultimately an empirical question, and the existence of flow-of-funds and balance-sheet accounts for the first time makes it subject to operational verification. It is possible to add somewhat further to our understanding of this issue on *a priori* grounds by utilizing the analysis of the previous chapters.

Following the theory of asset management under uncertainty developed in Chapter 2, wealthowners may be regarded as having some *preferred* portfolio composition for every set of financial asset prices. Economic change is continually pushing wealthowners out of portfolio balance, and their behavior may be interpreted as an attempt to maintain or move toward some preferred position of portfolio equilibrium. The critical behavioral assumption concerns the rate of this adjustment process. Two polar cases may be identified.

At one extreme it is possible to postulate an instantaneous adjustment period. This implies that assetholders continuously reappraise decisions to hold existing stocks in the light of current market opportunities, and continuously buy and sell out of their existing stocks so as to maintain a moving position of portfolio balance. Such behavior would result in a set of market prices that satisfy stock equilibrium at every point in time, so that assetowners desire to hold exactly the existing asset stocks.

Toward the other extreme one may conceive of a variable adjustment period, which may be indefinitely long, through which assetholders refrain entirely from the sale of existing assets, and rely solely on the allocation of gross cash inflows to achieve their preferred portfolio position. In the polar case wealthowners are completely indifferent to asset stock diversification considerations, at least within a wide range of portfolio composition, and formulate their behavior solely in terms of maintaining preferred saving and investment flows. Such behavior would produce a set of market prices that satisfies current flow equilibrium, while stock excess demand persists indefinitely, or is irrelevant.

More generally, wealthowner behavior may be expected to lie somewhere between these extremes. In this general case movement toward a preferred portfolio composition operates both through sale of existing holdings and through reallocation of current savings, but the rate of adjustment is not instantaneous, so that only a tendency towards clearance of excess stock demand may occur in any period. Under such circumstances current market price is influenced by both, yet satisfies neither, stock and flow equilibrium conditions. It may be represented by some distributed lag function of excess stock or flow demands existing over previous periods.

This may be shown as follows. Let P_t represent an asset's price at the end of the tth period, and Q_t the stock of the asset outstanding at the end of the tth period. Ignoring other variables in the demand function, the unlagged stock hypothesis may be represented:

$$P_t = f_1 (Q_t) \tag{1}$$

The unlagged (net) flow hypothesis may be represented:

$$P_t = f_2 (Q_t - Q_{t-1}) \tag{2}$$

The equality of Equation (1) is unchanged by taking the first difference of both sides:

$$P_t - P_{t-1} = f_1 (Q_t - Q_{t-1}) \tag{1a}$$

The *unlagged* stock hypothesis therefor implies that current net flows are more closely associated with the current *change* in asset prices (Equation 1a), while the *unlagged* flow hypothesis implies that current flows determine the current *level* of asset prices (Equation 2).

Once it is admitted that stock adjustment need not be completed within the measurement period chosen, it is necessary to introduce *lagged* stock values into Equation (1):

$$P_t = f_1 (Q_t, Q_{t-1}, Q_{t-2} \ldots) \tag{3}$$

This is operationally extremely difficult to distinguish from a *lagged* flow hypothesis:

$$P_t = f_2 (Q_t - Q_{t-1}, \quad Q_{t-1} - Q_{t-2}, \quad Q_{t-2} - Q_{t-3}, \ldots) \tag{4}$$

Both contain the same explanatory variables. The discriminatory power of empirical evidence is reduced to different predicted values for the coefficients of the lagged (and autocorrelated) variables.

Little theoretical or empirical work has been done on the question of an *optimum* rate of adjustment of actual to desired asset holdings in response to portfolio disequilibrium. The cost of increasing the speed of adjustment of an existing portfolio composition to a preferred position includes all the expenses of asset exchange costs and brokerage fees, any cost effects on customer relations, the costs of collection and analysis of contemporary information inputs, and the costs of decision making. The return from more rapid portfolio adjustment is the higher expected future income and/or lower risk associated with the preferred portfolio position. The optimal rate of adjustment will therefore in general not be identical among assetholders and debtissuers, nor among asset and debt forms.

The foregoing remarks illuminate the question of whether current excess flow or stock demand more satisfactorily explains the observed level and variation in a particular financial asset price and yield. The flow *versus* stock dichotomy is clearly incorrectly posed. Financial asset markets differ from commodity markets most importantly in the fact that existing stocks typically are very large relative to current flows over any arbitrarily chosen period of time, e.g., one year. It is frequently stated that where existing stocks are large relative to annual flows, and substitutability between newly created and previously existing assets is high, stock relationships are dominant in the determination of price. But over what period ought flows to be measured? What is "large" or "small" in this context? The ratio of outstanding stocks to current flows clearly has a different significance in determining price in different markets, for example houses and equities.

Given total stocks outstanding relative to current net flows, the importance of trading in existing assets (stock relationships) relative to purchases of currently created assets (flow relationships) can be shown to depend on the speed of portfolio adjustment to disequilibrium by holders of existing asset stocks. The relative share of net flow to gross transactions in determining a change in price may be expressed:

$$P_t - P_{t-1} = f\left[(d_t - s_t) + a_t(D_t - S_t)\right] \qquad (5)$$

where $(P_t - P_{t-1})$ represents the change in price in period t, f is some function that satisfies the condition $f(0) = 0$, $(d_t - s_t)$ represents flow excess demand in period t, $(D_t - S_t)$ represents stock excess demand at the beginning of period t, and a_t is a constant, representing the proportion of portfolio adjustment completed over the period t $(1 \geqslant a_t \geqslant 0)$. Given the stock of assets outstanding, the shorter the period t required for complete portfolio adjustment to occur $(a_t = 1)$ the more important will be current stock relations $(D_t - S_t)$ relative to flow relations $(d_t - s_t)$ in determining price, since the shorter the period the smaller will be flow magnitudes. For example if portfolio adjustment were completed in one week, for $a_t = 1$, $t = 1/52$, so that assuming flow relations are expressed in annual values, Equation (5) would appear:

$$P_t - P_{t-1} = f[1/52 (d - s) + (D - S)] \tag{5a}$$

If portfolio adjustment were completed only after many years, or the question concerns the determination of price over a long period, flow magnitudes become predominant.

Diagrammatic analysis of conventional supply and demand relations to illustrate the interrelationship of stock and flow magnitudes can easily be unhelpful and misleading. The sometimes suggested simple aggregation of stock and flow supply and demand relations to portray equilibrium price is valid *only* in the case of a once-and-for-all change, for which the period selected to comprise the flow relationships is not arbitrary, e.g., one year, but rather the complete portfolio adjustment period (so that $a_t = 1$). The critical question concerns the duration of this stock-adjustment period for different assets.

It is important to remember that the flow supply s_t of a financial asset also represents movement towards some preferred total portfolio composition, including both assets and debt, on the part of financial asset issuers. It therefore is dependent on debtor units' speed of adjustment to disequilibrium:

$$s_t = b_t (Q_t^* - Q_{t-1}) \tag{6}$$

where Q_t^* is the stock of debt the unit desires to have outstanding at the end of period t, Q_{t-1} is the amount outstanding at the beginning of the period, and b_t again represents a constant rate of adjustment coefficient over the period t $(1 \geqslant b_t \geqslant 0)$. Since adjustment and exchange costs ordinarily are much higher for debtors than for creditors, it may be expected that for most financial assets $a_t > b_t$ for all periods t over which adjustment is incomplete.

As a result of diverse adjustment rates the relative explanatory importance of stock and flow magnitudes over any given period may be expected to vary widely among different markets. But in all markets their relative importance will depend on the conceptual time period chosen over which equilibrium price—no tendency to change—is defined. Real-world economies are always in disequilibrium. As Equation (5) indicates, in general and for all assets, over the short-run stock relations $(D_t - S_t)$ play a *relatively* more important role in determining price movements, while over a longer-run flow relations $(d_t - s_t)$ explain a larger proportion of price variation.

This suggests a convenient analytical approach to the determination of financial asset prices. As a heuristic device two equilibrium prices may be distinguished, even though neither is ever achieved in real economies. For all financial assets where existing stocks are large relative to quarterly or annual flows, and where organized secondary markets exist, variations in price over the short run may plausibly be assumed to be determined primarily by stock relationships, that is by a portfolio demand function and the actual stocks of the asset in existence. Stock disequilibrium will be completely eliminated only within the adjustment period of assetholders, which will vary among different assets. A position of stock equilibrium, in which wealthowners are content to hold exactly the existing stocks of financial assets, has been termed a position of *Portfolio Balance*. It represents a *nonstationary* dynamic solution, and may be termed *temporary equilibrium*.

Such a price is ordinarily accompanied by flow disequilibrium, which over a longer period of time gradually changes the underlying stock relationships, so that a new stock equilibrium price is determined, and the process continues in this manner. It is possible to postulate over the long run the existence of a *stationary* dynamic solution, which again may never be realized in actuality, in which flow as well as stock relationships are in equilibrium. Such a conceptual event may be termed *full temporal* equilibrium. In both cases equilibrium price satisfies stock relationships, but only in the latter case are flow relationships simultaneously satisfied.

This general-equilibrium dynamic formulation of the determination of financial asset prices, with some simplifications to confine the analysis to two dimensions, may be presented diagrammatically. Consider an economy in which only two financial assets exist, money M, and a nonmonetary interest-bearing security S. In Figure 5-1a the horizontal distance OO represents the total existing stock, and in Figure 5-1b the total existing flow (incremental supply), of financial assets in real terms which must be held by wealthowners. In both figures the share of monetary assets in total financial assets $M/(M + S)$ is measured from the left origin rightward, and the share of non-monetary securities $S/(M + S)$ from the right origin leftward. The vertical axis measures the return r_s on nonmonetary securities. The anticipated marginal return r on the stock of tangible capital K is assumed given at any moment in time, and the interest rate on monetary assets is assumed to equal zero.

In Figure 5-1a the asset relationship $A^T A^T$ indicates the relative value of the currently existing *stocks* of money and securities in total financial assets. It is positively sloped, since as the return on fixed-interest securities falls, their price rises, increasing their relative proportion of total assets as well as the real value of the total wealth.

In Figure 5-1a the Portfolio-Balance relationship PP indicates the alternative combinations of portfolio composition and interest rate on securities that satisfy general equilibrium in financial asset markets. At different interest rates (r_s) wealthowners in the aggregate desire to hold the indicated proportions of monetary and nonmonetary securities in their financial portfolios, given the stock of tangible assets (K), and the return on money (0) and tangible assets (r). Points to the right of PP represent situations of excess stock supply of monetary assets, while points to the left of PP represent positions of excess stock demand for monetary assets.

Temporary equilibrium in financial asset markets is satisfied where the PP and $A^T A^T$ curves intersect. This situation is represented at E_T in Figure 5-1a, at which point the demand for financial assets by wealthholders exactly equals the stocks of money and securities in existence. For portfolio balance in the short run security prices must adjust until all assetholders have reached their desired portfolio

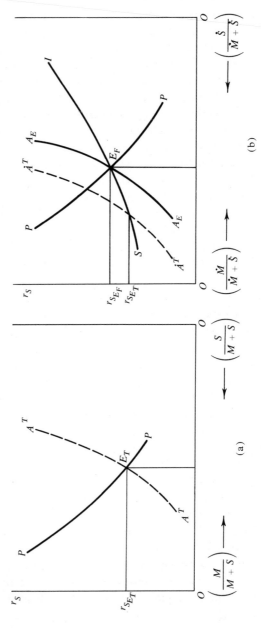

Figure 5-1

composition. Only if all households had identical preferences with regard to return and risk, and identical return expectations, would each prefer to hold the proportion of money and securities in its portfolio of financial assets shown in Figure 5-1a.

In Figure 5-1b the full-employment aggregate demand or saving-investment relation SI shows the incremental (flow) portfolio composition that results from different interest rates on securities consistent with aggregate demand equal to full-employment aggregate supply in the markets for current output, given the return on tangible assets (r) and on money balances. At all points on this curve total new issues of financial assets by deficit-spending units (businesses and governments) equal total new acquisitions of financial assets out of current saving by wealthowners. At higher interest rates on securities planned private deficits fall and planned private surpluses rise, as investment and consumption spending is reduced due to both interest and wealth effects. If aggregate demand is to be maintained this must be offset by greater cash-financed government deficits, and so results in a greater incremental supply of monetary assets and a lower incremental proportion of securities and debt in wealth portfolios. As shown in Chapter 3, saving and investment expenditures by households and firms are dependent on the *composition* of financial assets and debt in existing wealth portfolios, in addition to total wealth, total income, and rates of discount. The area below SI represents situations of excess demand for current output and excess flow supply of securities, while the area above SI represents positions of excess flow demand for securities where aggregate demand falls short of full-employment output.

The temporary equilibrium interest rate established by current stock relationships ($r_{S_{ET}}$ in Figure 5-1a), together with the SI relationship, determine the current incremental (flow) supply of money balances and securities forthcoming at full employment equilibrium in the markets for current output. This incremental supply of money balances and securities is shown by $\dot{A}^T\dot{A}^T$ in Figure 5-1b, drawn where $r_{S_{ET}}$ from Figure 5-1a intersects the SI relationship. This flow composition will not in general be identical to the stock composition of existing portfolios outstanding (A^TA^T in Figure 5-1a). As a result over time A^TA^T will gradually shift, causing the temporary equilibrium interest rate to change. In the particular situation illustrated the $A^T A^T$ curve will shift leftward over time, raising the temporary equilibrium interest rate, and increasing the incremental flow of money balances relative to securities (a rightward shift of $\dot{A}^T \dot{A}^T$ in Figure 5-1b).

A position of *full temporal equilibrium* is defined as that configuration where there is no tendency for the interest rate to change over time. This will only be attained when the temporary equilibrium interest rate established by stock relationships in financial asset markets (the intersection of the PP and $A^T A^T$ curves in Figure 5-1a), generates a composition of incremental (flow) supply of financial assets identical to the then existing composition of financial asset stocks. Full temporal equilibrium is shown in Figure 5-1b at E_F, and is defined by the intersection of the SI and PP curves. Only at this interest rate $r_{S_{E_F}}$ are the stock and flow compositions of financial assets $(A_E A_E)$ identical. In full temporal equilibrium asset stocks have adjusted so that the AA, SI, and PP relationships all pass through the same point. Alternatively expressed, only at full temporal equilibrium interest rates do the portfolio preferences of financial asset-holders exactly conform to the portfolio preferences of financial assetissuers, so that *both* debtors and creditors are simultaneously in full portfolio balance.

Once the assumption of flexible prices and full employment is relaxed, it is possible to construct in Figure 5-1b a whole family of SI curves. The curves lying above the full employment SI relationship each represent some frictional disequilibrium position in the market for current output coexistent with a particular level of unemployment and excess capacity. The curves lying below the full employment SI relationship represent some frictional disequilibrium position in the market for current output consistent with a particular level of excess demand. Similarly, once the assumption of a constant expected return from investment in tangible assets r is removed, it is possible to construct a whole family of PP curves, each appropriate to a different rate of return on real investment.

Combining Figures 5-1a and 5-1b, it follows that an indefinitely large number of financial asset prices and yields are consistent with portfolio balance at different levels of employment and income. But in general there is only *one* temporary equilibrium set of financial asset prices and yields that satisfies both portfolio balance *and* a full-employment level of output at constant prices. The uniqueness of the solution is assured because a rise in financial asset prices and a fall in financial asset yields increases aggregate demand through both wealth and interest rate effects, while conversely a fall in the level of financial asset prices depresses the level of private expenditure on current account.

Since Keynes it has been recognised that, in the absence of perfectly flexible prices and wages in output and factor markets, there is no automatic assurance that the equilibrium price and yield of financial assets determined in financial markets necessarily results in a level of aggregate demand in product markets equal to that level of output at which all factors of production are fully employed at stable prices. But since a rise in financial asset prices (fall in yields) will stimulate deficit spending and discourage surplus spending, there is, in all economies, some level of financial asset prices sufficiently high (yields sufficiently low) to support a level of aggregate demand consistent with the full employment of all productive factors.[1] This full-employment temporary equilibrium level of financial asset prices represents a lower limit or "floor" return on financial assets, rather than any "normal" or "natural" level. It is a floor in the sense that if financial asset yields fall below this level, over-full employment and inflation will ensue, driving yields upward.[2]

Concentration on interest cost and yield effects of a rise in financial asset prices on consumption and investment spending, and failure to consider wealth and portfolio effects, misled Keynes and many of his followers to conclude incorrectly that full employment might under some circumstances necessitate a zero or even negative return on financial assets. This cannot occur since as the rate at which expected future income-streams are discounted falls, the real present market value of long-lived tangible and financial assets becomes indefinitely large.

1. Market imperfections may of course preclude the compatibility of full employment with price-level stability, so that the relevant alternatives become various combinations of unemployment and inflation. For presentational simplicity "full employment" is used in a qualified sense, implying the highest level of employment consistent with "approximate" price level stability.

2. A downward structural shift in an economy's opportunity (Philip's) curve between inflation and unemployment consequently *reduces* the temporary-equilibrium level of returns on financial assets consistent with full employment.

Temporary Equilibrium Determination of Financial Asset Prices

The general short-run theory of financial asset price determination in competitive markets may be briefly stated. Given an initial distribution of wealth and income among economic units, and given the preferences of wealthowners with regard to return, risk, and other asset characteristics, the stocks of assets already in existence will uniquely define a temporary equilibrium set of asset prices and asset holdings. At every moment of time wealthowners must somehow, whether in equilibrium or not, hold all existing assets in their portfolios. Portfolio balance will be attained only within assetholder adjustment periods to portfolio disequilibrium, so that at any moment in time stock equilibrium conditions may not be fully satisfied. The determination of financial asset prices in the *short run* is thus analogous to the Marshallian *market period* determination in the theory of price, in which commodity stocks are assumed given.

Ceteris paribus, the temporary equilibrium price of any particular asset A will be higher if:

(1) The desire to hold A is increased as a result of a change in preferences,
(2) The distribution of ownership of total assets by those economic units whose desire to hold A is greater than average is increased,
(3) The total income or total wealth of assetholders is increased
(4) The relative stock of A is reduced.

The inclusion of wealth as a variable in asset demand functions underscores the interdependence of stock demand and supply in the determination of asset prices. The temporary equilibrium price and yield on all financial assets where stock relationships dominate "hang from their own bootstraps," in the sense that supply and demand are interdependent. There is a large element of thinking makes it so in the temporary equilibrium determination of financial asset prices. But the same can be said for tangible assets in inelastic supply, e.g., the price of Picassos. Furthermore if speculators make up an important share of the demand for a particular financial asset, for example corporate equities, then their concern must include speculation on one another's behavior, and the range of uncertainty concerning future prospects is likely to be increased. The incremental supply and demand forces determining full temporal equilibrium financial asset prices and yields affect temporary equilibrium values importantly, though indirectly, through present portfolio preferences, which are shaped by expectations of future financial asset prices and yields.

Holders of financial assets for which organized secondary markets exist are able to adjust their portfolio holdings of particular assets relatively quickly, with typically low exchange costs. Issuers of financial assets, with the exception of central governments, are much more restricted in the types of securities that they can create. Moreover they incur much higher exchange costs in any attempt to switch the composition of their outstanding obligations. It is because in the short-run asset stocks are relatively fixed that movements in temporary-equilibrium asset prices and yields are necessarily dominated by demand factors. Over the longer run, as additional outstanding obligations are incurred, deficit spending units have some latitude in selecting from among alternative contractual forms a finance mix that will minimize the return paid to wealthowners for the use of their funds. Consequently a long-run tendency exists for incremental supply of particular financial asset types to adjust outstanding stocks, so that the temporary equilibrium solution successively approaches some (changing) full temporal equilibrium price and yield.

Wealthowners have different asset preferences, and are faced with a variety of nonfinancial assets and financial instruments each possessing widely diverse characteristics. The reward required to induce wealthowners to hold their wealth in the form of particular financial assets, rather than to hold tangible assets directly or to increase current consumption, varies with the composition and risk of existing asset stocks, the distribution of wealthownership between economic units of differing portfolio tastes, and the relative desiredness of alternative asset characteristics.

Financial assets are characterized by an extreme diversity of properties, each more or less attractive to different wealthowners. With regard to marketability and certainty, currency and bank deposits impose no restraint on the disposal of purchasing power that ownership represents, and low or zero exchange costs. As a low-risk asset with zero or low explicit income yield, they are subject to uncertainty of future capital value with changes in the general level of prices. Short-term marketable bills possess inferior convenience and liquidity in comparison to currency and deposits, but are characterized by only slightly greater capital uncertainty, and yield a greater if uncertain future income return. Bonds possess greater income certainty but considerably less capital certainty, due to changes in their realizable market value with future movements in interest rates. Corporate equities are subject to both substantial capital and income uncertainty, but offer greater protection against future movements in the general price level vis-à-vis financial assets whose values are fixed in money terms. Bills, bonds, and equities exhibit to various degrees lenders' risk due to the contingency of borrower default or failure. Nonmarketable household and business debt is characterized by substantial illiquidity and inconvenience due to the cost and difficulty of cash realization before maturity, as well as being subject to lender's risk.

Obligations of financial intermediaries possess little income uncertainty and minimum lender's risk. Differences in expected income return among primary securities possessing different asset properties offer a potential source of profits to financial intermediaries, who are able to endow their own secondary obligations with properties attractive to wealthowners but not possessed by primary securities.

The temporary equilibrium formulation of the determination of financial asset prices described above bears a clear family resemblance to liquidity-preference theories of interest. Both are formulated in terms of stock supply and demand relationships. The return on non-monetary financial assets is described by liquidity preference theorists as the reward required in an uncertain world to overcome wealthowner preference for liquidity, and induce wealthowners to hold assets other than money. Such a formulation rather totally ignores the behavior of assetissuers. But even on the demand side it oversimplifies and distorts the complexities of asset choice, since it implies that differences in a single asset property, liquidity, provide a one-dimensional scale upon which all assets may be ranked. While liquidity or money-ness is important, there exist a multiple of asset characteristics—capital certainty, income certainty, assymetry of return expectations, form of return services, marketability, divisibility, carrying costs, etc.,—all of which affect the utility from wealthownership and so portfolio demand, yet do not lead to identical asset ranking.

Full Temporal Equilibrium Determination of Financial Asset Prices

In full temporal equilibrium, market-determined financial asset prices that satisfy stock equilibrium must simultaneously satisfy flow equilibrium, so that incremental demand equals incremental supply of financial assets. This long-run stationary dynamic solution must be analyzed quite differently from the temporary equilibrium case, since a different set of supply and demand functions are relevant, and the complications introduced by the presence of asset stocks and portfolio considerations disappear. Full temporal equilibrium determination becomes in fact a variant of the loanable funds theory of interest. It is heuristically convenient to consider initially the forces determining the general *level* of financial asset prices and yields, as if all financial assets were homogeneous, before identifying some factors affecting the relative price and yield structure of heterogeneous financial assets.

Financial assets are supplied (loanable funds demanded) by deficit-spending business, household, and government units. The household sector is on balance a surplus-spending sector, and it is convenient to consider household supply of financial assets along with the factors determining net household saving. Supply of and demand for financial assets by governmental units will be examined in Chapter 9 under the discussion of financial policy. It will there be shown that government monetary, fiscal, and debt operations exert an important independent influence on the level and structure of financial asset prices.

The supply of primary financial assets by deficit-spending nonfinancial business units is governed by the distribution of marginal return opportunities available to the business sector from operating tangible assets, relative to the size and distribution of business saving. The cost of capital that business units are obliged to pay for borrowed funds depends upon the price at which they can sell primary securities to intermediaries and surplus-spending units. In a world where the future is uncertain and markets are imperfect, business units will undertake only those investment opportunities for which the expected return exceeds by some risk margin the expected yield they must pay to nonadministering wealthowners. This necessitates a brief summary of the determinants of investment spending and the cost of capital to business firms as developed in Chapter 3.

A management acting in the best interest of stockholders will continue to undertake investment projects so long as the result is expected to increase the market value of the corporation's stock. This required cutoff rate of return if real investment is to be undertaken has been termed the *cost of corporate capital*. It represents the opportunity cost, expressed as an annual percentage of the principal, that a business must pay to obtain additional financing.

Business corporations obtain funds both internally, from depreciation charges and retained earnings, and externally, from issue of new debt and equity securities. At any moment in time a firm is faced by a rising and typically discontinuous cost of capital function, since after a point additional external financing can be obtained only at higher rates. Corporate financial policy, by varying retention and leverage ratios, consists in finding the optimum mix among various sources of financing so as to minimize the cost of capital schedule.

For any particular investment project an expected rate of return can be calculated that equates the present value of anticipated cash outflows and inflows. It is then possible to rank in descending order complementary and alternative investment opportunities by their expected internal rate of return, and reject those below the cutoff rate. Alternatively and preferably, it is possible to discount future alternative cash flows at a rate equal to the corporation's cost of capital, and select those investment projects that yield the largest present value.

The composite incremental supply price of primary financial assets by deficit-spending business units is thus governed by their expected future marginal return opportunities from operating tangible assets, and by their existing balance-sheet position. As discussed in Chapter 3, critically important portfolio characteristics concern the liquidity of their financial asset position, and the amount of debt previously issued relative to firms' existing financial and tangible asset stocks.

Incremental demand for financial assets by the household sector represents the excess of incremental demand by surplus-spending household units over incremental supply by deficit-spending household units. As described in Chapter 3, a large proportion of household saving is invested directly in the accumulation of tangible assets and human capital, as well as in financial assets. As a result total household saving considerably exceeds the total current account surplus of the household sector available for the purchase of financial assets.

National gross saving undertaken in any period, an accounting identity conventionally defined as total current earned income minus total current consumption expenditures, may be classified as *"voluntary"* or personal, and *"involuntary"* or institutional. "Voluntary" or personal saving is that part of national gross saving accounted for by the purchase of tangible and financial assets by ultimate economic units. "Involuntary" or institutional saving is composed of gross saving by business units, in the form of depreciation allowances and retained earnings, plus total government saving, which equals public investment expenditure plus or minus current budgetary surpluses or deficits realized by government units. "Involuntary" saving is not determined by the proportion of their personal income that individuals who ultimately own the wealth of an economy directly chose to save, but represents the decisions of wealth administrators. In developed countries total involuntary saving ordinarily far exceeds voluntary saving.

"Voluntary" or personal saving may be subdivided further into *"rational"* and *"automatic"* saving. The mass of household income recipients may be regarded as "rational" savers, whose saving decisions represent a weighing of current against future utility of income, based on expected future needs and receipts. Gross saving by currently working rational savers is largely offset by current dissaving of other rational savers at the initial or terminal stage of their lifetime expectancies. In the case of a constant population with constant working and retirement life expectations, net national rational saving would be positive only if planned lifetime income exceeds planned lifetime consumption. This would occur if life spans were over-estimated, or provision were made for passing on of estates, while economic myopia would tend to depress net national saving toward a negative amount. The bulk of voluntary saving historically has been accounted for by "automatic" savers, those upper-income individuals whose expected lifetime wealth and income considerably exceed their lifetime consumption.

It is now possible to consolidate and summarize the factors which determine the full temporal equilibrium price that must be paid to persuade nonadministering wealthowners to yield up to wealth administrators the disposal over tangible wealth and to accept property claims in return. The full temporal equilibrium level of financial asset prices and yields is determined where incremental supply of financial assets equals incremental demand for financial assets. These flow supply and demand functions of financial assets are influenced by the expected profits and quasi-rent opportunities from tangible asset ownership made available by generalized claims over purchasing power, and by total consumption expenditure out of earned income. In addition they are affected by changes in taste for risk, unearned capital gains or losses, operations of financial intermediaries, and the properties of financial assets, debts, and alternative asset and consumption forms to which wealth increments may be applied. The stability of this equilibrium requires that a rise in financial asset prices induces an increase in incremental supply and/or a reduction in incremental demand for financial assets, while a fall in financial asset prices induces a reduction in the amount incrementally supplied and/or an increase in incremental demand.

In view of the fact that total investment exceeds by a considerable and variable margin incremental supply of financial assets, and total saving similarly exceeds incremental demand for financial assets, it is incorrect to state that the full temporal equilibrium price and return on financial assets is determined at the intersection of saving and investment. Total saving or investment, both *ex ante* and *ex post*, can shift without any necessary change in the equilibrium level of financial asset prices and yields. Conversely, the latter can change independently of any movement in total saving and investment schedules.

The full-employment equilibrium level of saving, investment, and marginal return on the operation of tangible capital is determined, within any institutional framework, by the "real" forces of resource endowment, technology, innovation, and time and risk preferences, which the classical economists properly emphasized. But it is profit rates, the gross return to productive agents who administer tangible assets, rather than yields on financial assets, the return to contractual claimants to income who own property rights, that are determined essentially by "real" factors. Even these may be shown to be affected importantly by financial factors in the short-run.

Given the institution of private property, financial assets enable the administration of tangible assets to be separated from the distribution of ultimate ownership of an economy's wealth. Wealthownership is more unequally distributed than personal income in all countries where the institution of private property exists, and the distribution of personal savings is even more concentrated. The long-run equilibrium return on financial property, which is received in a large part by upper-income savers who are also leaders in per capita consumption, cannot realistically be regarded as a measure of the reward required for the real psychic or social cost of abstention from consumption, even for a particular institutional setting. Although national saving does necessitate social abstinence, in the sense of lower current per capita consumption as resources are devoted to capital formation, most saving is *involuntary* and *automatic*, and the return on financial assets depends importantly on the distribution of wealthownership, and the rights and obligations attached to financial property. Otherwise expressed, the return on financial assets is a reward largely for past saving, and comprises a large element of economic quasi-rent, even though the marginal dollar allocated to saving by "automatic" and "voluntary" savers is not perfectly inelastic to yield.

As a scarcity reward to ownership *per se*, the return on financial assets may be viewed meaningfully as a tribute levied on present activity by past achievements. It is in this sense that interest payments represent the dead hand of the past upon the present. A permanent increase in the level of interest rates, which operates to increase the share of rentier property income in total income, *increases* the present value of past achievements in the same manner as it *reduces* the present value of future achievement.

Analogous to the temporary equilibrium case, a large number of financial asset prices and yields are consistent with full temporal equilibrium at different levels of income and employment. Given the stocks of tangible and financial assets outstanding, only one is compatible with a full-employment level of output at constant prices. This full-employment level of full temporal equilibrium financial-asset yields must again be regarded as a *floor* rather than a *normal* long-term equilibrium level, unless all wages and prices are perfectly flexible. Lower financial asset prices and higher financial asset yields, as shown in Figure 5-1b, are consistent with less than full employment equilibrium in output markets. The full temporal equilibrium level of interest rates is affected in addition by financial intermediary behavior, and by all government monetary and fiscal operations that change the incremental supply and demand functions for financial claims. The effects of intermediary and government operations on the temporary and full temporal equilibrium level and structure of financial asset prices and yields form the subject of Chapters 7, 8, and 9.

Relative Financial Asset Prices

It is now appropriate to consider some of the factors affecting the relative price and yield structure of heterogeneous financial assets. As has been stressed there exist multiple dimensions of financial asset characteristics, many of which may be adopted to debtor and creditor preferences. One of the most important properties is the expected risk attached to holding a particular asset. With the help of a few simplifying assumptions it is possible to formulate some general principles governing the structure of asset yields as ranked by the risk, i.e., the uncertainty of future return, associated with different assets.

As has been shown the risk associated with holding a particular asset varies among different assetholders. If all investors had identical marginal return-risk preferences, and identical investment opportunities and expectations, each investor would desire to hold the same portfolio composition. Suppose this preferred portfolio mix was not identical to the composition of existing asset stocks. All assets must somehow be held in investor portfolios, since an asset without an owner is as a general situation inconceivable. The prices of those assets making up this desired portfolio mix would then rise, reducing their expected return, while the prices of other assets would fall, increasing their expected return and attractiveness. As asset prices adjust to eliminate excess demand and supply, the opportunity frontier from different asset portfolios illustrated in Figures 2-4 and 2-5 would flatten out. At the limit the opportunity frontier would degenerate into a straight line, with a slope equal to wealthowners' common (constant) marginal rate of substitution between return and risk.

Such a linear opportunity curve would imply that, due to the adjustment of asset prices, the expected return on each asset is perfectly positively correlated with the expected return from every other asset. Under such conditions it would not be possible to reduce collective portfolio risk by diversification below the average of the independent asset risks. This is not to imply that assetholders would be indifferent to portfolio composition. The slope of the straight line would represent the market price of risk, and assetholders could still vary their total portfolio risk by holding more or less risky assets. The risk structure of asset returns would fall along a straight line, whose slope reflects the (constant) degree of risk aversion (in terms of additional return demanded) common to all wealthowners.

The foregoing analysis suggests that in the real world the opportunity frontier is not linear, but convex. The magnitude of differences in the return-risk ratio of different assets will depend upon the distribution of wealth among assetholders with different tastes for risk, and differences in investment opportunities and expectations envisaged by wealthowners. But to the extent that in the real world a large proportion of total asset risk is systematic, so that expected asset returns are highly correlated with some index of economic activity, and so with one another, diversification cannot reduce portfolio risk below average individual asset risk. The opportunity frontier must then be flat rather than highly convex from above. Irrespective of differences in taste, the market price of risk (in terms of additional return required) will be more nearly invariant to the degree of risk undertaken.

Differential risk from financial assetownership is related to differences in asset exchange costs, differences in the probability of borrower default (lender's risk) in the case of fixed-income securities, and in the likelihood of dividend increases or decreases in the case of variable-income securities. The expected risk from holding any particular asset is also associated with the *maturity* of the future stream of receipts that ownership of the property right in question confers. The magnitude of this maturity-related risk for a particular asset will vary among investors, depending upon the time-shape of their accumulation objectives, the maturity composition of their existing portfolios, and of course their future expectations.

Most explanations of the term structure of interest rates are based on a modified version of the expectations hypothesis. In its unmodified form this states that long-term interest rates are simply the "average" of expected future short-term rates over the intervening period. This implies that expected return over any given holding period, including capital gains or losses, must be equal on "comparable" securities of different term to maturity. The theory does not require, as sometimes claimed by its critics, that investors actually attempt to predict short-term rates over extended future periods. It is sufficient that some investors (speculators) are able to bring expected holding-period yields on "comparable" assets of different maturities into equality.

If expectations were uniform and held with certainty, and exchange costs were zero, securities of different term would become perfect substitutes for one another. Under such circumstances a change in the mixture of outstanding securities between long and short term could not affect the term structure of interest rates unless it changed expectations. The difficulty in testing this hypothesis is of course that of measuring expectations. Holding period returns do not empirically turn out to be equal over time on securities of different term. Does this imply bad forecasting or bad theorizing?

As soon as the above assumptions are relaxed, short and long-term securities cannot be regarded as perfect substitutes for one another. The holding of long-term securities is characterized by greater uncertainty of future capital values, due to their greater price variability, while the holding of short-term securities involves greater uncertainty of future income streams. Assetholders are not in general indifferent to capital and income risk. Some will demand a premium in the form of higher yields in return for holding long-term securities possessing greater capital uncertainty. Similarly, other investors, not concerned with short-term changes in capital value over the life of an investment that they plan to hold to maturity, will offer a premium for long-term securities in the form of higher prices in order to avoid the cost and trouble of frequent reinvestment and to enjoy the greater income certainty.

To the extent that short and long-term securities are imperfect substitutes in investor portfolios the expectations theory must be modified. The term structure of interest rates will depend, in addition to future expected levels of interest rates, on the composition of shorts and longs currently outstanding and issued, relative to the distribution of assetholders with diverse portfolio preferences. Costs of operation and capital limitations operate to prevent speculators from eliminating differences in holding period returns by moving across the term structure, even for assets that they regard as close substitutes.

This modified version states that long-term rates will equal the average of expected short-term rates over the intervening period, plus some positive or negative market premium for lending on long term. A number of recent empirical estimates, calculated for periods where it seemed plausible to assume that forward rates indicated expected rates, suggest that in recent American experience liquidity premiums have been positive and substantial for short-term bills, averaging in the neighborhood of a 0.67 per cent interest yield below expected future rates over the period, but diminish rapidly, and possibly even become negative, as maturities extend beyond three to five years. There is, in addition, evidence that the liquidity premium for short-term securities is positively related to the level of interest rates.

While the magnitude of this normal premium is patently an empirical question, it is possible to outline the general principles governing the full temporal equilibrium relationship of the term structure of yields by considering the factors determining the incremental supply and demand for short- and long-term claims.

1. While *some* lenders will be adverse to the greater capital uncertainty of long-term claims, virtually *all* borrowers will be indifferent to the greater capital uncertainty of long-term contracts. Unlike creditors, as long as debtors continue as operating units they will never be *forced* to repurchase their debt at high prices, though they may have the *option* of repurchasing it at low prices. As a result of this asymmetry, the greater income certainty advantages of long-term debt are offset to a much lesser degree for debtor units than for creditor units by its capital uncertainty disadvantages.

2. The existence of exchange costs increases the preferences of both borrowers and lenders for long-term contracts. To the degree these costs are borne disproportionately by borrowers, this differentially increases borrower preference for long issues.

3. Financial conventions restrict the extent it is possible for most debtors, with the exception of central governments, to take advantage of even very substantial yield differentials in order to finance long-term capital requirements on short-term contracts. Creditors ordin-

arily are not externally constrained from increasing the proportion of short-term securities in their portfolios, but convention or regulation frequently prevents them from increasing the proportion of long-term securities held.

4. Both borrowers and lenders are in general able to reduce capital uncertainty by tailoring their debt and asset maturity to the uncertain time path of their future cash requirements. The time horizon of corporate borrowers is ordinarily longer than that of household, and many although not all, institutional lenders.

The above four factors suggest a basic asymmetry in full temporal equilibrium incremental demand for and supply of short and long-term obligations. To the extent that this asymmetry exists, full temporal equilibrium long-term rates must *exceed* short-term rates by some premium sufficient to induce borrowing for terms shorter than debtor preferences, and lending for terms longer than creditor preferences, so as to equate incremental demand and supply for each maturity in financial markets.

This basic asymmetry between asset and debt maturity preferences of ultimate wealthowners and tangible wealth administrators provides a *raison d'etre* for both government debt operations and private financial intermediation. Governments, by increasing the relative supply of shorter-term obligations, and intermediaries, by lending on longer terms than they borrow, operate to reduce, and may even reverse, the full temporal equilibrium maturity yield differentials.

With regard to the actual (disequilibrium) and the temporary equilibrium term structure of yields, expectations may widen, eliminate, or reverse the full temporal equilibrium relationship. If future financial asset prices are expected to fall, (future interest rates expected to rise) creditors will prefer to hold shorter-term securities, in order to avoid capital losses. At the same time borrowers will prefer to borrow at longer term, in order to avoid increased future interest costs. The result is to increase the normal spread between short and long rates. Most of the positive slope of observed yield curves over the post-war period may be explained within the expectations hypothesis by the rising level of interest rates.

The existence of wealthowner expectations concerning some "normal" level of interest rates prevents long-term yields from varying proportionately as much as short-term yields. Under such circumstances a rise in the current price of longs at the same time enhances the expected likelihood of a fall in their future price, and conversely. For example if bond prices were generally expected with perfect confidence to return to their normal level after five years, a rise of at most 5 per cent in the *price* of perpetuities is sufficient to offset the effect of a fall of 1 per cent in the current yield on bills. In consequence the interest rate on perpetuities (r) would not fall by more than $r/105$ per cent for each 1 per cent fall in the bill rate. This holds even if the current level of the bill rate were expected to persist for five years.

The more dispersed, uncertain, or unstable are expectations of future yields and prices, the greater will be movements in long-term bond prices and yields in response to changes in current short-term rates, since the force of the deterrent of offsetting expected future capital losses or gains is so much the weaker. A large number of empirical studies indicate that market forecasts tend to hug present values, and so consistently underestimate the magnitude of future changes. This holds for interest rates as well as for other economic variables.

APPENDIX TO CHAPTER 5
A Brief Survey of the Literature

The portfolio approach to asset price determination developed in this chapter bears a close family resemblance to a number of different theories of interest rate determination. The diverse attempts made over the last few hundred years to develop a theory of interest defy any neat comprehensive classification. In the interests of presentational simplification it is convenient for the following comparison to distinguish nonmonetary from monetary theories, partial and general equilibrium from disequilibrium analysis, and flow from stock formulations.[3] Preclassical, classical, neoclassical, Keynesian and neo-Keynesian systems may all be examined within these categories.

The preclassical writers were men of affairs immersed in the daily events of markets and politics. Writing in the 18th century they were forced to consider the disturbances caused by the great influx of gold and silver from the New World. This conjunction of place and time probably accounts for their emphasis on monetary factors, that is changes in the supply and demand for money, in explaining levels of and movements in interest rates. Cantillon, for example, after distinguishing the two meanings of the value of money, the amount one can get for it when buying goods (purchasing power), and when lending it (interest rate), described how an increase in the quantity of money would in the short run either raise or lower the interest rate, depending upon whether it is injected into the economy by lenders or borrowers. The preclassicists did not confine their examination to equilibrium situations. Their still inchoate verbal analysis failed to distinguish clearly between stock and flow relationships. Yet writers such as Cantillon developed a theory of interest comprising both monetary and real influences that was highly suggestive of later loanable-funds doctrines.

The classical writers following Adam Smith developed in contrast largely nonmonetary theories of interest. Their rather complete disregard of monetary elements, and much else that was valid in

---

3. For an excellent brief review of interest theory, see J. Conard, *An Introduction to the Theory of Interest* (California, 1959).

earlier thought, may be explained partially by the fact that they were asking different questions from their predecessors. As philosophers of political economy rather than participants in the economic game, they were primarily interested in those fundamental or basic forces which determine the long-run level of interest rates. Consequently they tended to regard as unimportant those events of temporary and "secondary" nature that were characteristic of short-run disequilibrium situations. They most emphatically did not deny the importance of monetary factors in practical life, but rather their relevance to the long-run equilibrium states with which they were concerned. It may however be doubted whether most classical economists fully appreciated the quantitative importance of transitory "disequilibrium" phenomena relative to permanent "underlying" forces in determining actual market interest rates, nor the extent of the interrelationship between the two.

The classical economists typically if understandably identified the entrepreneur as the supplier of both capital and entrepreneurial effort. Consequently their theory of interest and profits appear at times virtually indistinguishable. The rate of interest was regarded by the early classical writers as approximately and permanently governed by the rate of profit, after deducting some institutionally determined and relatively constant allowance for an entrepreneurial reward for risk-bearing and superintendence. The chief force behind the demand for borrowed funds was held to be the physical productivity of present capital goods. The supply of funds was regarded as governed by a preference for present over future goods. This was explained by differences between the relative scarcity and so the marginal utility of present versus future goods, and by underestimation of future needs ("myopia"). From these grounds it was deduced that abstinence or waiting demands a return.

In its most developed form, as in the writing of Eugene von Bohm-Bawerk and Irving Fisher, the market rate of interest was regarded as fluctuating around an equilibrium level. This level satisfies the condition that the demand to borrow purchasing power, which is dominated by current investment opportunities, the latter dependent in turn upon technology, the rate of innovation, and the stock of capital in existence, is exactly equal to the supply of purchasing power offered by lenders, which is governed by the distribution of income and wealth, the character of expected future income streams, and time preferences of wealthowners between present and future goods.

This long-run equilibrium level of interest rates was usually formulated with reference to full employment of labor and capital. Short-run phenomena, such as business booms or recessions, changes in the quantity of money, governmental finance, etc., were held to produce only temporary effects on the market rate of interest, so that after some lag interest rates would return to their former level. The classical writers did not regard monetary factors as influencing the underlying long-term level of interest rates, and neglected to analyze the dynamics of disequilibrium processes. They did however recognize that both flow and stock relationships influence the normal level of rates, and they attempted to formulate the interest problem in general-equilibrium terms.

There have been two major attempts to synthesize nonmonetary and monetary theories of interest over the last fifty years. They may be grouped under loanable funds theories, most closely associated with Knut Wicksell and D. H. Robertson, and liquidity preference theories, developed by J. M. Keynes and his followers. According to the neoclassical loanable funds formulation, the equilibrium rate of interest is that rate which equates the supply of and demand for loanable funds, i.e., the demand for and supply of interest-bearing securities.

While supply and demand for securities may in principle be conceived in either stock or flow terms, loanable-funds theorists chose to adopt the framework of a flow analysis, directing attention to a period of time rather than a moment of time. In addition to borrowing to finance deficit investment and consumption expenditure, borrowing to build up cash balances (hoarding) was now explicitly recognized by neoclassical writers as a source of demand for loanable funds. Similarly, in addition to current saving, dishoarding of existing money balances and newly created money were recognized as sources of supply of loanable funds. Transactions in existing securities, and in other existing nonmonetary assets, were regarded as representing simultaneously both supply and demand for loanable funds, and so as cancelling out one another. Unfortunately this treatment, which continues to appear in the literature, implicitly eliminates by assumption the effect of stock relationships on security prices.

According to the Keynesian liquidity-preference theory, the equilibrium interest rate is that rate which equates the demand for and the supply of the stock of money balances. As stated by Keynes, "The rate of interest is not the price which brings into equilibrium the demand for resources to invest with the readiness to abstain from present consumption. It is the price which equilibrates the desire to hold wealth in the form of cash with the available quantity of cash."[4] The stock of money is regarded as determined by the monetary authorities through the banking system. The demand for money comprises the need for working balances (transactions motive), for unforseen opportunities and necessities (precautionary motive), for future movements in financial asset prices (speculative motive), and finally for contemplated future projects (finance motive).

Liquidity-preference theorists adopted the framework of a stock analysis, although again supply and demand for money can be conceived in flow terms. Keynes initially argued that the rate of interest was determined independently by the supply and demand for money, and that the intersection of the savings and investment functions determined the equilibrium level of income, but J. R. Hicks almost immediately suggested a general-equilibrium formulation.[5]

In Figure 5-2 the LM and SI curves illustrates the simultaneous interdetermination of both interest rate and the level of income. The return on securities r_s is measured on the vertical axis, and the level of money income pY on the horizontal axis. The price level p is assumed constant. The LM curve shows those combinations of interest rate and level of income at which the demand for money equals the stock of money in existence. Assuming a constant stock of money, a higher level of income involves a higher demand for transaction balances, which must be offset by a high enough interest rate to force an offsetting reduction in the demand for speculative and precautionary balances. For these reasons the LM curve is positively sloped. The IS curve presents those combinations of interest rate and level of income that equate planned saving and investment. It is conventionally drawn negatively sloped, implying that lower levels of

---

4. J. M. Keynes, *The General Theory of Employment, Interest, and Money*, (New York, 1936), p. 165.

5. J. R. Hicks, "Mr. Keynes and the 'Classics'; A Suggested Interpretation," *Econometrica*, 5 (1937), pp. 147–159.

interest are required to induce sufficient investment spending to equal the large savings generated by higher levels of income. It becomes positively sloped whenever planned investment expenditures increase more rapidly than planned savings as income rises.

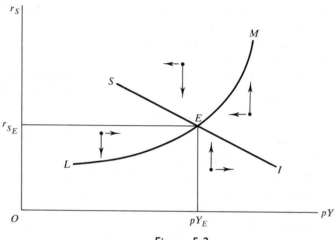

Figure 5-2

Only at the point of intersection E is general equilibrium in both the money and output markets attained. Whenever E lies in the vicinity of M on the LM relationship (where the LM curve is vertical), changes in saving and investment plans (which shift the IS curve) result only in changes in the interest rate, as the "pure" classical model suggests. Whenever the equilibrium point E lies in the vicinity of L (where the LM curve is horizontal) changes in saving and investment preferences produce only movements in the level of money income, as the "pure" Keynesian model concludes.

The classical nonmonetary theories previously described essentially state that the equilibrium rate of interest will be somewhere along the IS curve, and for this reason provide full determination of the rate of interest only when the level of income is assumed exogenously given. Preclassical and "crude" Keynesian monetary theories focus attention on the fact that the equilibrium rate of interest is determined somewhere along the LM curve, and again some income level must be assumed in any partial equilibrium presentation. Neoclassical loanable funds theories, and neo-Keynesian liquidity preference theories, both incorporate the interdependence of real and monetary variables. The first is formulated in terms of the supply and demand for securities, and the second in terms of the supply and demand for money. But as implied in Figure 5-2, in the special case of general equilibrium E, never achieved in reality, *both amount to the same thing*, since equilibrium in all markets must be satisfied.

The loanable funds formulation as a partial-equilibrium theory has the virtue of relating each rate of interest, or the price of any security, to the supply and demand for that security. This is a simple extension of the most basic tenet of traditional demand theory. In contrast the liquidity preference formulation relates the price of securities in general (the level of interest rates) to the supply and demand of a close substitute, money.

Formulating a supply and demand relation for each security has the additional advantage of emphasizing that there is no single rate of interest, and that the structure of interest rates may be expected to vary over time. However, the two presentations are clearly not exclusive. The relative explanatory importance of the supply and demand for the security itself, versus the supply and demand for a close substitute, as the single most significant set of variables in determining price is patently an empirical question. Because of the *ceteris paribus* assumption partial equilibrium analysis is much less satisfactory for interest theory than for price theory. A more general formulation, that includes both sets of variables, is preferable and clearly more appropriate.

A more basic distinction between the two approaches is that the liquidity preference theory conventionally is expressed in terms of stock relationships, while the loanable funds theory typically has been presented in terms of flow relationships. One contribution of this chapter has been to show that this dichotomy may be resolved upon examination of assetholder behavior under uncertainty. Both stock and flow relationships influence price. Stock relationships (liquidity preference) are more important in the short-run determination of financial asset prices, while flow relationships (loanable funds) play a greater role in explanations of long-run price determination.

In Figure 5-2 disequilibrium in output and financial markets is represented by points off both the *IS* and *LM* curves. Four possible disequilibria positions are represented. The transition path followed will depend on the speed at which prices adjust to clear each market. If financial asset prices adjust to eliminate excess demand or supply in financial markets more rapidly than the general price level and the level of income adjusts to restore equilibrium in output markets, in the short run the movement of the system will be predominantly toward *LM*, and only over the longer run toward *IS*. This is indicated in Figure 5-2 by the length of the rate-of-adjustment vectors. These transition paths correspond to the previously discussed temporary and full temporal equilibrium adjustment periods.

The reader has perhaps already realized that Figures 5-1a and 5-1b, and Figure 5-2, represent alternative two-dimentional presentations of a simple system of three equations in three unknowns. Such a system is stated below. Each equation represents the condition for zero excess demand in the market for current output, securities, and money respectively.

$$Y\ (Y, S/p, M/p, K, r, r_s) - Y = 0 \qquad \text{Current outputs markets (1)}$$

$$S\ (Y, S/p, M/p, K, r, r_s) - S/p = 0 \qquad \text{Securities markets} \qquad (2)$$

$$M\ (Y, S/p, M/p, K, r, r_s) - M/p = 0 \qquad \text{Money markets} \qquad (3)$$

Givens: S, M, K, r (For purposes of short-run analysis).
Unknowns: Y, p, r_s

By Walras' Law one equation may be dropped. In Figure 5-1a the level of income Y and prices p are assumed given, equation (1) is dropped, and Equations (2) and (3) are combined and solved for the alternative combinations of r_s and M/S. In Figure 5-1b, full employment income and prices are assumed given, Equations (2) and (3) dropped, and Equation (1) is solved for the alternative combinations of r_s and M/S. Combining Figures 5-1a and 5-1b, the temporary equilibrium levels of r_s and M/S that satisfy Equations (2) and (3) are compared with the full temporal equilibrium levels of r_s and M/S that satisfy full-employment equilibrium in output markets (Equation (1)). In Figure 5-2 the price level p and the stock of wealth $(M/p + S/p + K)$ are assumed given, Equation (2) is dropped, and

Equations (1) and (3) are solved for r_s and Y. Alternatively, full employment income may be assumed given and the system solved for r_s and p.

Recent empirical work in financial analysis has centered with a few exceptions on estimating the demand for money. There has been little agreement on the appropriate definition of monetary assets, but at least a general concensus seems to have been reached that the dependent variable is the *stock* of monetary assets, however defined, and that the determinants of quantity demanded are own-price, price of substitutes, and a wealth or income variable. The lack of agreement as to the specification of the explanatory variables is largely due to the statistical problems that plague regression analysis of economic time series—multicollinearity of all economic variables over time, serial correlation in the unexplained residuals, and the precise identification of supply and demand influences. Hopefully the large number of empirical studies currently underway will shed further light on the nature and speed of the adjustment process in different asset markets.

RECOMMENDED READING

John Gurley and Edward Shaw's, *Money in A Theory of Finance* (Washington, 1960), Don Patinkin's, *Money, Interest, and Prices* (New York, 1965), and Ralph Turvey's, *Interest Rates and Asset Prices* (London, 1960) all make important contributions to the recent development of a general theory of asset price determination.

A masterful summary of the extensive literature on monetary theory, plus a comprehensive bibliography, may be found in Harry Johnson's review article, "Monetary Theory and Policy," *American Economic Review*, Vol. LII, No. 3 (June 1962). For a classic discussion of stock and flow considerations and the time period of equilibrium, see W. Fellner and H. Somers, "A Note on 'Stocks' and 'Flows' in Monetary Interest Theory," *Review of Economics and Statistics*, Vol. 31 (May, 1949); L. Klein, W. Fellner, H. Somers, and K. Brunner, "Stock and Flow Analysis in Economics," *Econometrica*, Vol. 18 (July 1950); and W. Baumol, "Stocks, Flows and Monetary Theory," *Quarterly Journal of Economics* (February 1962). Also valuable are Don Patinkin, "Liquidity Preference and Loanable Funds: Stock and Flow Analysis," *Economica*, New Series Vol. 25 (November, 1958), and Warren Smith, "Monetary Theories of the Rate of Interest: A Dynamic Analysis," *Review of Economics and Statistics*, Vol. 40 (February 1958).

Joan Robinson's, "The Rate of Interest," *Econometrica*, Vol. XIX (April 1951) represents an early but incisive treatment of interest rate determination along the lines developed in this chapter.

An alternative treatment of the disequilibrium adjustment process in financial markets is suggested by George Horwich, *Money, Capital, and Prices* (Homewood, Ill., 1964).

William Sharpe has made a number of important contributions to a general theory of asset prices based on the principles of portfolio selection under risk. See particularly "Capital Asset Prices: A theory of Market Equilibrium Under Conditions of Risk," *Journal of Finance*, Vol. XIX, No. 3 (September, 1964). Also valuable is John Lintner's, "Security Prices, Risk, and Maximal Gains from Diversification," *Journal of Finance*, Vol. XX, No. 4 (December, 1965).

The results of a number of important recent investigations of the term structure of interest rates are lucidly summarized in Joseph W. Conard, *The Behavior of Interest Rates* (New York, 1966), Ch. 7.

6

Money and Banking

It is sometimes supposed that the banks mysteriously 'manufacture' credit . . . In fact it is not really the banks which lend, except in name. The banks are intermediaries. They bring borrowers and lenders together. And the lenders are the bank depositors. . . . All the borrowers are, then, the debtors, through the banks as intermediaries, of all the depositors. . . . Yet each depositor is in the position of a lender only so long as convenience dictates.

Harry Gunnison Brown
Economic Science and the Common Welfare, 1923

Introduction

Money has long commanded a central role in financial analysis due to the special significance of changes in the supply of monetary assets on the demand for other economic goods. This chapter reexamines the traditional analysis of commercial bank behavior as a necessary precondition to an exploration of the interrelationship between monetary change and real phenomena.

Money may be defined functionally as all financial assets that are directly acceptable as a means of payment. Section one reviews the special implicit services of monetary assets that explain why they are demanded at all in wealth portfolios in the absence of an explicit income yield. These properties may be summarized as *exchange convenience*, due to money's low transfer costs in the exercise of command

153

over purchasing power, and *capital certainty*, due to the high short-run predictability of money's future value. Together they provide monetary assets with an implicit yield in kind.

The second section takes up the murky question whether commercial banks, whose secondary securities are the most important type of monetary asset, are properly to be considered as merely one type of financial intermediary. Banks are shown to be *functionally* completely analogous to nonbank intermediaries, in serving to bring borrowers and lenders together. The lenders to a bank are the bank's depositors, who lend to the bank cash (legal tender) in return for deposit claims.

As is the case with nonbank financial intermediaries, the expansion of bank lending is shown to be limited by the supply of the primary securities that they purchase and the demand for the secondary securities that they issue. But because bank deposits, unlike the liabilities of nonbank intermediaries, are directly acceptable as a means of payment, it will be shown in the next chapter that the equilibrium volume of unregulated bank intermediation that profit-maximizing banks seek to establish will ordinarily not be consistent with general price level stability. Alternatively expressed, given the level of wealth, income, and asset returns, the demand for bank deposits is always determinate in real terms, but not necessarily in nominal terms.

Discussion of the forces determining the equilibrium volume of bank and nonbank intermediation and the effects of government regulation of bank output are deferred until the following chapter. Before developing the supply function for monetary assets it is necessary to review the operations of individual commercial banks considered as financial intermediaries to replace the mechanical reserve-deposit multiplier approach. Section three represents a straight-forward application of the theory of the firm under uncertainty to the determination of individual bank lending and borrowing operations and the level and composition of bank asset portfolios. For heuristic purposes two broad classes of bank portfolio decisions are distinguished, one pertaining primarily to liquidity, the management of bank reserves, and the other profitability, the management of bank earning assets.

In the appendix a model of bank operations is suggested which interprets bank behavior as that of utility-maximizing price discriminators faced by imperfect markets. The manner in which banks respond to changes in their cash reserves under such conditions is shown to differ considerably from the simple multiplier model.

Some Peculiarities of Monetary Assets

Money as a financial asset requires separate discussion. Both the properties of monetary assets, and the conditions governing their demand and supply, are somewhat special. Money may be defined functionally as those economic goods that are generally accepted as a *means of payment*. In addition a unit of money is usually the unit of account. The innovation of money permits the single transaction of barter, which requires an inverse dual coincidence of wants if exchange is to occur, to be broken into two separate transactions of purchase and sale. Since these two transactions are separated in time, exchange ratios can more efficiently equate demand and supply, because the necessity for a double coincidence of wants is eliminated.[1] The time separation of purchase and sale makes it desirable that the payments media used also be capable of serving as a temporary store of purchasing power or value.

The specific assets that are invested with general acceptability as a medium of exchange is partly a matter of social and legal convention, and anthropology testifies to the large number of unlikely objects that have been used. Although the selection of a monetary asset is largely self-justifying, in the sense that its monetary value derives from its general acceptability, the last section of Chapter 8 will demonstrate that the particular assets that may be chosen to serve as money possess important and distinct economic consequences.

It must first be emphasized that the generic term money denotes a whole class of financial assets that share a common characteristic— general and direct acceptability as a means of payment. In all modern economies there exist competing media of exchange, which complicate the task of financial analysis as well as financial control. Only the state has the authority to designate what shall be legally sufficient in settlement of debt, and in all modern economies legal tender is conferred only on currency (including coin), a non interest-bearing debt

1. Significantly, "barter" is etymologically derived from the Old French "bareter," meaning to cheat.

of the state itself. But obligations of the state are typically not the only assets that are generally accepted as a means of payment. The authority to invest debt with the properties of monetary assets is granted to select private economic units, most importantly commercial banks.

At the same time, primarily because of the evident causal relationship between the *total* stock of nominal monetary assets outstanding and the money value of aggregate expenditures, and so the purchasing power per unit of money, the social desirability of maintaining a stable price level has in all modern economies induced the state to develop a number of techniques to regulate the quantity of all or most monetary assets outstanding, and the manner and terms on which they may be issued. The characteristics of the supply function of monetary assets will be examined in a later chapter. Since the effects differ, a change in the supply of or demand for different types of monetary assets must be distinguished carefully.

Monetary assets like other assets are held for the services that they provide. In a position of portfolio balance the expected utility at the margin to an investor unit contributed by holding monetary assets must equal that from holding the last dollar of any other asset in the portfolio. Monetary assets ordinarily yield a zero or low income return. What then are the services of monetary assets which offset a low or absent explicit income yield and enable them to compete with other assets in wealthowner portfolios? There are two important properties of monetary assets that distinguish them, albeit in degree rather than in kind, from all other financial and nonfinancial assets in wealth portfolios.

Exchange convenience. A distinctive attribute of monetary assets is their general acceptability at zero or near-zero transactions cost in exchange for other economic goods. Monetary assets are the most *marketable* and the most *reversible* of all asset forms, reversibility being defined as the difference between buying and selling price (realizable value) at an instant of time. This confers on monetary assets a differential transfer cost advantage over other highly realizable assets which alternatively may be held as a temporary store of purchasing power. This transfer cost advantage may be termed the *exchange-convenience yield* of monetary assets, and accounts for a demand to hold money balances for transactions purposes. Strong theoretical arguments based on inventory theory suggest that important economies of scale exist in holding transactions balances.

The most important monetary assets, currency and bank demand deposits, are themselves characterized by different exchange-convenience yields. Currency carries the risk of loss either by accident or theft, and, if in large enough quantities, a nuisance cost. Bank deposits carry a service charge for making payments by check, that may be waived, and a slight risk of deposit loss arising from bank failures. Currency is generally accepted in payment of purchases with no questions asked. Checks are frequently accepted only after the presentation of satisfactory evidence of identity, and this imperfect acceptability rises as transactions with strangers increase. Travel has therefore encouraged the development of new types of money— traveler's checks and credit cards, which have low identification costs and are protected against loss. Another implicit cost of bank deposits is the convenience of conversion into currency, which is associated with the accessibility of commercial bank offices. Small purchases are more cheaply and conveniently financed with currency, but bank deposits provide bookkeeping service in recording all transactions. For some purposes, for example, illegal activity, and in particular income tax evasion, the lack of traceable records itself yields an implicit return to currency holdings.

In an uncertain world working asset balances, which may be defined as the excess of total realizable assets over expected minimum realizable assets within the future time horizon of an economic unit, are maintained because of the irregular and stochastic nature of the rate and timing of receipts and expenditures of economic participants. The share of monetary assets in working asset balances is not constant, and may be expected to vary directly with their differential exchange-convenience yield, and inversely with the explicit income yield conferred by ownership of other realizable assets.

The composition of currency and demand deposits in monetary assets is much less stable than generally believed. Currency in the United States is currently about 25 per cent of bank demand deposits, but this ratio has varied between 18 and 37 per cent over the last 50 years. Quarterly and even annual changes in currency are not closely correlated with changes in demand deposits.

Capital Certainty. In addition to their share in working asset balances, monetary assets are also demanded for the permanent wealth portfolios of investor units. This is attributable to the superior short-run predictability of future capital value (asset uncertainty) associated with holding monetary *vis-à-vis* other financial and tangible wealth forms. Holding monetary assets entails for all practical purposes zero risk of future loss apart from changes in the general level of prices, since changes in relative prices leave the real purchasing power of a unit of money for the average economic unit comparatively unaffected. Because changes in the average level of prices, which determine the exchange value of monetary assets, are ordinarily smaller and more predictable than changes in the price of other individual assets, monetary assets are demanded in wealth portfolios as investors diversify their asset holdings in order to reduce portfolio risk.

Other assets, particularly those whose value is fixed in money terms or whose future price is firmly expected not to fall, are to a greater or lesser degree money substitutes in reducing portfolio risk. The share of monetary assets in permanent wealth portfolios will vary directly with their differential capital certainty yield, and inversely with the explicit income yield conferred by the ownership of alternative wealth forms. The relative capital certainty advantage associated with holding monetary assets declines with the remoteness of future expenditure requirements. Since investor risk can be reduced by tailoring the time-shape of expected future receipts from wealth-ownership to the time-distribution of expected future expenditure, other assets will frequently be regarded as less risky than money by wealthholders whose time-horizon is long.

It is now possible to summarize the factors behind the demand function for money. Monetary assets are demanded for working asset and permanent wealth portfolios in direct proportions to their differential advantage over other assets in providing the exchange *convenience* and *capital certainty* services in which money excels, and inversely with the differential income return expected from holding nonmonetary assets. For analytical purposes, in order that changes in these implicit services of monetary assets will not be overlooked, it will prove convenient to regard money's own rate of return in kind as measured by a proxy variable expressed as an explicit percentage yield. The total return from holding a monetary asset is therefore this implicit convenience and certainty yield, any explicit income yield, plus any change in its real value caused by a change in the general price level.

Are Commercial Banks Financial Intermediaries?

A long-accepted dichotomy in traditional financial theory maintains that commercial banks are creators of loanable funds, while nonbank intermediaries are rather loanable funds brokers or middlemen. More recently recognition of formal similarities in the operations of commercial banks and other financial institutions has provoked an extended controversy concerning whether the traditional dichotomy is substantial or merely terminological, and reopened an older debate on the nature of commercial banking transactions.

The present section attempts to demonstrate that the activity of commercial banks is from a functional viewpoint precisely analogous to the operations of other financial institutions, and that be regarding banks as intermediaries their behavior can be more fully understood. At the same time the properties of commercial bank liabilities give bank intermediation a special significance in any examination of the interrelationships between financial activity and markets for current output and productive factors.

Financial intermediaries have been defined broadly as all economic units whose principal economic activity is the holding of and trading in financial assets. In consequence of economies of scale in lending and borrowing such institutions are able to intervene profitably in the flow of funds between nonfinancial lenders and borrowers (Intermediation Effects). In addition, by making possible the indirect ownership of primary securities, financial intermediaries were shown to effectuate a reduction in the subjective risk and inconvenience of wealth holding to ultimate wealth owners (Asset Transmutation Effects). Such a definition of financial intermediaries clearly includes the banking system. Commercial banks acquire the primary securities of borrowers, loans and bonds, and provide their own indirect securities, demand deposits, for the portfolio of lenders.

The creation of legal money or currency, at least in its modern token form, is unique in that by virtue of the legal authority of the state alone the State's noninterest-bearing obligations become legally acceptable in settlement of debt. All financial assets other than currency are *created* in the act of borrowing, which may be defined as the promise to pay currency (legal tender) in the future in return for a certain amount of currency in the present. Borrowing by an economic unit describes the act of sale of a newly created debt against itself in return for currency, lending the act of purchase of a debt against another economic unit in exchange for currency. Financial assets are simply legally binding acknowledgments of debt, that is, promises to pay currency or its equivalent.

Total financial assets other than currency outstanding in an economy can be increased only by an act of borrowing, which is always proximately reflected in an increase in the total assets and liabilities of the borrower. Total assets and liabilities of the lender always remain proximately unchanged, though the composition of his total assets is altered, since currency balances fall while holdings of financial assets rise by an identical amount. This is illustrated below for the case where both lender and borrower are nonfinancial units.

Table 6-1

Nonfinancial Borrower			Nonfinancial Lender		National Balance Sheet	
Currency +	Primary Security +	←	Currency −		Currency 0	Primary Security +
		→	Primary Security +		Primary Security +	
Total ——	Total ——		Total ——		Total ——	Total ——
Assets +	Liabilities +		Assets 0		Assets +	Liabilities +

As previously described, financial institutions occupy an intermediate position between nonfinancial borrowers and lenders. In their activity as borrower, all provide lenders with their own indirect securities in exchange for currency. Acting as lender, they acquire the primary securities of borrowers with the currency proceeds they have received from lenders. Nonfinancial economic units issue primary securities against themselves in return for currency. This process is illustrated below for the case where a financial intermediary is interposed between a nonfinancial lender and borrower. In their activities as borrower financial intermediaries create financial assets, since, as has been shown above, this is the prerogative of borrowers alone. All financial intermediaries dispose only of the currency lenders entrust to them, and make a profit insofar as they can charge borrowers a higher rate than they must pay lenders for currency received.

In addition to their role as intermediary in bringing borrowers and lenders together and so facilitating the transfer of currency balances from nonfinancial lenders to nonfinancial borrowers, financial institutions effect a transmutation of financial assets. This is shown by a comparison of the composite national balance sheet changes in Tables 6-1 and 6-2. The only difference between the two final situations is

Table 6-2

a. Borrowing Operations

Financial Intermediary		Nonfinancial Lender		National Balance Sheet (Excluding Financial Units)	
Currency +	← Currency −			Currency −	
	Secondary	→ Secondary		Secondary	
	Security +	Security +		Security +	
Total —	Total —	Total —	Total —	Total —	Total —
Assets +	Liabilities +	Assets 0	Liabilities 0	Assets 0	Liabilities 0

b. Lending Operations

Nonfinancial Borrower		Nonfinancial Intermediary		National Balance Sheet (Excluding Financial Units)	
Currency +	Primary	← Currency −		Currency +	Primary
	Security +	→ Primary			Security +
		Security +			
Total —	Total —	Total —	Total —	Total —	Total —
Assets +	Liabilities +	Assets 0	Liabilities 0	Assets +	Liabilities +

that in the case of indirect lending of currency through a financial intermediary, the nonfinancial lender gains possession of a secondary security of the intermediary rather than a primary security of the nonfinancial borrower. The foregoing analysis is completely general and applies to all economic units. As a comparison between Tables 6-1 and 6-2 indicates, any differences in the effects of direct versus indirect finance on the behavior of economic units, or differences between different types of indirect finance, must be attributable either to the type of borrower accommodated and primary security which is created, or to differences between the properties of the secondary securities acquired by nonfinancial lenders in exchange for currency.

Commercial banks, like all other financial intermediaries, conform to the process outlined in Table 6-2, and can lend to borrowers only currency entrusted to them by their depositors. In their role as borrower they issue deposits in return for currency, while other financial intermediaries issue various other forms of secondary securities in return for currency. The lenders to a bank are the bank's depositors, and all the borrowers from a bank are the debtors, through the bank as intermediary, of all the depositors. While no one depositor need remain a continuous lender to a bank for a longer period than he desires, depositors as a whole, considering the entire banking system, do in fact remain continuous lenders. As long as checks received are held or redeposited upon receipt, and not cashed in for currency, fluctuations in individual deposit accounts are offsetting for the system as a whole. As total deposits outstanding of any individual bank exhibit a much higher degree of stability than individual deposit holdings, total deposits outstanding of the banking system exhibit a higher degree of stability than total deposits of any individual bank.

While the operations of all financial intermediaries are functionally analogous, the *effects* of their operations may be shown to differ insofar as the secondary securities that they create in their role as borrower possess different properties, and so are conducive to differential behavior on the part of their holder. Secondary securities that financial institutions create yield a wide variety of future services, and product differentiation results in differing liquidity, realizability, reversibility, predictability, and divisibility characteristics of the instruments offered.

Deposit balances, the indirect securities issued by commercial banks, are a substitute for currency *par excellence*. Although claims against other intermediaries approach deposits in many of the attributes of currency, bank deposits historically have been unique in being acceptable for direct transfer by check without encashment in settlement of debt. The form of product differentiation adopted by commercial banks—ready and convenient convertibility at par into currency, provision of an instrument (check) by which deposits may be transferred within the banking system, and bookkeeping services on deposit accounts—encourages the widespread acceptance and use of checks drawn against bank deposits for settlement of debt in most transactions. Consequently depositor-lenders to commercial banks, in return for lending their currency, receive a secondary security that itself serves directly as a payments medium. The liquidity of depositor portfolios is not reduced by the act of lending to a bank, since there is no sacrifice of disposal over current purchasing power for most transactions, and no imposed necessity to defer current expenditures, except for those transactions payment of which cannot be settled by means of check. Such a form of wealth holding requires a minimum reward to wealthowners for the act of lending.

The previous section discussed the demand to hold monetary assets for working and portfolio balances in terms of convenience, certainty, and return. Commercial banks enable the convenience waiting entailed by holding currency to be put at the disposal of borrowers. In addition to the facilities involved in maintaining and administering the deposit transfer mechanism, banks provide safety of principal, financial advice, credit references, edifying edifices, attractive tellers, and a host of other desirable services which combine to produce a return on bank depoits higher than that attainable from holding currency balances. The result is that bank deposits dominate currency for many purposes, particularly for portfolio balances.

The fact that bank deposits are maintained at considerable cost as a close and for some purposes superior substitute for currency lends a special significance to bank intermediary operations. When an individual bank makes a loan to a nonbank borrower, the banking system as a whole ordinarily finds that its total assets and liabilities increase by the same amount, less a fractional cash drain to nonbank currency balances. Since *only* the act of borrowing can result in the creation of intangible assets, this indicates that the banking system simultaneously increases its borrowing by an amount approximately equal to the increase in lending by an individual bank. The causal chain linking the borrowing and lending operations of nonbank intermediaries is complex and tenuous, while for the commercial banking system the causal relationship is immediate and direct. This relationship is indicated in Table 6-3.

If a bank borrower is content to hold a bank deposit rather than currency, *the act of borrowing from the bank at the same time involves an act of lending to the banking system*, so that the roles of nonfinancial lender and borrower are performed simultaneously by the same economic unit. As shown in Table 6-3b, the two transactions of borrowing and lending merge in a single contract, so that borrowing from a bank becomes in effect a barter exchange of debts.

It is now possible to examine the validity of the conventional dichotomy with some precision.

"Creator" versus "Middlemen". It has been customary to regard commercial banks as unique among financial institutions in possessing

Table 6-3a

Borrowing and Lending Operations
Functionally Related

Nonfinancial Borrower

Currency	+	Primary Security +
		Total Liabilities +
Total Assets	+	

Commercial Banking System

Currency	0	Deposit +
Primary Security	+	
Total Assets	+	Total Liabilities +

Nonfinancial Lender

Currency	–	Deposit +
Total Assets	0	Total Liabilities 0

National Balance Sheet (Excluding Financial Units)

Currency	0	Primary Security +
Deposit	+	–
Total Assets	+	Total Liabilities +

Table 6-3b

Borrowing and Lending Operations
Simultaneous

Commercial Banking System

Currency	0	Deposit +
Primary Security	+	
Total Assets	+	Total Liabilities +

Nonfinancial Borrower and Lender

Currency	0	Primary Security +
Deposit	+	
Total Assets	+	Total Liabilities +

National Balance (Excluding Financial Units)

Currency	0	Primary Security +
Deposit	+	
Total Assets	+	Total Liabilities +

an ability to create money "like thousands of little private mints." The analogy is unfortunate. The analysis of the previous section indicates that commercial banks are not categorically different from other financial institutions by virtue of their ability to "create" deposits. All financial as well as nonfinancial institutions "create" secondary securities in their role as borrower. Commercial banks create demand deposits when they borrow currency; other intermediaries create various forms of indirect debt when they borrow currency. Credit "creation," in the sense of an increase in financial assets, occurs whenever one economic unit, financial or nonfinancial, borrows from another. Differences between financial institutions lie not in the fact that some can create debt and others cannot, but in the properties with which each endows its debt obligations.

It has been argued to support the dichotomy between bank deposits and other indirect securities that a significant operational criterion of monetary assets is that their total remains unaffected by a payment made in any of their components. The bank deposit balance of an individual economic unit increases or decreases as a result of surpluses or deficits in its money payments and receipts, without altering the aggregate stock of monetary assets and without having any effect in the market for loans. Reduction of individual deposit balances with nonbanks, it is argued, reduces the total quasi-money stock in existence. Conversely, it is often maintained that the decision to save and to hold bank deposits does not increase total deposits, and so does not make any more funds available than would the decision to spend instead.

Such arguments fail to appreciate the significance of the banking function as an intermediator between lender and borrower. The above statements are logically correct only for the case in which the recipient of a check drawn against a bank deposit is always willing to increase his deposit balance, and so his lending to the banking system, by an identical amount. *The decision to hold bank deposits does make more funds available to borrowers than the decision to hold currency balances,* and the latter is the relevant comparison as well as the demonstration of banks' intermediary function. Only legal money or currency satisfies the operational criterion that the aggregate outstanding remain invariant to decisions of private spending units to reduce or increase their individual component balances.

The Multiple Expansion of Bank Deposits. The dichotomy between commercial banks and other financial intermediaries is conventionally related to well-established differences in the role of the community's asset preferences in determining the size of secondary claims outstanding. Aggregate bank deposits are proximately determined by the volume of assets that banks may create from a limited reserve base, and not by the preferences of assetholders. The implication of the bank credit multiplier is that banks, if uncontrolled, would possess an unlimited ability to expand deposits, since the latter are determined only by the amount of primary securities that the banking system purchases. For nonbank institutions, it is argued, the causal direction is reversed. The amount of primary securities that nonbanks can purchase is limited by the amount of indirect securities they can lodge in the portfolios of lenders. Not possessing the multiplicative faculty of commercial banks, they are confined to the brokerage function of simply transmitting to borrowers the funds entrusted to them by lenders.

As previously noted, the feedback relationship between bank lending and borrowing operations is much closer than is the case for most nonbanks. The banking system is truly distinctive both in the high proportion and in the speed with which lending to the banking system increases in consequence of an increase in bank lending to nonbank spending units. Whenever a bank borrower is content to hold his loan in the form of a bank deposit, the restoration is instantaneous and occurs within a single transaction. Due to the general practice of redepositing checks in a bank after receipt, whatever the intended disposition of funds by the recipient, currency lent by an individual bank is retained as cash reserves for the banking system, minus only a fractional drain to currency in circulation outside of banks as deposit balances expand.

For nonbank intermediaries the drain is much larger, and only a small proportion of currency lent is returned in the short run by lenders to any particular intermediary type, Nonbank lending and borrowing operations are related within the average income-turnover period of spending units. An act of lending by a nonbank institution increases total financial assets of borrowers, which subsequently increases aggregate expenditure and aggregate demand for financial assets, including demand for the obligations of that particular intermediary.

Changes in both bank and nonbank liabilities reflect portfolio management decisions in response to changing financial asset prices, As a result the increase in secondary obligations of an intermediary class in any particular period may be but tenuously related to the current saving flow (an increase in net worth). An increase in lending to an intermediary may also be financed out of past savings, that is by the sale of existing assets, and, in the case of banks, by new borrowing.

This important distinction with regard to the feedback relationship between lending and borrowing operations has commonly been interpreted to imply that banks if unregulated possess an *unlimited* ability to expand total deposits. Conventional presentations of the bank deposit multiplier process frequently appear to deny the existence of an effective demand schedule to the market for bank deposits. The factors determining the volume of bank and nonbank intermediation will be considered in the next chapter. Without anticipating the argument there, the close association between total lending and borrowing by the banking system does *not* imply the absence of transactions and portfolio demand functions for bank loans and deposits, and so the existence of an equilibrium level of bank output. All financial assets are to a greater or lesser degree substitutes in wealth portfolios. The general acceptability of bank deposits as a means of payment, because expensive to provide and maintain, has its cost in terms of income yield, so that wealthowners prefer to hold some desired and finite proportion of deposit balances and bank loans to income and wealth. As will be explained in the subsequent chapter, the equilibrium level of unregulated bank output will be consistent with price level stability only under certain limited conditions.

The multiplicative relationship of bank deposits to bank reserves merely reflects the institutional fact that bank expansion is anchored, as other financial intermediary expansion is not, to a regulated base. *The multiplicative faculty is more accurately regarded not as a distinctive feature of bank intermediation, but as a consequence of government regulation of the volume of commercial bank assets and liabilities at a disequilibrium position, below the level that it would be profitable for banks to supply in the absence of controls.* The input-coefficient relating bank reserves to bank deposits is specified, and since bank reserves are rationed the level of bank intermediation is exogenously determined. If nonbank intermediaries were similarly subject to effective quantitative regulation, they too would be able to create liabilities by a multiple of their allotted legal reserves.

Governmental policy perpetuates commercial banks as a disequilibrium system. But it does not eliminate the influence of the demand schedule for bank deposits on the volume of bank intermediation. Once the policy goal of the government is stipulated—whether it be a particular interest rate structure, general price level stability, rapid growth, full employment, balance of payments, or any other objective or combination of objectives—and the techniques of monetary control are directed to this end, the government losses control of the volume of bank deposits in an effective rather than a technical sense. The supply of deposits becomes a tap issue, and the amount outstanding is effectively determined by the asset preferences of spending units.

As it is more accurate to attribute the multiplicative relation between bank reserves and deposits to the regulations to which banks alone are subjected, rather than to the special nature of the banking function, it is incorrect to conclude that an unregulated banking system possesses an unlimited power to expand its assets and liabilities. The banking system can best be understood as an industry prevented by quantitative limitation from expanding to its equilibrium size. Banks like all other business firms make a profit by selling their product above cost, and this necessity of operating at a profit, combined with a downward sloping demand curve for bank loans and deposits, serves to restrict output expansion even in the absence of deposit control through reserve manipulation.

As will be developed in the following chapters, the traditional view of the way a central bank works is that it supplies some volume of reserves, which, given existing reserve requirements and certain leakages, determines the stock of money. The public must hold that stock whether it wishes to or not. The foregoing analysis suggests that it is more useful to think of open-market operations as affecting financial asset stocks and interest rates, and by this route affecting the preferred portfolio composition that banks and the public desire to hold, and so the volume of bank and nonbank intermediation. Only so long as bank intermediation is exogenously restrained below its equilibrium output, and relative asset returns remain unchanged, will banks increase the supply of deposits *pari passu* as their reserves increase.

Asset Transmutation Effects. Financial intermediaries effectuate the indirect ownership of primary securities by ultimate wealth units, and in the process affect a transmutation of financial assets in the portfolios of nonfinancial spending units. Differences in the significance of intermediary activity for economic behavior are attributable primarily to the different properties which they endow their various secondary securities in comparison to the properties of the primary securities that they acquire.

The purchase of primary securities by all intermediaries in their role as lender enables the seller to increase current expenditure by an identical amount. Borrowers find their total assets and liabilities proximately increased by the amount of the loan, while intermediaries experience a change in the composition of their total assets as a result of the transaction. The sale of secondary securities by all intermediaries in their role as borrower increases intermediary total assets and liabilities, while lenders to intermediaries experience a change in the composition of their total assets. The extent to which lenders experience an offsetting reduction in their disposal over current goods and services depends on the properties of the secondary securities they receive in exchange for currency balances.

It has been emphasized that each type of financial institution creates its own unique form of indirect debt which it makes available to lenders. Commercial bank demand deposits are unlike most other secondary securities in that they are generally accepted as a means of payment. If money is defined to include only commercial bank demand deposits plus currency outside of banks, commercial banks are by definition unique among financial institutions in creating "money." But if monetary assets are defined functionally to include all claims generally accepted as a means of payment, commercial bank time and savings deposits, and deposits of some other financial institutions, must in many countries be included if directly transferable by check.

Once money is recognized as a generic term denoting a collective of financial assets, the question arises how inclusive ought the operational definition of general acceptability as a payments media to be? Checks drawn against demand deposits do not command general acceptability when the payee cannot be certain they will be met. Deposits payable on demand at a variety of financial institutions may be directly transferred for some purposes, and may be indistinguishable from bank deposits in possessing the certainty and store of value properties of currency. Even unused lines of credit are similar to bank deposits in that they represent potential command over goods and services that can be exercised on demand.

In view of the abundance of "near-money" substitutes, it cannot simply be assumed *a priori* that a sharp discontinuity exists between bank demand deposits and other financial assets. A delineation of monetary assets to include commercial bank demand deposits but no other secondary securities requires empirical evidence that bank demand deposit balances are related to the current spending behavior of their owners in a manner significantly different from holdings of other secondary obligations. Such evidence is unlikely to be forthcoming in all those countries where bank savings deposits and other intermediary claims possess high exchange convenience and are directly transferable by check.

As a result of such considerations some experts have argued that *no* satisfactory operational criterion exists for distinguishing between "money" and "quasi-money". While the appropriate empirical counterpart remains in dispute, the functional definition of monetary assets previously developed, as all claims generally accepted as a means of payment irrespective of the issuing institution, appears *a priori* likely to be most significantly related to current expenditure. Similarly, a class of monetary intermediaries may be distinguished which borrow, possibly to a varying degree, by the issue of instruments directly acceptable as a means of payment.

Monetary assets so defined represent a form of wealth holding that requires from wealthowners no contractually imposed postponement of disposal over the purchasing power that wealth represents. They are therefore an acceptable form of lending by deficit as well as surplus spending units. Lenders to monetary intermediaries, which in all countries comprise primarily commercial banks, find that the composition of their assets has been changed in such a fashion that a claim generally regarded as a means of payment is substituted for a currency balance. Such claims are an acceptable and even preferred substitute for currency balances for most purposes, and the lender to monetary intermediaries finds his balance sheet position but imperceptibly changed. Since an act of lending to a monetary intermediary does not reduce the total amount of means of payment available to the depositor-lender, it does not impose even a temporary external restraint to current expenditures by the depositor.

The secondary securities received by lenders to nonmonetary intermediaries are to varying degrees less close substitutes for currency balances. While they may be a very satisfactory store of temporary purchasing power, they cannot ordinarily be bartered directly for economic goods, but must first be encashed at some exchange cost or inconvenience for currency or bank deposits. Lending to nonmonetary intermediaries therefor imposes a varying restraint to current expenditure, depending on the procedure of exercising the purchasing power which the loan represents, since such claims cannot be directly transferred to other spending units but must first be encashed. Sale of secondary securities by most nonmonetary intermediaries is consequently much more likely to be associated with an accompanying decision to postpone expenditure and to increase current saving on the part of nonbank lenders, in contrast with lending to a monetary intermediary which is much less likely to imply an accompanying decision to increase *ex ante* saving.

It may be concluded that an expansion of monetary intermediation is generally associated with a greater increase in aggregate demand than an equal expansion of nonmonetary intermediation. The act of borrowing results in the creation of debt and the transfer of currency to borrowing units, who presumably intend to spend it. Lending of currency to monetary intermediaries imposes no obstacle to current expenditure on the part of the depositor. Lending to nonmonetary intermediaries imposes a penalty to nonpostponement of current expenditure on the part of the lender, varying with the contractual period specified for which the secondary security must be held and on the transactions costs and inconvenience of encashment. *Individual* depositors, as long as they maintain a positive balance outstanding, do in fact temporarily refrain from current expenditure by an amount equal to their lending, but this may be regarded as "convenience" waiting. Depositors *in the aggregate* remain continual lenders to monetary intermediaries, but do not of course continually refrain from current expenditure. Individual holders of nonmonetary claims similarly refrain from expenditure during the period that such secondary securities are held, but the turnover of such claims is much lower. Lending to nonmonetary intermediaries represents to a greater extent imposed contractual or "inconvenience" waiting, and demands a correspondingly larger reward.

To the extent that readily encashable claims against nonmonetary intermediaries are regarded as convenience lending by their holders, their turnover will be high, reflecting a wealth-expenditure relationship that may approach that of demand deposits. For nonmonetary claims that can be encashed quickly, with certainty, and without expense, the fact that they are not *directly* transferable in settlement of debt undoubtedly recedes in importance. Flow of funds data on *gross* inflows and outflows to nonmonetary institutions would make it possible to calculate the extent to which expansion of nonmonetary intermediation is associated with an increase in the level of aggregate expenditure. The expansionary effect is smaller than an equivalent expansion of monetary intermediation, but the distinction is a matter of empirical degree rather than kind.

In the presence of shifts in the composition of asset portfolios, an increase in holdings of nonmonetary secondary securities cannot categorically be identified with *ex ante* decisions to increase saving out of current income by an equivalent amount. Conversely an increase in monetary deposits need not reflect an intention to increase *pari passu* current consumption or investment expenditure, although to the extent increased lending to the banking system is financed by increased borrowing, rather than sale of other assets, this is likely to be the case.

Commercial Bank Operations

Before considering the determination of bank and nonbank intermediation it is necessary to examine in greater detail the behavior of individual banking firms. Commercial banks, like other financial institutions, derive their profits from the differential between the average rate they are able to charge borrowers and the average rate they are required to pay lenders to induce them to acquire an equivalent amount of secondary obligations. Bank earnings are obtained primarily from interest charges on two broad types of primary securities—nonmarketable secured or unsecured loans to business and household units, and marketable bonds of business and government units. Bank expenses consist of interest payments to depositors, remuneration to employees, and other current operating expenses largely allocable to the servicing of deposits, and to a lesser extent to the cost of granting and administering loans and securities.

Commercial bank management is commonly described as the art of balancing liquidity against profitability. Although practicing bankers are faced with a spectrum of possible assets, with divergent liquidity and risk characteristics and varying chance of gain, it is a convenient simplification to distinguish three broad asset categories, reserves, investments, and loans.

Bank reserves are composed of assets of high liquidity and predictability, and are either legal money, i.e., currency and central bank deposits (primary reserves), or readily convertible into legal money without large inconvenience to their issuer or substantial risk of capital loss to the holder, i.e., treasury bills and other highly liquid assets (secondary reserves). Bank secondary reserves include realizable assets that yield some income return, but they are held not primarily as a source of profit but as a pool of liquid assets to be used for transactions purposes.

Bank earning asset portfolios provide the main source of bank income. The investment portfolio consists of intermediate-term marketable securities held for income and diversification purposes. It is in effect a means for speculation against future changes in the level of interest rates. The nonmarketable loan portfolio is held for income purposes, and is composed of illiquid assets considered unavailable for meeting expected net deposit withdrawals.

The portfolio problem concerns the manner in which commercial banks, in order to maximize their expected utility, allocate their total assets among these three asset categories. In view of the short-term nature of banking liabilities, and the relatively small size of bank capital accounts, banks are conventionally regarded as risk-averting investors. The share of total funds in portfolio balance allocated to each asset group may then be expected to vary positively with expected return, and negatively with expected risk.[2] While the magnitude of

2. The ratio of bank loans to total deposits on a cross-section basis has been found to be negatively related to loan rates charged. While this result conceivably could be explained by an income effect dominating the substitution effect for high risk averters, a more persuasive explanation as will be shown lies in terms of the differing structure of banking markets.

shifts in bank preferred portfolio composition in response to changes in these variables, and the speed of adjustment to portfolio imbalance, can only be discovered by empirical estimation, it is fruitful to specify further the nature of bank preferences and the institutional and legal constraints that shape the response mechanism.

Corresponding to the three broad asset categories, it is possible to distinguish two distinct types of bank operating decisions, pertaining first to the quantity of the primary and secondary reserve portfolio as a proportion of total bank assets (liquidity), and secondly concerning the optimum size and composition of the earning asset portfolios between investments and loans (profitability). These two types of operating decisions will now be considered in turn. Although the distinction is of some analytic convenience, strictly speaking both considerations are involved in most decisions.

Present bank attitudes to liquidity are in part the product of a long historical evolution. Commercial banking began when Italian goldsmiths first discovered that they could lend out the coin of others and still remain in business. The possibility of operating with claims against themselves exceeding coin in their vaults was found to be compatible with maintaining bank notes or deposits continuously convertible on demand into coin only so long as creditors remained confident that bank liabilities will always be freely exchangeable into coin. Once apprehensiveness developed that a banker could not pay his liabilities on demand the public attempted to exchange its holdings of his notes and deposits into cash, and a "run" on the bank developed that frequently resulted in a "bankruptcy" (literally, breaking the money changer's bench or table). Early bankers learned from experience to be very cautious about the type of operations in which they engaged, since their whole position depended upon the maintenance of this "confidence trick". In order to remain above suspicion the successful banker attempted to cultivate an image of conservative prudence, to confine his activities to the purchase of financial assets from "credit-worthy" borrowers, to require ample collateral on loans granted, and to acquire only such primary securities as are repayable fairly quickly (the tradition of the self-liquidating loan).

Caution about the kinds of loans made was found to be a necessary but not sufficient guarantee of solvency. The final safeguard of a banker's position was that he should avoid making too many loans, but always maintain sufficient holdings of cash balances in reserve to be able to deal with any conceivable "run." This customary cash ratio originally was determined largely by painful experience. In deciding the volume of their loans and investments bankers were forced to protect themselves against the consequences of large, even though improbable, deposit withdrawals. The penalty was the inability to honor demand obligations, so that the bank would fail, not because its loans and investments were bad, but because they were illiquid. In many countries bank imprudence about cash ratios led to legal provisions to reinforce bankers' self-discipline so as to protect depositors. Banks are now universally legally required to hold a minimum proportion of their total note and deposit liabilities in the form of cash reserves, or some other suitable liquid asset.

Commercial bankers traditionally were thus compelled to be extremely conscious of their liquidity position—much more so than other economic units. This tradition has remained, even though the cushion against insolvency due simply to illiquidity has been rendered very nearly obsolete. Governments have chosen not to confer legal tender upon bank deposits, but the central bank, by acceptance of its role as "lender of last resort", can prevent banks from failing from lack of funds to meet deposit withdrawals. If the central bank were prepared to rediscount long-term credit instruments acquired by commercial banks, and for longer periods, the distinction between reserves and earning assets disappears, and the possibility of a contagious loss of confidence in a particular bank or banks due to a liquidity crisis would be completely removed. Carried to its logical conclusion, such government policy would eliminate entirely the function of required cash reserves as a protection against insolvency, as well as any self-imposed confinement to short-term lending on the part of commercial banks. Any loan or investment becomes as liquid as the central bank's readiness to accept it for rediscounting, and in a crisis no other financial assets are liquid. Under such conditions a bank could conceivably fail as a result of poor management or bad judgement in making loans and investments, not because its assets are illiquid but because they are of insufficient value to cover deposits even if held to maturity.

The historic function of required cash reserves as a cushion of safety for bank depositors against insolvency having become anachronistic, their contemporary purpose is to provide a fulcrum for central bank control over the volume of commercial bank intermediation. Primary reserves are now held because they are legally required. Paradoxically, in view of the original function of reserve requirements, primary reserves are now largely or completely unavailable to meet unanticipated deposit withdrawals, depending on the manner in which they are calculated. Secondary reserves are held to avoid the additional special costs of borrowing, liquidation of higher-yielding assets, inconvenience, and damage to prestige involved in failing to pass the reserve test in consequence of net deposit withdrawals, as well as to protect against the disaster of insolvency.

An increase in earning assets relative to total reserves increases the probability of having to incur special costs in order to meet the required reserve test. An increase in secondary reserves relative to earning assets reduces this probability, but at the same time reduces the net profit rate earned on total bank assets. For any set of expected yields on reserves and earning assets, bank preferences between risk and profitability will define an optimum composition of the reserve portfolio, and an optimum ratio of total reserves to total assets. Since this preferred liquidity position describes a state of bank portfolio balance between risk and profitability, it will not in general remain invariant to changes in asset yields and in the cost of failing to meet the reserve test.

In an uncertain world a bank is not able to predict with certainty its future transaction needs. Given the current volume of bank earning assets, a bank must regard its total deposits on future dates as governed by some probability distribution of expected net deposit withdrawals and accretions. Analysis of the transactions demand for money have indicated that the desired reserve-asset portfolio should vary positively but less than proportionately with the volume of deposit transactions. The larger the proportion of large and erratic deposits, and the larger the penalties involved in being caught with insufficient reserve assets, the larger will be the desired reserve asset portfolio. Such penalties include the cost of borrowing and the expenses involved in the purchase and sale of investment assets. For all these reasons the proportion of total assets allocated to reserves may be expected to differ widely among individual banks in different size classes.

Assuming that a preferred ratio of reserves to total assets has been selected on portfolio principles, how is the composition of earning assets between the investment and loan portfolios determined? Investment assets are intermediate with respect to the other two portfolio groups in terms of expected return, liquidity, and risk. The existence of relatively high brokerage fees and large possible variations in price make them ill-suited to meet unexpected transaction movements. The possibility of a large capital loss, combined with an extreme risk-averting preference function, deters most banks from holding long-term securities. Loans have the highest expected rate of return, the greatest risk, including risk of default, and the least liquidity. Unlike the other two groups, the return, risk, and terms on loans are subject to significant control by the bank, and the demand for loans is subject to considerable cyclical variation.

The markets in which investment and loan assets are purchased are distinct and separate, in that funds loaned in one do not readily flow into the other. Due largely to the costs of information, markets for nonmarketable debt instruments are restricted geographically. Many bank borrowers have access to few alternative sources of credit. Moreover interest expense is quantitatively a small item in determining the overall desirability of most short-term borrowing decisions. As a result individual banks are faced in local markets for nonmarketable loans by typically interest-inelastic supply schedules of primary securities.

Individual banks are faced with a much more elastic supply of securities in the well-organized markets for marketable bonds. Banks must compete for the existing stock of marketable securities with a wide range of other institutional and private investors on national markets. New issues of many such obligations represent long-term borrowing more sensitive to interest expense. For smaller banks the supply elasticity of most marketable securities purchased approaches infinity, while for certain issues and for larger banks the elasticity is large though finite.

In the case of imperfect markets the previous analysis of portfolio selection must be reconsidered, since the price and return on alternative assets can no longer be regarded as *given* to individual portfolio managers. The circumstances described above in fact provide the standard preconditions for price discrimination. Banks are able both to control the risk and to establish the return on a large proportion of assets in their loan portfolios. The degree of risk accepted will depend on the utility functions of individual banks, so that the nature, composition, and return of loan portfolios may be quite diverse among different banks. The situation is complicated by the fact that the markets for bank loans and the markets for bank deposits are not independent. The terms and availability of loan credit offered to individual borrowers are also used as an instrument in the competition for bank deposits.

Given the characteristics of the loan portfolio, its share in total earning assets may then be expected to vary widely, both over time for the banking system as a whole and among individual banks at a moment in time, depending on the relative strength of loan demand.[3]

3. This suggests an explanation for the negative relationship observed between loan-deposit ratios and loan rates. Lower loan rates increase the amount demanded, which result in higher loan-deposit ratios, while higher rates result in lower ratios.

APPENDIX TO CHAPTER 6

A Model of Commercial Bank Asset Selection in Imperfect Markets

Regulatory authorities, primarily through restrictions on branching, entry, and merger, have sought two somewhat conflicting objectives—the attainment of a "failure-proof" banking system that is also "efficient". The relationship between the structure of geographically separate banking markets and bank performance has been the subject of considerable recent empirical research by economists. The typical small community or large city banking market in the United States has been found to be highly oligopolistic, with the three largest banks controlling 60 to 95 per cent of the total deposits.

Commercial banks, like other financial institutions, may be regarded as a firm whose multiple products are particular types of credit, and whose chief nonlabor factor inputs are funds obtained from lenders. Traditional theory of the firm then enables a static price discrimination model of an individual bank's behavior to be formulated with some precision.

Banks may be regarded as multiple-product firms that separate their markets and customers in order to practice price discrimination. A bank's profits are the difference between its total revenue from all markets and its total cost of production. In order to maximize profits, a bank will set its marginal revenue in each market equal to the marginal cost of its total output. Whichever markets have the lowest elasticity of demand will also have the highest interest rates.

Figure 6-1 provides a graphical formulation of bank lending and investment operations.[4] The short-run cost of funds for bank lending operations is the net rate banks must pay to attract an equivalent quantity of deposits, adjusted for "dead-weight" reserve holdings. Once the quantity of bank reserves is established by the monetary authorities the supply of nominal deposits for the banking system as a whole is relatively inelastic, since changes in total deposits

4. Although on first glance rather formidable, Figure 6-1 is simply an adaptation of the supply and demand curves for monetary intermediation of the next chapter (Figure 4) to the case of an individual bank operating in separable and imperfect markets.

can only occur as a result of variations in bank liquidity ratios. For individual commercial banks the short-run marginal cost curve of deposit balances is much less steeply rising, since they are able to bid deposits away from other banks and so to increase their share of the given total of reserves available to the banking system.

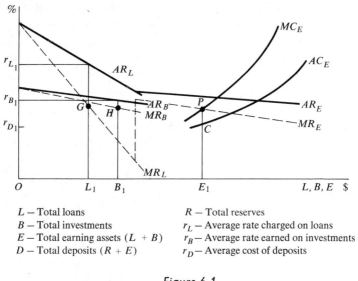

L — Total loans	R — Total reserves
B — Total investments	r_L — Average rate charged on loans
E — Total earning assets $(L + B)$	r_B — Average rate earned on investments
D — Total deposits $(R + E)$	r_D — Average cost of deposits

Figure 6-1

The short-run average and marginal cost of funds to acquire earning assets are shown as AC_E and MC_E in Figure 6-1. They represent the average and marginal costs of increasing outstanding deposits, adjusted for the load factor (earning assets/total deposits) minus any return earned on bank reserves.[5] For most unit banks, institutionally restricted to a local and oligopolistic deposit market, average cost curves will be first flat and then steeply upward sloping, so that marginal cost curves exhibit a vertical discontinuity at the

5. If L is the ratio of total reserves to total deposits (R/D), r_D is the average net cost of deposits, and r_R the return earned on reserves, the average cost of funds equals $[r_D/(1-L) - r_R L]$. A recent cost study estimated gross annual expenses of handling demand deposits at 2.3 per cent of total deposits outstanding. Revenue from service charges was estimated at 35 per cent of total deposit expenses, reducing the net costs of demand deposit funds to 1.5 per cent. *New England Business Review*, October, 1961, Federal Reserve Bank of Boston.

point where excess cash is used up for a given level of services to depositors.

The demand for bank loans (supply of nonmarketable debt) is represented by AR_L, and the supply of marketable bonds is represented by AR_B. The single interest rate shown at each level of loan and bond holdings is to be interpreted as the expected return from an optimally diversified loan or bond portfolio, given the individual bank's aversion to risk. The position of the curves may therefore differ among banks in the same market due to differences in the attitude of management to risk bearing. Lending rates of return are regarded as measured net of all costs of purchasing and administering primary securities, including a deduction for estimated bad-debt loss ratios. The marginal revenue schedules from loan and bond portfolios are labeled MR_L and MR_B, respectively. The average revenue schedules from bank lending and investment operations may then be aggregated and average and marginal revenue curves applicable to total bank earning assets constructed (AR_E, MR_E).

Postulating that it is legitimate to attribute utility functions to banking firms, individual bank behavior may be described as maximizing a utility function that is related to expected profits and risk. The model of Figure 6-1 simultaneously depicts the total volume of earning assets, and the total volume of reserves and deposits, that an individual bank will maintain, given the optimum reserve ratio. It also shows the preferred composition of bank earning-asset portfolios, between loans and bonds, and the rates that the bank will charge for different types of bank credit and will pay on bank deposits.

Commercial banks operating in two or more distinct credit markets will maximize their utility function by expanding earning assets until total marginal revenue and marginal cost are brought into equality at a desired degree of risk bearing. This intersection (P) determines the total volume of earning assets (E_1) at which profits are maximized for a given degree of liquidity. Once the marginal cost of earning assets is estimated (E_1P) banks will so manage their earning asset portfolios between loans and bonds that the marginal revenue from each type of credit is equal to the marginal cost of providing earning asset funds. These intersection points (H and G) determine the amount of loans (L_1) and investments (B_1) in bank portfolios, and the representative rates charged and received by banks (r_{L_1} and r_{B_1}) for the two types of credit. Total reserves and total deposits are simultaneously determined, providing a unique liquidity ratio exists appropriate to the degree of risk and alternative return opportunities available $(D_1 = E_1/[1 - (R_1/D_1)])$. Similarly, from the average cost of that volume of earning asset funds $(E_1 C)$, it is possible to derive the average return $[r_{D_1} = (1 - L) (E_1 C) + (1 - L)r_R L]$ in terms of cost of services and interest payments that the bank must pay to attract that level of deposits.

The above framework could easily be extended to include price discrimination among other types of primary securities, for example mortgages and consumer credit, that banks purchase in more or less separate markets with distinct supply and demand characteristics. Differential lending rates charged by size of borrower may also be partially explained by such a price discrimination model. Observed interest rate differentials by size of loan reflect in addition lower per-unit costs of granting and administering loans of larger amounts, due to the fixed costs involved in loan extension, so that identical net yields are consistent with substantial differences in gross interest charges.

The foregoing explanation of the determination of bank lending and borrowing operations and the level and composition of bank asset portfolios possesses some important advantages over the more customary deposit-multiplier approach. As an application of conventional theory of the firm both supply and demand factors are introduced. The volume of individual bank assets and liabilities are determined not by any mechanical multiple expansion process but by behavioral relationships derived from utility maximization. The apportionment of deposit expansion between banks is not a random process but is determined by spending units' relative supply of deposits to and demand for credit from individual banks, which in turn is partially dependent on individual bank preferences with regard to profitability and risk.

A model of bank behavior in which banks are regarded as rational price discriminators offers a persuasive explanation for the often-observed persistent differences in profit margins on loan and investment portfolios. Adjustments to changes in monetary control, which operate by shifting the average and marginal cost of funds schedules, is shown to fall primarily on bank investment portfolios, while loan volume may be expected to be little affected. Figure 6-1 provides strong justification for the well-honored tradition that granting of loans is the primary function and obligation of commercial bank management, while investment operations are relegated to the subsidiary role of providing an outlet for residual funds after all loan demands have been accommodated.

If banks operate as oligopolists in the loan market the average revenue curve from loans may be drawn as kinked at the current administered rate. This creates a discontinuity in the loan marginal revenue schedule, so that the terms of bank loan operations are likely to be responsive only to *signal* changes in central bank control. The rational price-discriminator model offers one explanation why in particular periods commercial banks have been observed to purchase securities at a rate below the average cost they must pay for deposit funds. Such behavior is particularly likely to the extent that due to economies of scale in bank intermediation banking is a decreasing cost industry, so that the *long-run* marginal costs of earning-asset funds remain below average costs as banks expand the volume of their lending and borrowing operations.

The relationship between the structure of banking markets and bank performance also applies to banking markets that are separated geographically or by legal boundaries. Bank pricing in unit-bank areas is as might be expected less uniform than in areas where branch banking is permitted. Even though banking is a highly regulated industry, bankers are still subject to the competitive pressures of the market. A number of studies have found that the concentration ratio (the proportion of business accounted for by the largest two, four, eight, or more firms) and branching are related to observed differences in bank performance. While the evidence is not conclusive, more highly concentrated banking markets appear to pay lower average rates on time and savings deposits, to charge higher average rates on loans, and to earn higher profits on total assets. Size is also important. Large banks have higher loan-deposit ratios than small banks, in part because they are able to reduce their liquidity requirements by diversifying risks more widely, but also because they may have more competent, professional and aggressive management and a lower disutility from risk-taking. To the extent that economies of scale occur as bank size increases, the usual judgement has to be made about the extent to which the benefits of lower average costs are likely to be offset by diminished competition.

RECOMMENDED READING

Transaction and portfolio motives for holding money balances are examined rigorously in two articles by James Tobin, "The Interest-Elasticity of Transactions Demand for Cash," *Review of Economics and Statistics*, Vol. 38 (August 1956) and "Liquidity Preference as Behavior Toward Risk," *Review of Economic Studies*, Vol. 25 (February 1958).

A large number of articles have been written on the question as to whether commercial banks are properly to be regarded as financial intermediaries. The "new" view is presented succinctly in James Tobin, "Commercial Banks as Creators of 'Money'," in *Banking and Monetary Studies*, D. Carson, ed. (Homewood, Illinois, 1963). For a valuable summary of the controversy, which also contains some excellent insights of its own, see John A. Galbraith, *The Economics of Banking Operations* (Montreal, 1963), Chapter 1.

An excellent introduction to bank operations may be found in Roland Robinson, *The Management of Bank Funds* (New York, 1951). An imaginative application of theory of the firm to commercial banking is the pioneering study by David A. Alhadeff, *Monopoly and Competition in Banking* (Berkeley, 1954). Chapter two of the Galbraith book mentioned above makes a number of original contributions to this discussion.

A large number of studies have been undertaken recently on problems of banking structure and performance. Especially to be recommended are Paul Horvitz, "Economies of Scale in Banking," and Deane Carson and Paul Cootner, "The Structure of Competition in Commercial Banking in the United States," in *Private Financial Institutions*, Commission on Money and Credit (New Jersey, 1963). Also important is Donald Hodgman, *Commercial Bank Loan and Investment Policy* (Illinois, 1963). For an excellent recent summary that includes some new statistical evidence, see Franklin Edwards, "The Banking Competition Controversy" *National Banking Review*, Vol. 3 No. 1 (September, 1965).

7

Monetary and Nonmonetary

Financial Intermediation

*The principal function of financial intermediaries is to purchase
primary securities from ultimate borrowers and to issue indirect
debt for the portfolios of ultimate lenders. . . . All financial
intermediaries create financial assets.*

—J. Gurley and E. Shaw
Money in a Theory of Finance, 1960

Introduction

The previous chapter concluded that while commercial bank
operations are functionally analogous to those of other financial intermediaries, the direct and general acceptability of bank secondary
securities as a payments medium may prevent market forces from
uniquely determining a nominal volume of deposits outstanding. The
conditions that define an equilibrium volume of bank and nonbank
intermediation constitute the subject of this chapter.

Section one considers the market supply and demand forces that
in the absence of government regulation determine the volume of
financial intermediation. Nonmonetary intermediaries are considered
first. The expansion of total assets and liabilities of different intermediary groups are shown to be constrained by the asset and debt

185

preferences of surplus- and deficit-spending wealthowners. In competitive equilibrium the rate that an intermediary group charges borrowers exceeds the rate it pays to lenders by a premium just sufficient to cover the average costs of intermediation plus a normal rate of profit.

The situation is formally similar for monetary intermediaries. But because their liabilities are readily acceptable as a means of payment, and so impose no constraint on the exercise of purchasing power, bank intermediaries unlike nonbanks need not increase the return paid on notes and deposits to induce wealthowners to increase their *nominal* lending to the banking system. Since the supply price of providing deposits is positive, the unregulated *real* volume of monetary intermediation is determinate, at the intersection with the downward sloping demand function for bank credit. It is shown that, depending on the prevailing marginal return earned on tangible assets and the degree of price flexibility, this market-determined volume of monetary intermediation will not in general be consistent with general price level stability.

Section two then considers the effects on the banking industry of government regulation of the volume of monetary intermediation. In general regulation impedes financial intermediaries from making full portfolio adjustment. Monetary control typically constrains bank total assets and liabilities below the volume that banks would find it profitable to establish if freed from quantitative reserve requirements. By regulating the expansion of monetary intermediation monetary control is shown to affect the differential between bank lending and borrowing rates, and so the profitability of the commercial banking industry. Competition among banks for deposits operates to eliminate any supernormal differential between bank lending and borrowing rates by transferring scarcity rents to bank lenders and, to a lesser extent, bank borrowers.

Financial intermediaries enable borrowers who wish to expand their investment in real and financial assets to borrow at lower rates and easier terms than if they had to borrow directly from nonfinancial lenders. Nonbank intermediaries are also subject to rules and regulations supervised by Federal and state regulatory authorities. Section three considers some of the most important implications of this supervision for the allocation of saving among competing users and uses, and for the short-run response of intermediary behavior to monetary controls.

For interested readers, the economic function of net worth in financial intermediaries, with particular attention to the special case of commercial banking where profit rates are affected by output regulation, is considered briefly in the appendix. The economic function of equity capital is shown to diverge widely between financial and nonfinancial business corporations. Although government economic policy has enormously reduced the risk assumed in monetary intermediation, bank capital ratios have increased over the postwar period. Explanations for these trends are suggested, and alternative institutional changes are considered that would reduce the price to the community of banking services and alter the preference functions of banking firms.

Determination of the Unregulated Volume of Monetary and Nonmonetary Intermediation

The recognition of commercial banks as one particular species of the genus financial intermediary implies that the behavior of the banking system, in particular the determination of the volume of bank intermediation, is explainable by the same general principles of supply and demand as are applicable to other financial institutions. Both monetary and nonmonetary financial intermediaries exist on the differential between the lending rate they are able to charge borrowers and the borrowing rate that they must pay to lenders. In the absence of external controls the total assets and liabilities of different intermediary institutions are therefore determined by asset preferences of deficit and surplus spending units. In a regulated world expansion of commercial bank assets and liabilities is subject to an additional restraint—a legal requirement that a certain proportion of bank deposit liabilities be held in the form of a reserve base controlled by the monetary authorities. This cash reserve requirement, originally instituted as a protection for bank depositors, has become the fulcrum for monetary control over the volume of bank deposits. Nonmonetary intermediaries are also subject to regulation of the composition and terms of their assets and liabilities.

In order to compare the operation of an uncontrolled banking

system with the operation of uncontrolled nonmonetary intermediaries, it will prove instructive to eliminate these constraints, that
is to hypothesize a situation in which the volume of bank reserves is
not exogenously restricted, and nonmonetary intermediaries are free
of all restrictions. To simplify the analysis the fiction of a pure credit
economy will be resorted to. In such a world bank notes and deposits
are acceptable as legal tender. For simplicity it will be assumed that
currency as a debt of the government disappears. Banks no longer find
it necessary to hold some portion of their notes and deposits as cash
reserves. Since bank notes and deposits are legal tender, the problem
of maintaining convertability is nonexistent. The total of bank assets
and liabilities will be assumed no longer subject to quantitative control
by the government, so that the very concept of a multiple expansion
of deposits on a limited reserve base vanishes. Under such circumstances in what manner do the effects of unregulated bank behavior
differ from that of other unregulated intermediaries? How do the
consequences of unregulated bank intermediation provide a rationale
for the singling out of the banking system alone for special governmental control?

Before the introduction of financial intermediation the temporary
equilibrium prices of primary securities at any point in time are
determined, as described in Chapter 5, by the existing stocks of
primary securities and the portfolio demand for such securities by
wealthowners. In full temporal equilibrium these prices also satisfy
flow relationships, so that the incremental supply of primary securities
offered by deficit-spending units in any period equals the incremental
demand for primary securities by surplus-spending units. If the
analysis is confined to long-run full temporal equilibrium solutions,
in which both stock and flow equilibrium are satisfied, the argument
may be presented in flow terms throughout. This avoids the complications of the adjustment process. To simplify the exposition
further primary securities will be regarded as homogenous, in order
that the effect of intermediation on the structure of financial asset
prices may be temporarily deferred. All financial markets will be
treated as perfectly competitive.

Figure 7-1 illustrates the determination of the full temporal
equilibrium return r_{P_0} and the flow of primary securities P_0 that
exist in the aggregate before the introduction of financial intermedia-

tion. Given the expected return r_0 on the stock of tangible capital K_0, and community preferences with regard to present versus future income and to risk bearing, the incremental demand for primary securities by surplus spending units is represented by $D_S D_S$, and $S_D S_D$ represents incremental supply of primary securities by deficit spending units.[1]

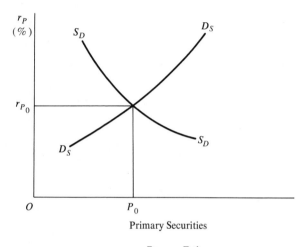

Figure 7-1

Next consider the full equilibrium situation after the introduction of nonmonetary financial intermediation. In a position of competitive general equilibrium a total volume of intermediary assets and liabilities is established at which the rate charged borrowers exceeds the rate paid to lenders by a premium just sufficient to compensate financial institutions for the cost of intermediation. Were the differential to exceed this normal premium, competition between intermediaries and entry of new firms would produce expansion of intermediary aggregate assets and liabilities. To expand loans *ceteris paribus* it would be necessary to lower the rate charged borrowers. To expand liabilities

1. The supply and demand curves in Figure 1 are reversed from their standard positions because quantity is related to return, which varies inversely with price. Were price to be plotted on the vertical axis demand would be downward sloping and supply upward sloping.

Nonmonetary Intermediation

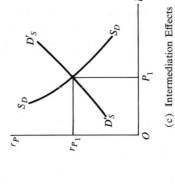

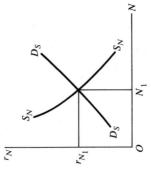

(a) Lending Operations

(b) Borrowing Operations

(c) Intermediation Effects

Figure 7-2

ceteris paribus it would be necessary to raise the rate paid lenders. As a result the process of intermediary expansion would operate to reduce profit margins to the normal level. A reverse process would operate to contract the volume of intermediation were profit margins to fall below the normal premium.

It is important to recognize that all financial intermediaries are to a varying extent competitive with one another in the purchase of primary securities from nonfinancial borrowers, and in the sale of secondary securities to nonfinancial lenders. The relative size of each intermediary type in full temporal equilibrium in an unregulated world depends upon the asset preferences of surplus and deficit spending units.

This full equilibrium position is represented in Figure 7-2, where for presentational simplicity all nonmonetary intermediaries are considered as a homogeneous group. In Figure 7-2a the incremental supply of primary securities L by nonfinancial deficit units to intermediaries (demand for intermediary loans) is represented by $S_D S_D$, while $D_N D_N$ represents incremental demand for primary securities by nonbank intermediaries. Similarly in Figure 7-2b, $D_S D_S$ represents incremental demand for secondary securities N by nonfinancial surplus units, and $S_N S_N$ represents incremental supply of secondary securities by intermediaries. Incremental demand for primary securities by intermediaries ($D_N D_N$ in 7-3a) is equal to the incremental demand for secondary securities by nonfinancial surplus units ($D_S D_S$ in 7-3b), adjusted upward by the normal profit margin A on financial intermediation. Similarly, incremental supply of secondary securities by intermediaries ($S_N S_N$ in 7-3b) is derived from incremental supply of primary securities by deficit-spending units to intermediaries ($S_D S_D$ in 7-3a), adjusted downward by the same normal supply price of intermediation.

It follows that in this simple formulation, with no intermediary capital accounts, $L_1 = N_1$, and the differential between the full equilibrium lending rate r_L and borrowing rate r_N charged and paid by intermediaries represents the normal profit margin (A) for nonbank intermediation. The volume of intermediation is thus uniquely determined. Any attempt to expand intermediary borrowing and lending activities beyond this level can occur only at the expense of a less than normal profit margin. Similarly any lesser volume of intermediation would result in above-normal profits, inducing further expansion of intermediary activities.

As described in Chapter 4 intermediation enables incremental demand for secondary securities by nonfinancial units to be *transformed* into incremental demand for primary securities by intermediaries. This conversion of incremental demand for secondary securities into incremental demand for primary securities by financial intermediaries is illustrated in Figure 7-2c. Full equilibrium may now be regarded as determined where total incremental supply of primary securities by deficit spending nonfinancial units, represented by $S_D S_D$, intersects $D_S' D_S'$, the sum of direct incremental demand for primary securities by surplus spending units plus the transformed incremental demand for secondary securities by surplus spending nonfinancial units.

Since secondary securities N possess properties, most importantly income and capital certainty and marketability, that make them more attractive to ultimate wealthowners than the primary securities L in intermediary portfolios, demand for secondary securities plus primary securities by surplus-spending units after intermediation ($D_S' D_S'$ in Figure 7-2c), exceeds their demand for primary securities alone before the introduction of intermediation ($D_S D_S$ in Figure 7-1). As a result, r_{P_1} in Figure 7-2c, the return on primary securities after the introduction of intermediation, will be *lower* than r_{P_0} in Figure 7-1, the return on primary securities before intermediation. This must follow providing that the downward-sloping incremental supply function of primary securities $S_D S_D$ remains unaffected, or more specifically does not increase, as a result of the introduction of intermediation.

The result of intermediation is thus to encourage more indirect wealthholding at every level of technology, time preference, and risk aversion. Intermediaries permit nonfinancial borrowers to be accommodated at lower rates and/or easier terms than would exist if debtor units were confined to borrowing directly from nonfinancial lenders. If the creditors of financial intermediaries were to be induced to hold an equal amount of primary securities instead, they would require higher rates and stricter terms. It is for this reason that any financial innovation producing an autonomous increase in the volume of lending, borrowing, and financial intermediation in an economy has an expansionary influence. A lower return on primary securities in full equilibrium after intermediation $(r_{P_1} < r_{P_0})$ implies a larger capital stock $(K_1 > K_0)$ and a lower marginal efficiency of investment $(r_1 < r_0)$, in order that equilibrium in financial markets be consistent with stable prices in factor and product markets.

The operations of commercial banks, as one type of monetary financial intermediary, conform to the above general framework. Bank notes and deposits must compete with other financial assets in the portfolios of wealth holders, since the advantage of direct transferability in settlement of debt can be overcome by sufficient differences in yield and other services. The size of the banking system relative to other intermediaries similarly depends on the asset preferences of surplus and deficit spending units.

But while asset preferences determine the desired *proportion* of bank notes and deposits in total wealth portfolios, given the return structure on other financial and tangible assets, the commercial banking system, unlike other financial intermediaries, does not find it necessary to increase the return paid on deposits in order to induce wealth owners to increase their *nominal* lending to the banking system. In a pure credit world an increase in nominal bank notes and deposits can occur only as a result of bank purchases of earning assets. Bank notes and deposits are always acceptable to deficit spending units *without any concomitant increase in deposit yield*, since such notes and deposits by definition can readily be exchanged for desired real goods and services. Consequently, in contrast to nonbank institutions, the demand *to accept though not to hold* nominal secondary securities faced by commercial banks, both individually and in the aggregate, is infinitely elastic.

This does not imply that banks "create" deposits simply by the stroke of a pen in a manner analogous to government mints or private counterfeiters. The cost of maintaining the direct acceptability of deposits is the significant expense of managing the payments mechanism for the economy. The supply price of bank deposits and hence of bank credit is not zero, as traditional banking theory at times seems to imply when it attributes to the banking system unique and quasi-necromantic powers of "money creation." The postulation of bank monetary creation at zero cost would be a more accurate description if bank notes, rather than bank deposits, circulated as the chief payments medium. In this sense, the doctrine was more appropriate at its birth one hundred and fifty years ago than it is today.

The above analysis reveals that it is necessary to distinguish the demand for bank notes from the demand for bank deposits, even where both are legal tender in a pure credit world. The demand *to accept* both notes and deposits in payment on the part of borrowers is infinitely elastic. If bank notes were the only form of bank secondary securities in existence, individual commercial banks as well as the banking system as a whole would be faced by a perfectly elastic demand curve *to hold*, as well as to accept bank notes, as long as individual banks were able to maintain public confidence in their solvency. This is because, once issued, *such notes would never be redeemed, but simply transferred among assetholders.* If the cost of issuing bank notes were very low, the supply price of bank credit would also be very low, and similarly perfectly elastic.

The case of bank deposits is somewhat different. *Unlike notes, deposits can be transferred to another bank at the option of the holder.* While the demand to accept deposits in payment for financial assets on the part of bank debtors is perfectly elastic, from the point of view of an individual bank the demand of the public to *hold* its deposits is not perfectly elastic. Even though for the system as a whole, or for a one-bank system, the demand to hold *nominal* deposits is perfectly elastic, for an individual bank the demand to hold its nominal deposits is upward sloping. Consequently although commercial banks in an unregulated competitive pure credit have no incentive to pay an interest yield on bank notes, they do individually have an incentive to pay interest on demand deposits, since by so doing they are able to attract deposits away from other banks. In the absence of the preconditions for perfect competition, in particular the presence of barriers to entry, this suggests that individual banks have a strong incentive to prescribe collectively the maximum interest rate individual banks shall pay on deposit obligations.

Even in a one-bank system the existence of a perfectly elastic demand for nominal notes and deposits does not *necessarily* imply that the nominal volume of unregulated bank intermediation is indeterminate, since as has been seen the supply price of bank notes and deposits is positive. Just as in the case of other financial institutions the profit calculus may be relied on to determine an equilibrium level of nominal commercial bank total assets and liabilities. Even though an unregulated one-bank system is able to supply nominal deposits indefinitely at constant cost, the negative slope of the supply of primary securities offered by borrowers (i.e., the demand for bank credit) would appear to be sufficient to ensure a determinate nominal output based on profit considerations. This is *a fortiori* true for a multi-bank system, where individual banks face an upward-sloping demand for total nominal deposits. Expansion beyond this equilibrium point reduces the profit margin below the normal premium, while a smaller volume of bank intermediation would entail larger than normal bank profits.

This process is illustrated for the polar case of a one-bank system in Figure 7-3. Bank secondary securities are demanded by both surplus and deficit spending units. In Figure 7-3b, $D_{SD}D_{SD}$ represents incremental demand by surplus and deficit units for nominal bank deposits D. In a multi-bank system $D_{SD}D_{SD}$ would be upward-sloping. In Figure 7-3a, D_BD_B represents bank incremental demand for primary securities L. As indicated in Figure 7-3a, D_BD_B is equal to the demand for bank deposits ($D_{SB}D_{SB}$ of Figure 7-3b) adjusted upward by the normal profit margin A on bank intermediation. In Figure 7-3a, S_DS_D represents the incremental supply of primary securities by deficit units to the banking system, from which S_BS_B in Figure 7-3b, the incremental supply of deposits by the banking system, is similarly derived.

Figure 7-3 differs from Figure 7-2 in that incremental demand for *nominal* bank deposits $D_{SD}D_{SD}$ faced by a one-bank system is perfectly horizontal at a yield r_{D_2} that is determined by the cost of providing checking facilities and other services on deposits and notes. Consequently incremental demand for *nominal* primary securities by a one-bank system D_BD_B (the supply of bank credit) is also perfectly elastic.

Since as shown in Figure 7-3a and 7-3b the nominal volume of monetary intermediation appears to be determinate even for the case of a one-bank system, and the same conclusion holds *a fortiori* for a multi-bank system, where then at this level of abstraction lies the necessity for the singling out of the volume of commercial bank intermediation for quantitative government regulation? Two separate grounds may be distinguished.

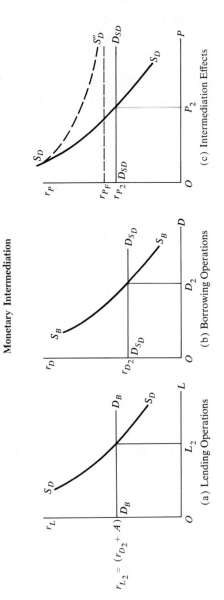

Monetary Intermediation

(a) Lending Operations

(b) Borrowing Operations

(c) Intermediation Effects

Figure 7-3

The introduction of bank intermediation, analogous to the previous introduction of nonbank intermediation, reduces the offer price necessary to induce wealthholders to hold financial assets, and so, given the supply schedule of primary securities, reduces the real return on primary securities below the rate that had prevailed before the existence of bank intermediation ($r_{P_2} < r_{P_1}$). For this yield to be consistent with full equilibrium in the factor and product markets, the marginal efficiency of investment must fall accordingly ($r_2 < r_1$). *If the return from holding tangible assets does not fall by the required amount, the incremental supply of primary securities will increase indefinitely when the cost of borrowing falls sufficiently below the marginal return from holding tangible assets.*

The existence of a large stock of long-lived investment opportunities that become profitable at very low interest costs provides in normal circumstances a floor r_F to the real return on tangible assets. The marginal efficiency of investment may thus be prevented from falling continuously, even in the face of large increases in the stock of tangible capital. This in turn provides a floor to the supply price of primary securities, so that the demand for bank credit becomes increasingly elastic at some positive return. Such a situation is illustrated in Figure 7-3c, where r_{P_F} ($r_{P_F} < r_F$) is the floor yield on primary securities, at which rate the supply of primary securities, shown by the dashed line $S_D S_D''$, becomes infinitely elastic.

Under these conditions the market is no longer capable of exercising discipline over the *nominal* volume of bank intermediation, since $D_{SD} D_{SD}$ and $S_D S_D''$ do not intersect. As banks continue to expand total assets and liabilities by increasing their purchases of primary securities, borrowing and expenditure by deficit units increase continuously as wealthowners attempt to spend their excess supply of nominal deposits to accumulate tangible assets. This is not consistent with price stability in factor and product markets, and the price level rises persistently.

While the above discussion refers explicitly to a one-bank system, the same analysis and conclusions are applicable to a multi-bank system if mutual agreement or government legislation imposes a zero or low ceiling to the rate payable on demand deposits. Under such circumstances, even if individual banks are faced by an upward-sloping demand for nominal deposits $D_{SD} D_{SD}$, the maximum supply price of bank credit may be held below the floor return on primary securities (r_{P_F} in Figure 7-3c). As a result the nominal volume of unregulated bank intermediation remains undetermined.

While the level of *nominal* bank deposits under such circumstances is indeterminate, the existence of transactions and portfolio demand for deposits in real terms always limits the *real* volume of bank assets and liabilities demanded. Even though incremental demand for nominal bank deposits is perfectly elastic in a one-bank system, the demand for real bank deposits (not illustrated in Figure 7-3) is upward sloping. This is because a higher return must be paid to induce wealthowners to increase the real share of deposits held in their wealth portfolios. Were lending and borrowing operations to have been presented in real rather than nominal terms, the demand for deposits would be upward sloping, and Figure 7-3 illustrating monetary intermediation would appear similar to the determination of the volume of nonmonetary intermediation in Figure 7-2.

The second ground for regulation stems from the degree of price flexibility prevailing in the economy. If all prices were perfectly flexible in an upward and downward direction, an unregulated banking system would be unable to reach a position of competitive equilibrium even when the intersection of $D_{SD}D_{SD}$ and $S_D S_D''$ lies well *above* the previously described floor level of returns on primary securities. Under such circumstances the market is again unable to exercise effective determination of the nominal quantity of bank deposits.

Consider the effects of a change in resources, technology, or tastes that alter the marginal efficiency of investment, and so the supply price of primary securities, from a position of full employment general equilibrium in such an economy. The banking system and nonbank intermediaries are induced to increase or reduce the volume of their lending and borrowing operations in response to the changed differential between their lending and borrowing rates. Even when the new nominal volume of intermediation would otherwise be determinate, if prices were instantaneously flexible in all markets any change in nominal deposits would cause an immediate and proportionate change in price levels, maintaining the volume of bank intermediation unchanged in real terms, and preventing bank profit margins from adjusting.

Perfect price flexibility is thus incompatible with a stable price level.

In such an economy there is no mechanism to get a grip on the profit rate from bank intermediation and force it to conform to the normal competitive premium. Real profits in banking are unaffected by the nominal size of the banking system. Any deviation of real profits from the normal competitive premium would result therefore in a continuous expansion or contraction of nominal deposits. This indeterminacy remains even when the assumption of a perfectly competitive multi-banking system is removed. Any attempt to increase bank profits in real terms by changing the volume of inter-mediation will be frustrated by a proportionate change in the price level, which maintains real bank deposits and so profit margins in banking unchanged.

Once the quite unrealistic assumption of instantaneous price flexibility, with its consequent neutrality of nominal deposit change, is relaxed this paradox disappears, and the system is no longer left in an aimless drift. To the extent that the price level is less than perfectly flexible upwards or downwards changes in the supply of nominal deposits do produce *some* change in the level of real bank inter-mediation, in the marginal efficiency of investment, and in the return on primary securities, which affect the differential between bank lending and borrowing rates and operate to push the system into an equilibrium position. Increasing costs in banking will also operate to force the profit rate more rapidly towards the normal premium, but decreasing costs have the opposite effect, and tend to perpetuate the differential above or below the normal level.

In the general case of imperfectly flexible prices, depending on the speed at which the price level adjusts to eliminate excess supply or demand in markets for current output, changes in bank lending opportunities may provoke very substantial changes in the price level before the determinate equilibrium level of real bank assets and liabilities is attained. Otherwise expressed, the nominal volume of bank intermediation determined by the intersection of the $D_{SD}D_{SD}$ and $S_D S_D''$ relationships may not be consistent with a stable price level. The external costs of price level instability may then be held sufficient to justify government regulation in the public interest.

In conclusion, because lending to the banking system imposes no deferment to the exercise of purchasing power on the part of the lender-depositor, changes in the nominal volume of bank intermediation produce accompanying changes in the level of aggregate expenditure. To the extent that such changes result in movements in the general price level, the equilibrating operation of the market mechanism that brings bank lending and borrowing rates towards equality is partially frustrated. Nominal changes in the level of bank assets and liabilities then result in much smaller movements in the volume of bank intermediation in real terms, and it is the latter that determines the reward at the margin for bank intermediation. In the extreme case, in which no price inflexibility exists, the level of nominal deposits is necessarily indeterminate.

There have been isolated historical periods when the marginal efficiency of investment has temporarily fallen below its long-run floor level, while at the same time market imperfections have restrained the downward flexibility of the price level. When both conditions are met, the return of primary securities may fall to a level at which it is no longer profitable for the banks to expand further their total assets and liabilities (r_{P_2} in Figure 7-3c), in which case the market mechanism is sufficient to determine a unique level of nominal bank deposits D_2. In such circumstances, as in the late 1930's in America, increases in the reserve base by the monetary authorities will merely result in the accumulation of excess reserves in bank asset portfolios.

It is possible to visualize an economy in which capital accumulation has so outdistanced technological change that the marginal return on tangible assets is permanently reduced to a level at which unregulated bank intermediation happens to be compatible with price stability in factor and product markets. Until this stage is reached an additional restraint on bank intermediation must ordinarily be introduced to supplement the operation of the market in the interests of price level stability. The fundamental rationale for the quantitative restriction of bank intermediation may then be summarized as follows. Monetary intermediation normally reduces the reservation price of holding wealth in the form of monetary financial assets substantially below the return expected from holding tangible assets. In consequence banks find it profitable to expand their nominal loans and deposits to a degree incompatible with price level stability, as spending units on balance persistently desire to borrow from the banking system in order to increase their holdings of real assets. As a result in the absence of regulation aggregate current expenditures exceed aggregate current income and output valued at stable prices.

The Regulation of Monetary Intermediation

It is now appropriate to reintroduce the reserve restraint over the volume of monetary intermediation. Since bank deposits are not legal tender, checks drawn against deposit balances retain their general acceptability as a payment medium only for so long as banks are able to maintain the continuous and ready convertibility of their deposits into currency at par. The necessity that bank deposits be freely interchangeable into legal money forces individual banks to maintain sufficient cash balances to protect themselves at all times against large if improbable net deposit withdrawals. Under these circumstances the determination of the total stock of legal money by the government constrains the total amount of primary securities that the banking system is willing to purchase, and so the total quantity of bank liabilities. The techniques by which the expansion of monetary intermediation is controlled are considered in the following chapter, but some of the consequences of monetary regulation may be illustrated with the aid of the foregoing analysis.

The commercial banking system may usefully be regarded as an industry operating at a disequilibrium output, in the sense that total assets and liabilities are quantitatively restrained by government regulation below the volume banks would find it profitable to establish if freed from reserve requirements. Figure 7-4 reproduces Figure 7-3c for a multi-bank system, where $S_D S_D$ again represents the supply of primary securities by deficit units, and $D_{SD} D_{SD}$ the upward-sloping demand for nominal bank deposits by surplus and deficit units adjusted upward by the normal competitive supply price of bank intermediation. The limit to the expansion of monetary intermediation permitted by the controlled cash reserve base R is represented for simplicity by the vertical line $D_C D_C$, at which output the competitive lending rate charged by commercial banks to clear the markets for primary securities must equal r_{L_c}.

As Figure 7-4 indicates, the competitive rate banks charge borrowers at this permitted scale of monetary intermediation r_{L_c} considerably exceeds the rate that the banking system must pay lenders (the r_{D_2}

rate of Figure 7-3) in order to *attract* this level of nominal deposits. While the maximum effective supply of nominal deposits for the banking system as a whole may be regarded as perfectly inelastic at the ceiling value of $D_C = d(R)$, ignoring for the moment all supply complications that produce variability in the actual ratio of reserves to deposits, *individual* banks can always obtain additional reserves at a higher cost by bidding deposits away from competitors. Consequently the demand schedule for nominal deposits, that is the cost of deposit funds, becomes sharply positively sloped *as seen by individual banks* in consequence of the scarcity of reserves, and therefore similar to the demand curves faced by nonmonetary intermediaries.

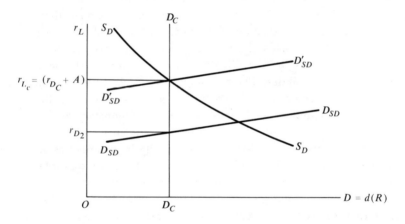

Figure 7-4

Competition among banks forces the differential between borrowing and lending rates towards the normal premium A. This occurs primarily through reductions in service charges and increases in services and income return r_D offered to bank depositors, but lending terms r_L may also be sweetened in the competition to attract deposits. In controlled *competitive* equilibrium the demand schedule for nominal deposits for the banking system as a whole has shifted upward to $D'_{SD}D'_{SD}$, and bank lending and borrowing rates are established in competitive equality ($r_{L_c} = r_{D_c} + A$).

In an economy in which the supply of legal money is restricted, it is competition in banking that eliminates the resulting differential between bank lending and borrowing rates $(r_L - r_{D_2})$ by transferring the scarcity rents created by output restriction, primarily to bank depositors. The total cost of administering the deposit payments mechanism then exceeds considerably the total net revenue in service charges received from depositors, and the latter may even be negative if interest payments on demand deposits are permitted. The cost of providing checking facilities on deposits are borne therefore in large part by bank borrowers. Since at the margin the cost of providing settlement of debt by deposit transfer ordinarily exceeds the price to depositors of using checking facilities, this conflicts with the Pareto price-equal-to-marginal-cost criterion for optimum resource allocation. Settlement by check rather than currency is encouraged, and trans-actions demand for bank deposits is increased. From an efficiency point of view it would be preferable to combine service charges equal to the marginal cost of deposit transfer with an explicit income yield on deposits.

Restrictions on competition among banking institutions, most significantly legal prohibitions or ceilings on payment of interest on deposits, explicit or implicit agreement among bankers to refrain from price competition for deposits or loans, restrictions on entry into banking, and a wide variety of other institutional arrangements all serve in the real world to maintain the differential between bank lending and borrowing rates $(r_L - r_D) > A$, and thus permit part of the scarcity rents arising from the limitation of monetary inter-mediation to be captured by bank shareholders. A lower return on bank deposits, whether due to a reduction in the legal interest ceiling or to a change in the competitive situation, reduces demand for bank deposits in the wealth portfolios of economic units relative to other financial assets (a leftward shift in the PP relationship of Chapter 5). As a result the volume of monetary intermediation consistent with the stabilization goals of the monetary authorities is reduced. The permitted maximum expansion in bank loans and deposits ($D_C D_C$ in Figure 7-4) shifts leftward, and the relative volume of nonmonetary intermediation may be expected to increase.

Significantly, and at first glance somewhat paradoxically, an *increase* in the maximum interest rates paid on bank demand deposits may ordinarily be expected to produce a *fall* in the full-employment equilibrium level of returns on all nonmonetary primary and secondary securities, and not merely in the level of yields of those primary securities which banks purchase. This effect occurs because, although an increase in interest rates paid on bank deposits raises the average cost of providing bank credit, the total volume of monetary intermediation consistent with price level stability increases. Since even this now higher cost of lending by the banking system (derived from "wealthowners" supply price of "convenience lending" to the banks) will in normal periods be considerably *below the average borrowing rate on nonmonetary instruments* that nonfinancial borrowers or other intermediaries must pay for the loan of purchasing power by non-administering wealthowners. The economy's average reservation price of wealthownership, and so its aggregate supply schedule of loanable funds, will shift downward. Thus a very strong case can be made for removing all interest rate ceilings on bank deposits.

Monetary control, by regulating the expansion of monetary intermediation in relation to cyclical changes in demand, affects the differential between bank lending and borrowing rates ($r_L - r_D$), and reinforces cyclical changes in profitability of the commercial bank industry.[2] Restrictive monetary policy typically increases total profits in banking, at least in the short run, since rates received on earning assets and so the profit differential rise by a greater relative proportion than the restriction in earning asset growth. This will be more or less offset to the extent the rates paid on deposits are permitted to rise. Conversely expansionary monetary policy in the short run typically reduces total profits, since the fall in rates received on earning assets and in the differential exceeds the relative proportion by which earning assets expand. This cyclical variability of bank profits is lagged, since average yields earned on bank portfolios follow, depending on portfolio maturities, existing market rates of interest. In addition bank purchases of bonds at high prices and resale at lower prices to accommodate loan demand during periods of monetary restraint dampen cylical fluctuations in *reported* profits, due to the timing of realized capital gains and losses.

2. The differential between commercial bank total earnings and total expenses, whether expressed as a percentage of total assets or net worth, is closely correlated with the level of interest rates in American and Canadian experience.

These distributional consequences of monetary control, reinforced by the redistributional effects of inflation that reduce the real value of bank net worth and net profits as monetary values depreciate in real terms, and by the failure of nominal financial asset yields to adjust sufficiently to offset fully expected price level increases, suggest a substantive ground for the "sound money" preferences vociferously held by the banking community.

Over the long run, depending on the degree of effective competition in banking, a portion of the windfall scarcity rents from regulation may be expected to be passed on to bank lenders and borrowers. In addition a less restrictive monetary policy is compatible with a larger volume of bank intermediation in the long run.

The Regulation of Nonmonetary Intermediation

The previous sections have proceeded as if nonbank intermediaries were completely free to adjust their assets and liabilities toward their preferred portfolio positions in response to changes in the demand and supply price of financial assets. In practice nonmonetary as well as monetary financial institutions are subject to a plethora of regulations and restraints governing the composition and yield of their assets and liabilities. These regulations originated historically in a desire to protect the solvency and liquidity of financial institutions, frequently upon the discovery of flagrant financial abuse. They also must be recognized as an attempt to foster desired nonefficiency social objectives, such as the promotion of the habit of thrift, home ownership, and a politically desired distribution of income, wealth, and financial antonomy among regions and groups.

Regulation of nonmonetary intermediaries takes the form of specifying the assets and liabilities that particular institutions may acquire and issue, and the rates that they may charge or offer, as well as certain codes of behavior. One important effect of such supervision is to inhibit portfolio choice and so the ability to adjust to portfolio imbalance by forcing intermediaries to *specialize* in fewer types of financial assets and liabilities. The result of such enforced specialization and yield inflexibility from an efficiency point of view is in general to interfere detrimentally with the market allocation of resources.[3] By increasing the discrepancy between marginal cost and price charged or paid on intermediary credit or claims, a less efficient allocation of resources is ordinarily produced than would have occurred if intermediary portfolio adjustment to market-determined yield differentials had been unrestricted. Resources are channelled away from their highest opportunity use, and the allocation of funds among users and uses largely reflects the flow of funds to specialized institutions.

Misallocation of resources need not of course always occur in consequence of intermediary regulation. If important externalities exist, regulation of private behavior will not necessarily result in a greater misallocation of resources relative to the social optimum. To the extent intermediary specialization is incomplete, and some portfolio flexibility exists, financial institutions are ordinarily able to transfer funds directly to higher-yielding opportunities by shifting their holdings of some common asset, for example government bonds. Even in the case of the enforcement of complete specialization, misallocation would not result providing the rates paid by intermediaries on their own secondary securities were to follow closely the rates earned on their current investment opportunities, *and* if nonregulated nonfinancial assetholders were sufficiently sensitive to yield differentials to shift their holdings among competing intermediary claims.

Existing evidence on financial behavior in the United States in the postwar period reveals however a marked insensitivity in the composition of saving allocation among competing financial intermediary claims. Household ownership of nonbank intermediary claims have grown at impressively stable rates. When the strong trend factor is eliminated by comparing first differences (quarterly changes) in intermediary claims, the mutual association is very weak, and there is more evidence of positive than of negative correlation. Close examination of the Flow-of-Funds Accounts has failed to reveal any

3. An extreme example is the limitation of a savings and loan association to a primary lending area within fifty miles of its office, and the specification that its investments other than first-mortgage home loans be limited to less than twenty per cent of total savings. Another is the widespread prohibition or extreme limitation on the holding of corporate equities by financial intermediaries other than investment companies.

significant offsetting movements between claims on nonbank intermediaries and cyclical demand deposit variability in response to monetary control. Relative yields do appear to explain some of the limited variation in the composition of household saving left unexplained by income and wealth changes, but the interest rate coefficients in multiple regression demand estimates are generally very low, and frequently statistically insignificant.

There are a number of factors that account for this observed insensitivity in the composition of household financial portfolios among intermediary claims. The most important are not related to supervisory regulation. Most household investors do not have the knowledge, expertise, or sophistication to shift their portfolios in response to changing yield differentials. Many secondary securities, for example bank deposits or insurance policies, are frequently held in large part for the in kind and widely diverse services that they yield. The diversity of these services, plus the fact that these non-income characteristics do not vary over the short run, reduce the substitutability of intermediary claims from the viewpoint of asset holders.

In addition the explicit income yields on intermediary obligations are both inflexible and very highly positively correlated with one another. This occurs in part because the return paid by intermediaries on their secondary securities cannot follow closely the rate they are able to earn on their current investments. Financial institutions ordinarily must pay the same rate on both existing and newly issued claims. As a result the return they can pay is based on the *average* earnings on their total portfolio. To the extent that their existing assets are long term, the average portfolio return must vary very much less than the current return on new loans and investments. As a result intermediaries are not able to bid aggressively for new funds to take advantage of short-run increases in profitable investment opportunities.

Many nonbank intermediaries are organized on a mutual rather than a stock basis. Due in a large extent to legal requirements and prohibitions, additions to the surplus accounts of mutual institutions account for a substantial share of their net earnings. In addition the allocation of intermediary net income between return to holders of outstanding claims and additions to surplus or allocation to reserves varies substantially, both among different intermediaries at a point in time and among similar intermediaries over time. Since such additions to surplus do not provide the basis for capital gains as in a stock company, and are lost if shareholders withdraw their accounts, they interfere with the allocative function by forcing a gap between the net earnings rate and the rate received by lenders.

Finally, operating expenses, due to changes in variable and fixed costs, do not remain in a constant proportion of total assets or gross income as the discussion of the previous sections assumed.

These reasons combine to produce a very substantial and variable gap between the interest rate charged to new borrowers, and the implicit and explicit return paid to new lenders. In consequence misallocation resulting from legally enforced portfolio inflexibility of financial intermediaries will be only weakly if at all corrected by portfolio shifts among intermediary secondary claims on the part of nonregulated household and nonfinancial business assetholders.

With regard to the objective of capital mobility and an optimum allocation of resources, it is thus highly desirable that all legal restrictions on asset choice be eliminated to permit intermediaries greater flexibility in their portfolio policies. Such relaxation would reduce some of the barriers presently inhibiting the flow of funds among users and uses. A gradual elimination of regulatory restraints could be pursued to avoid any conflict with the goal of ensuring the solvency and safety of individual financial institutions. Such a policy would however necessarily affect the existing competitive position of different intermediaries, and tend to reduce existing differentials in the price and availability of credit to different borrowers. If these allocational implications of a more perfect capital market conflict with other social goals, they could be compensated for by direct selective incentive payments to borrowers, lenders, or intermediaries in those areas where the market allocation may be deemed undesirable, due for example to the existence of important external benefits or costs, or distributional goals.

With regard to stabilization objectives, the overall impact and effectiveness of a given degree of monetary restriction would be reduced to the extent capital mobility and so the partial substitutability of claims and credit of other financial institutions for commercial banks is increased by relaxing the enforced specialization of nonbank intermediaries. On the other hand the impact of a given degree of monetary expansion would be increased. The greater the substitutability among bank and nonbank intermediary claims and credit, the smaller the impact of a given degree of monetary control on the price and yield of those financial assets purchased by commercial banks. The enforced portfolio specialization of financial institutions, coexistent with legal ceilings on the return on certain classes of financial assets, have at times combined to produce severe disruptions in the flow of credit due to monetary control, and an uneven impact of monetary restraint on certain types of borrowers.

For the reasons previously considered the short-run flow of funds among bank and nonbank intermediary claims, even in the absence of legal portfolio restrictions, is unlikely to be disstabilizing nor seriously to offset the restrictive measures taken by the monetary authorities. For all unregulated intermediaries there would remain a substantial gap between the rate of return currently earned on new investments, and the rate they are currently able to pay to attract funds from other intermediaries.

There are of course reasons why it may be deemed undesirable to have to "increase the dosage of a diluted medicine".[4] Large open-market operations for example might be erratic or disstabilizing in their effect on "thin" bond markets, causing very large movements in financial asset prices. But if the effectiveness of monetary controls is measured by the magnitude of the response of some crucial policy variable, for example the money stock or the level of interest rates, a structural change which leads to a reduction in "effectiveness" in this sense is not necessarily undesirable. Any structural change that increases the allocative efficiency of capital markets is likely also to alter the response of real and financial behavior to the cyclical disturbances that the monetary authorities are attempting to offset.

As will be developed in the following chapter, the ultimate effectiveness of monetary control must be judged in terms of its effects on the real return at which wealth administrators are willing to add to their existing stocks of reproducable capital goods. The real rate of return on tangible assets required to encourage the production of new capital goods depends on the relation between desired and

4. William Brainard, "Financial Intermediaries and a Theory of Monetary Control," *Yale Economic Essays*, Vol. 4, No. 2 (1964) p. 451.

actual stocks of tangible assets held by wealthowners. For any given level of technology, tastes, and existing tangible and financial asset stocks, the magnitude of tangible asset portfolio imbalance produced by a particular level and structure of asset prices and yields is dependent on the effectiveness of financial markets and institutions in meeting the preferences and needs of lenders and borrowers.

There is one important area where there is no even potential conflict between allocation and stabilization goals. Removal of the restrictions that prevent commercial banks themselves from paying interest on demand deposits, place a ceiling on the rates that banks may pay on savings and time deposits or charge on loans, and limit bank portfolio holdings of important assets, for example mortgages and corporate stock, would all operate to increase the overall effectiveness of monetary control. At the same time, by increasing mobility among capital markets and reducing the discrepancy between marginal cost and the price charged or paid on bank credit and claims, such a relaxation of bank regulation would move toward a more efficient allocation of capital market resources.[5]

5. For a brief statement see Lawrence Ritter, *Regulation Q: Issues and Alternatives* (Chicago, 1965).

APPENDIX TO CHAPTER 7

The Question of Bank Capital

Monetary control, by regulating the quantity of bank total assets and deposits, necessarily affects the differential between bank lending and borrowing rates and so incidentally the profitability of bank intermediation, even though its central concern is a quite different objective.

Can criteria be developed to judge whether such windfall profits are too high or too low? From the viewpoint of the community the statistic relevant in assessing allocational efficiency of financial intermediation is the level of, and the differential between, lending and borrowing rates, which depend in turn on the ratio of total expenses and of net profits to total assets. The rate of return earned on equity capital is of greater ambiguity for judging the adequacy of intermediary earnings, since it is dependent in addition on the degree to which intermediaries trade on equity.

To what extent is it possible to formulate an optimum capital ratio for financial intermediaries? On one hand, the lower are intermediary capital-asset ratios, the lower is the differential between intermediary lending and borrowing rates consistent with a normal return on capital comparable to returns earned on equity capital in other similar-risk industries. As a result the lower is the price that the community must pay for intermediation. On the other hand the lower are capital-asset ratios, the lower is the cushion of protection to creditors against a decline in asset values provided by the owners of the institution. As a result the greater is the risk attached to wealthownership.

The economic function of equity capital diverges importantly between financial and nonfinancial business units. For most nonfinancial corporations additional equity capital, in practice primarily internally financed, provides a dominant share of the additional financial resources to permit an expansion of assets and operations. In contrast the bulk of funds for the acquisition of earning assets by most financial institutions is provided not from the issue of equities or from retained earnings but from the issue of secondary claims, in the case of banks demand and saving deposits. In the special case of a regulated commercial banking system an increase in equity capital does not even permit an increase in total deposits for the banking system as a whole. For most nonfinancial corporations the primary function of capital is to finance the purchase of buildings and equipment. Financial institutions' capital typically far exceeds the amount necessary to finance the acquisition of physical assets.

The primary function of bank capital has traditionally been regarded as the provision of a cushion or insurance fund to prevent bank failures, and to protect bank depositors against loss as a result of depreciation of bank assets due to mismanagement or to a liquidity crisis.[6] The existence of central banks as a lender of last resort has virtually eliminated the latter contingency, since as discussed in the previous chapter any private debt is liquid that the central bank is willing to accept as collateral, and in the last analysis, for the system as a whole, nothing else. While future net cash demands on the banking system remain unknown, the liquidity risk assumed in bank intermediation has thus been enormously reduced.

The divergence between private and social estimates of this risk could be further narrowed, and the real cost of risk-bearing in banking further reduced, were governments to choose to make explicit their ultimate responsibility for the satisfactory functioning of the payments mechanism and for the value of bank deposits. In contrast most governments have refused publicly to make such guarantees, and have maintained that bank solvency is the primary responsibility of bank managers and owners. This is largely because were governments to

6. Regulatory agencies commonly assess the adequacy of bank's capital by means of the relationship of capital accounts to various balance-sheet items. The most important of these have been the rates of capital to total deposits— the "10 per cent rule," and capital to "risk assets" (total assets less cash and U.S. government securities)—the "20 per cent rule". Significantly, statistical analysis of banks that have failed and banks that have survived has either failed to reveal any significant difference in the relative levels of these capital ratios in the two groups, or has found that the ratios are lower for nonfailing banks. The latter result is due to the fact that larger banks fail much less frequently, and have lower capital levels. "Either capital adequacy is a relatively unimportant factor in preventing bank failure, or, alternatively, these ratios do a relatively poor job of measuring capital adequacy". Richard Cotter, "Capital Ratios and Capital Adequacy". *National Banking Review*, Vol. 3, No. 3 (March, 1966), p. 345.

make such a commitment to bank depositors, the function of private equity capital in banking would be rendered completely otiose. In the absence of government or central bank guarantees the possibility of loss to depositors of individual banks, due to mismanagement, bad luck, or prolonged depression, remains.

As the foregoing discussion suggests, governmental fiscal and monetary policy has enormously reduced the risk assumed in bank intermediation, yet bank capital-asset ratios have risen in the postwar period. This may be explained in part by a *prisoner's dilemma effect* pushing individual banks to increase their capital-asset ratios. Even though the total amount of cash reserves available to the banking system is fixed by the central bank, for an individual bank an increase in shareholders' equity will be accompanied by an increase in its cash reserves. This redistribution of total cash reserves in its favor will enable an individual bank to make more loans, which enable it to capture a greater proportion of total deposits and so to grow at the expense of other banks. For large banks, which retain a significant proportion of their new loans as deposits, this effect is likely to be very strong, since an increase in capital accounts may then permit a multiple increase in total assets and liabilities.[7] Yet such a beggar-my-neighbor growth policy cannot succeed if the profit margins of other banks enable them to retaliate by strengthening their own capital positions. Additional equity capital for the system as a whole can result in an equal absolute increase in total earning assets, but no increase in total deposits, assuming the rate at which the central bank is willing to supply cash reserves is given. The result is simply to increase the cost of bank intermediation.

In the United States much of the blame for conservative bank lending policies, as well as the pressure to raise bank capital-ratios whenever profits permit, appears to be attributable to the quantity and fragmentation of bank regulation among separate authorities, each unempowered to take a wider view of allocational efficiency.[8]

7. This suggests an explanation as to why very large unit banks and branch banks have voluntarily increased their capital ratios in line with their higher profit margins, while for small unit banks the pressure of supervisory agencies seems to have been primarily responsible for the recent rise in capital ratios.

8. The following quotation is particularly interesting in this context:

"The capitalization problem has become confused with the question of

It is frequently asserted that a related function of bank capital is to induce banks to undertake the intermediary function of providing adequate risk capital to borrowers, yet still ensure the absolute solvency of the payments mechanism. In consequence banks in most countries have been permitted to build up tax-free reserves against future contingencies, in addition to shareholders' equity. These inner reserves are intended to cover all expected and unanticipated bad debt losses on the basis of experienced loss ratios. In many countries banks feel no compunction about long-term loans and equities dominating their portfolios.

This function clearly is critically important, but the unknown terms in the argument are the manner and degree to which higher bank capital-ratios affect the preference and utility function of banking firms and so influence bank lending behavior, particularly with regard to the risk, maturity, and diversity of the earning asset portfolio as discussed in the previous chapter. Do higher capital ratios in fact result in more aggressive banking? Since banking is a very highly regulated industry (many would insist over-regulated), does a larger cushion of capital protection permit less restrictive

---

bank liquidity. Indeed, it sometimes appears that capital is regarded as something held in the bank to meet the demands of depositors. Nothing could be further from the truth. The main issue in connection with bank capital, transcending such peripheral problems as the correct ratio or the character of bank assets, is whether or not we are sufficiently concerned about preserving the present unit system of privately owned banks. Serious questions are bound to be raised when the legal owners of a bank permit their equity in the enterprise to shrink so drastically that they have little stake in sound banking. They have degenerated to the level of self-appointed allocators of a large and vital segment of the nation's resources. If the enterprise happens to be profitable, the returns to the bankers in these situations are undeservedly large. If, on the other hand, losses are incurred they are limited to the amount of the small investment. To stretch the situation to, but not beyond, the breaking point appears to be the fond hope of bank owners who are disposed to view with complacency the decline in the capital ratio. Continuance of this situation is bound to breed suggestions that dilution of the private equity in banks has reached a point requiring the management of banking be socialized. They (the bankers) must realize that the erosion of capital may unwittingly cause them to lose control of their banking establishments."

E. H. Cramer (Chief of the Division of Research and Statistics, F.D.I.C.), "The Philosophy of Bank Capitalization," *Journal of Finance*, Vol. 6 (March, 1925).

regulation and greater operational freedom from supervisory control?

These questions have been but little explored. Unless they can be answered in the affirmative it must be concluded that a rise in capital-asset ratios above those functionally required to fulfill the intermediary function *actually undertaken* have the primary effect of raising the price that the community must pay for the services of bank intermediation, and so lowering the return from financial and tangible wealth ownership.

To the extent functional bank capital requirements have been substantially reduced, and providing that institutional preferences for risk bearing would not be adversely affected, a case can be made for permitting the mutualization of commercial banking, following the example of insurance and savings bank intermediaries. Alternatively, greater reliance on a deposit insurance fund would provide considerably more efficient protection to depositors than an equivalent amount of equity capital, since it is available to be supplied to the weakest bank in the system, rather than being compartmentalized among individual banks.[9] A less-drastic institutional change to reduce the price to the community of banking sources would be a general reduction in the regulation of bank behavior, including the simple permission of branch banking.[10] One insufficiently emphasized advantage of a branch banking system over a unit banking system is the lower capital-asset ratios required to provide an equivalent margin of protection to depositors against asset mismanagement.[11]

The economic function of bank equity capital is a cupboard which, upon current inspection, appears surprisingly bare. The vexed problem of "inadequate" bank capital ratios has, in the opinion of one perspicacious observer, long served rather as a "plausible, spurious apology for excessive bank earnings".[12]

9. In the period 1930 to 1936 in the United States losses on loans approached $2 billion, yet this was only 22 per cent of the capital of all operating commercial banks in 1929. In the period of 1930 to 1933 alone, losses to depositors amounted to $1.3 billion, and over 9,000 banks suspended operations.

10. For a recent appraisal see Paul Horvitz and Bernard Shull, "The Impact of Branch Banking on Bank Performance", *National Banking Review*, Vol. 2, No. 2 (December, 1964).

11. During the 1950's, capital-asset ratios for commercial banks in the United States averaged more than 50 per cent higher than in Canada, and nearly three times as high as in the United Kingdom.

12. Henry Simons "Debt Policy and Banking Policy," reprinted in *Economic Policy for a Free Society*, (Chicago, 1948), p. 234.

RECOMMENDED READING

James Tobin and William Brainard have applied the portfolio approach to the interrelationships between monetary and non-monetary intermediation in, "Financial Intermediaries and the Effectiveness of Monetary Controls," *American Economic Review*, Vol. LIII, No. 2 (May 1963). Consideration of a number of problems in this area by different authors may be found in Deane Carson, (ed.), *Banking and Monetary Studies*, (Illinois, 1963).

John Gurley and Edward Shaw used their conceptual framework to interpret American Financial history in, "Financial Intermediaries in the Savings-Investment Process," *Journal of Finance*, Vol. 11 (May 1956), and "The Growth of Debt and Money in the United States, 1800-1950: A Suggested Interpretation," *Review of Economics and Statistics*, Vol. 39 (August 1957). For a recent empirical study, which finds a low substitutability between bank and nonbank claims in the United States, see I. Friend, "The Effects of Monetary Policies on Nonmonetary Financial Institutions and Capital Markets," in *Private Capital Markets*, Commission on Money and Credit (Englewood Cliffs, N.J., 1964).

A detailed summary and criticism of the regulation of non-monetary intermediation may be found in Thomas Gies, Thomas Mayer, and Edward Ettin, "Portfolio Regulations and Policies of Financial Intermediaries," in *Private Financial Institutions, Commission on Money and Credit* (New Jersey, 1963). For a brief survey see David Fand, "Financial Regulation and the Allocative Efficiency of Our Capital Markets," *National Banking Review*, Vol. 3 No. 1 (September, 1965).

A comprehensive presentation of the scope of financial markets and institutions is contained in Raymond Goldsmith, *The Flow of Capital Funds in the Postwar Economy*, (New York, 1965).

Both the British "Radcliffe Report," *Report of the Committee on the Working of the Monetary System* (London, 1959), and the Canadian *Report of the Royal Commission on Banking and Finance* (Ottawa, 1964) emphasize the significance of the functional similarity of the operations of monetary and nonmonetary intermediaries for financial control. The Canadian report further recommends legal reserve requirements to control the growth of nonbank institutions.

8

The Dynamics of Monetary

Disturbance

The weakest and least satisfactory part of current economic theory seems to me to be in the field of monetary dynamics, which is concerned with the process of adaptation of the economy as a whole to changes in conditions. . . . In this field we do not even have a theory that can appropriately be called "the" existing theory of monetary dynamics."

—Milton Friedman
The Methodology of Positive Economics, 1953

Introduction

After having examined the origins and effects of the process of monetary intermediation (Chapter 6), and the effects of government regulation of the money stock on monetary intermediaries themselves (Chapter 7), it is finally appropriate to confront the general consequences of monetary change on aggregate economic behavior. The present chapter reexamines the traditional analysis of the effects of monetary change on the interrelationship between financial and real variables. By utilizing the model of assetholder behavior under uncertainty described in Chapter 2, and the theory of financial asset price determination developed in Chapter 5, it is possible to formulate with some precision the dynamic transition process provoked by monetary disturbance, and so extend the analysis beyond the confines of comparative static equilibrium formulation.

After a review of comparative static conclusions section one is devoted to a careful examination of the disequilibrium sequence propelled by a change in the nominal stock of money in a stationary economy. The proximate result of monetary change is always to alter the composition of wealth portfolios. Temporary equilibrium is ordinarily reestablished first in financial asset markets, while excess demand in product and factor markets persists. Throughout the subsequent transition period towards an equilibrium configuration in output and factor markets general portfolio imbalance forces a change in the *composition* of aggregate demand between investment and consumption goods. It is easy to demonstrate that only under the very limited and unreal assumption of instantaneous adjustment will monetary disturbance be neutral in its impact on the real contours of the new general equilibrium position.

The second section reconsiders the phenomena of monetary disturbance within the framework of a growing economy. A once-and-for-all change in the rate of money issue is shown to be similar to an increase or decrease in the money stock in a stationary economy, with the exception that a growing economy remains *perpetually* at some stage in the adjustment path. As a result the nonneutral consequences of nominal money change on the level of interest rates and the composition of output are increased. The admittance of expectations introduces an additional nonneutral consequence of failure of the nominal money stock to grow at the rate of growth of demand for real money balances. This is shown to result centrally from the fact that when the yield on money is fixed, nominal interest rates on fixed-income securities do not adjust sufficiently to offset completely future changes in the price level, even for the case in which such changes are completely anticipated with perfect foresight by all wealthowners.

The third section incorporates the fact that the transactions that bring about a change in the stock of monetary assets must also be incorporated into the analysis of monetary disturbance. Different monetary assets, all of which are acceptable as a means of payment, originate in different ways. The basic distinction between *inside* and *outside* monetary assets is described. It is then demonstrated that inside and outside money economies *ceteris paribus* have different characteristics. Irrespective of the monetary system in use, or the rate at which nominal money is issued, it may be shown that a change in the *mix* between inside and outside money can exert an important independent influence on the real profile of an economy. The chapter closes with a brief discussion of commodity money, an interesting economic anachronism.

Monetary Change in a Stationary Economy

One of the central tenets of neoclassical monetary theory was that in a competitive economy, where all prices are perfectly flexible, changes in the nominal stock of money are neutral, in the sense that in the final equilibrium position all real variables must remain unaltered. Keynesian monetary theorists in effect argued that changes in the nominal stock of money affected the level of interest rates because factor and commodity prices are not perfectly nor equally flexible in real-world economies. Both classical and Keynesian analysis treat the internal financial structure of an economy as being of secondary importance, netting out the assets and liabilities of the private sector. The central features of the relationship between financial and real variables are obscured or lost in these models, and the relationship between demand and supply of money is viewed as the essence of the linkage between financial and real activity.

The purpose of the present section is to reexamine the effects of monetary change, under both neoclassical and Keynesian assumptions, in a stationary economy in which asset stocks, uncertainty, and portfolio considerations are explicitly introduced. The attempt by wealth-owners to maintain a desired portfolio composition in the face of uncertainty will be shown to provide an explanation of the dynamic process by which the economy as a whole adapts to changes in monetary conditions, as well as an understanding of the direction and magnitude of the nonneutral consequences of monetary change.

A stationary state may be defined as a position of general equilibrium in a production economy in which the real capital stock, the labor force, productivity, and the level of output remain constant. If prices and wages are perfectly flexible full employment of factors is maintained continuously. The certainty and convenience yield on money balances (r_M) will be regarded as an exogenously determined constant. The assets that constitute money will remain unspecified until a later stage in the analysis. The price and yield on securities is assumed initially such as to satisfy temporary and full temporal equilibrium in competitive financial markets.

The neo-classical argument that changes in nominal money are neutral in such a system may be summarized as follows. Assume an instantaneous increase in the stock of nominal money M of x per cent in a stationary economy where all markets are perfectly competitive and resources perfectly mobile. The increase in real money balances creates excess demand for financial assets and current output, pushing up their prices, and causing the level of interest rates to fall temporarily. Debtor units respond by issuing additional bonds. The increase in the level of prices and the stock of nominal bonds continues until equilibrium is restored. In the new equilibrium position both the price level and the stock of nominal debt must have increased by exactly x per cent, and interest rates must have returned to their original level. For until this is the case real money balances would be larger than in the initial equilibrium, so that excess demand for goods would remain, pushing prices upward. Similarly, until interest rates have returned to their initial level debtor units would continue to issue nominal debt. Consequently in the final equilibrium position all real values must have returned to their initial levels, and the monetary disturbance is neutral in its effects.

The recognition of a variety of financial assets and liabilities within the private sector does not in itself invalidate the above analysis of monetary change, *providing* the additional assumption of no distribution effects is made. Netting out private obligations in effect implies that assets and liabilities have an identical converse effect on the real behavior of their holder. Economic units that hold fixed-income financial assets suffer a real capital loss in inflation, while those that have incurred fixed-income liabilities experience a real capital gain. If these groups have different marginal propensities to consume out of wealth or capital gains, neoclassical economists recognized that the composition of real output will be different in the final equilibrium position. These distributional effects are likely to be relatively small within a sector, but large among sectors, to the extent balance sheet positions are similar for most units within a sector eg. business firms, but very substantially among different sectors, eg. households versus firms.

The conclusions of comparative static analysis rest on the simplifying implicit assumption that the events of the disequilibrium process followed by the system do not itself influence the final equilibrium position, and so may be ignored. This is necessarily true only if all price adjustments are instantaneous, so that this disequilibrium period vanishes. In reality as was of course recognized the speed of adjustment to excess demand is not instantaneous, but takes place over some finite period that may be expected to differ among different markets. Nevertheless neoclassical economists felt justified in ignoring the effects of the transition period *per se* as of secondary importance. Their neutrality conclusion implicitly presupposes that any plans to increase new investment spending in response to lower interest costs are offset by simultaneous reductions in *ex ante* savings, that is plans to increase consumption expenditure. As a result any new real net investment is choked off before fruition by the general bidding up of prices. All redistribution effects have been eliminated by assumption. At this level of abstraction the operation of the wealth effect does not suggest any *necessary* alteration in the composition of output during the transition period. Because they had no theory of the dynamics of the adjustment process, they had therefore no reason to expect that the events of disequilibrium would alter significantly and systematically the real factors that determine the composition of aggregate demand for and supply of current output. The neglect of the adjustment process in comparative static analysis of macroeconomic models *under certainty*, apart from the questions of stability and convergence, would appear to be justified on the grounds of tractability and fruitfulness.

With the aid of the portfolio analysis previously developed it is possible to formulate an explanation of the dynamic disequilibrium process by which an economy adopts to monetary change *in an uncertain world*. The classical assumptions of perfect mobility and full employment of productive factors throughout the adjustment process will temporarily be retained. If price movements to eliminate excess demand are not assumed instantaneous, some assumption must be made with regard to the speed of price adjustment to disequilibrium in various markets. As discussed in Chapter 5 there is strong theoretical and empirical evidence to suggest that prices adjust most rapidly to eliminate excess demand in organized financial asset markets, and much less rapidly in markets for current output and factor services.

Consider an instantaneous increase in the nominal money stock brought about by government action. Any increase in real wealth and in disposable real income created by the nominal money issue creates excess demand for both consumption and investment goods as the neoclassical explanation recognized, pushing prices upwards. At the same time in an uncertain world the increase in the *proportion* of money balances in wealth portfolios throws assetholders out of portfolio balance, creating excess demand *for all other assets* in their portfolios. Depending on wealthowners' speed of adjustment to disequilibrium, financial asset prices established in organized financial markets respond relatively rapidly to excess demand. A *temporary equilibrium* position is thus restored initially in financial asset markets, with a higher level of financial asset prices and a lower level of asset yields. Higher liquidity ratios and higher financial asset prices (lower interest costs) further raise desired over actual holdings of tangible assets.[1] This induces debtors to issue nominal debt in order to adjust their actual stocks of tangible assets. As a result additional excess demand for capital goods is provoked, further shifting the composition of final demand for current output towards investment goods.

As a result of excess demand prices of current output and productive factors are pushed upwards. But throughout the adjustment period there is *a shift in the composition of aggregate demand* towards investment expenditure as a result of general *portfolio imbalance*. This induces a responsive shift in the composition of aggregate output in favor of reproducable capital assets throughout the transition path. Conversely, in the case of a reduction in the stock of nominal money, the composition of aggregate demand and output shifts away from reproducable capital assets throughout the transition period in which excess supply of output and productive factors force prices downwards.

The dynamics of monetary disturbance outlined above may be presented with greater precision diagrammatically. Figure 8-1 combines Figures 5-1(a) and 5-1(b) of Chapter 5. Total financial assets are represented by the horizontal distance OO'. The PP curve represents

---

1. Tangible assets, real assets, investment goods are used synonymously in the theoretical not the conventionally measured sense, as defined in Chapter 3, to denote all forms of nonfinancial capital assets, "real" and "intangible."

the combinations of interest rate and portfolio composition that satisfy financial portfolio balance. The AA curve represents the real value of existing stocks of money M and securities (S) at different interest rates r_s. The point of intersection of the PP and AA relationships represents a *temporary equilibrium* position of financial portfolio balance, at which point financial asset prices and yields (r_{S_E}) are such that the quantities of financial assets demanded exactly equal the stocks of financial assets in existence. This need not imply general portfolio

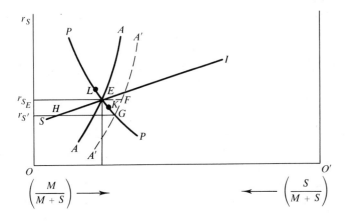

Figure 8-1

balance, since there may be excess stock demand or supply of tangible assets and debt. The curve SI represents the combinations of interest rate and incremental (flow) financial asset composition consistent with full employment in output markets. A position of full employment *full temporal equilibrium* is represented at E, where both asset and output market relationships are satisfied.

It is now possible to illustrate graphically the process by which an economy adapts to monetary change. An increase in the nominal money stock may be represented in Figure 8-1 by a rightward shift in the AA curve, e.g. to $A'A'$. At existing prices the resulting disequilibrium position F is characterized by excess demand in both financial asset and output markets. The increase in nominal money creates excess portfolio supply of money and excess portfolio demand for securities of EF through the Portfolio Balance Effect. Depending on the value of the speed of adjustment coefficients of wealthowners to disequilibrium, temporary equilibrium in security markets is reestablished relatively rapidly at G, with higher security prices and lower security yields (r_s'). Since G is further below SI than F, excess demand in the markets for current output increases, pushing up the price level. The lower interest cost of securities r_s' and the larger share of money balances in wealth portfolios at G induce debtor units to increase their issue of nominal debt in order to acquire tangible assets with the proceeds. The resulting composition of incremental (flow) supply of financial assets is shown in Figure 8-1 at H, as determined by the SI relationship at the lower temporary equilibrium interest rate r_s'. This gradually shifts the $A'A'$ relationship leftwards. *Throughout the transition period the composition of final demand is twisted toward tangible assets as wealthholders attempt to restore general portfolio balance.*

In response to any concurrent increase in real net wealth the IS relationship will shift upward to the extent the wealth effect operates. This will further accentuate the excess demand for current output. The ensuing rise in the price level will gradually push the IS relationship downward as the real value of private wealth falls. The rise in the price level also creates an intersectoral redistribution of real income and wealth from creditor to debtor sectors. This may further induce debtors to issue nominal securities in response to the fall in their real debt burdens, reinforcing the leftward movement of $A'A'$, and shifting further the composition of aggregate final demand and current output towards investment goods.

This process continues throughout the adjustment path until general equilibrium in output and asset markets is regained. If the adjustment period is not instantaneous, capital formation will occur *throughout the transition period* in response to the twist in the composition of final demand toward tangible assets. As a result real wealth and output will be higher in the new equilibrium. If investment is subject to diminishing returns the marginal return on tangible assets *ceteris paribus* will tend to fall. The new equilibrium position may again be represented at E, unless the marginal efficiency of investment has fallen as a result of the higher capital-labor ratio, in which case it will lie on PP below E. Due to the rise in real output and wealth, and the fall if any in tangible and financial asset yields in the new equilibrium, the price level will have risen less than proportionately to the increase in nominal money.

A converse argument is applicable to a reduction in the stock of nominal money, which creates excess portfolio demand for money and excess portfolio supply of other assets. As a result the composition of aggregate demand is shifted *away* from reproducable capital assets, and capital formation is depressed throughout the adjustment period.

In a more complicated world a more rapid rate of capital formation may conceivably raise, and a less rapid rate of capital formation reduce, the marginal return on capital goods. Whenever the capital goods sector has a sufficiently higher capital-labor ratio than the consumption goods sector, a relative increase in the demand for the more capital-intensive output of the capital goods sector will raise the marginal efficiency of investment for the economy as a whole, even though the stock of capital increases.

The forces shaping the adjustment process following monetary disturbance are more precisely revealed by the above diagrammatic presentation. If portfolio preferences are extremely sensitive to differential asset yields (the PP relationship more nearly horizontal in the neighbourhood of E), small changes in security prices will be sufficient to restore partial portfolio equilibrium among financial asset holdings. Debtor units then have a smaller interest-cost inducement to alter their debt and tangible asset positions. The shift in the composition of aggregate demand during the transition period is therefore likely to be reduced.

If wealthowners are indifferent to portfolio composition, at least within some relevant range, or exhibit extremely slow rates of adjustment of asset stocks in the short run to portfolio imbalance, the PP relationship may be envisaged as a broad band rather than a line. No portfolio imbalance or change in financial asset prices need then ensue from the change in the composition of wealth portfolios, and the wealth effect alone must be relied upon to restore equilibrium.

The foregoing analysis has proceeded as if a change in price were the only mechanism by which demand and supply are equated in securities markets as in other markets in the economy. But in all financial markets lending is rationed by a collateral requirement in addition to the interest charge. The price mechanism alone may be seen to be an insufficient regulator in the case of financial transactions because it does not provide a universally powerful exclusion principle. Risk-seeking borrowers would always be willing to pay a higher interest rate, providing they were assured of being able to borrow later to repay interest and principle, even if at a still higher rate, and so on *ad infinitum*. Since the probability of default rises with a borrower's debt-income and debt-asset ratio, credit rationing is introduced to supplement price rationing in all, even perfectly competitive, financial markets in order to satisfy risk-avoiding lenders. Once the degree of risk entailed in a property right to future income is specified, this establishes a debt limit beyond which borrowers may not trespass, irrespective of desired debt and the differential between expected real investment return and interest cost.

Depending on the initial position of the AA curve, to the extent debtor units are operating at or near their debt limits the interest elasticity of the incremental supply of securities, and hence of investment spending, may be expected to be considerably reduced. The recognition of collateral rationing as an effective constraint in securities markets supplementary to the price mechanism implies that the impact of nominal monetary change on the level and composition of aggregate demand and output will vary with the initial balance-sheet composition of wealthowner portfolios. Changes in portfolio demand for securities will still alter the yield structure and real value of the existing stock of securities outstanding. But the magnitude of any induced change in debt issue and real investment spending will depend in addition on the prevailing debt-asset position of potential borrowers. Financial asset prices may fail to respond rapidly to portfolio imbalance (the movement from F to G in Figure 8-1) in noncompetitive financial markets characterized by administered prices, or where no secondary markets exist.

The modification of neoclassical assumptions, in particular perfect competition and downward wage and price flexibility, considerably enhances the nonneutral impact of changes in the nominal stock of money on the real variables of an economy. This is because the result of dropping these assumptions is to prolong and accentuate the disequilibrium adjustment path. Anything that reduces the efficiency of changes in the general price level as the means by which nominal money balances are adapted to the desired real level increases the significance of the behavior of the nominal money stock.

In particular in a Keynesian world a reduction in nominal money will generate involuntary unemployment of labor and capital. In addition to the change in the *composition* of aggregate demand, the *level* of aggregate demand is reduced, with a subsequent loss of real output throughout the transition period. Even if financial asset prices are completely inflexible in the short run, so that the system remains at the initial point F in Figure 8-1, portfolio imbalance propels a change in the level and composition of aggregate demand throughout the longer adjustment period.

The explicit recognition of asset stocks and portfolio management considerations considerably improves the *stability* of macroeconomic models built on classical or Keynesian assumptions, since an additional equilibrating force is thereby introduced. Ignoring all redistributional effects between debtors and creditors, two conceptually distinct relationships now operate on aggregate demand to ensure a determinate price level in response to monetary or real disturbances. Changes in the price level cause an inverse movement in aggregate real cash balances, which through the *real balance effect* induces an increase or reduction in consumption and investment spending. Simultaneously, changes in the price level change the proportion of monetary assets in wealth portfolios, which through the *portfolio balance effect* operates to increase or reduce incremental demand for other asset forms. Conventional neoclassical and Keynesian analysis of money and commodity markets, due centrally to failure to treat adequately the fact of uncertainty, long overlooked and ignored the implications of portfolio diversification considerations.

Nominal monetary change can thus be regarded as neutral in an uncertain world only if the events of the disequilibrium path are ignored. The magnitude of the nonneutrality of monetary disturbance in a particular economy will depend on a number of factors, most importantly the elasticity and stability of portfolio preferences, and the duration of the price adjustment process. To the extent that wealthowners attempt to maintain a preferred portfolio composition, the portfolio balance effect, unlike the wealth effect, will generate excess demand for reproducible wealth forms, and hence for final output, of a magnitude large in relation to the initial change in nominal money balances. Given the desired ratio of money balances to total wealth $m = M/W$, a change in nominal money of ΔM will generate excess portfolio demand for all other assets of a magnitude $\Delta M(1 - m)/m$. For example with a value of $m = 0.1$, each dollar of monetary change would generate 9 dollars of excess portfolio demand for other assets. This suggests a very powerful route by which monetary control is able to influence investment expenditures.

To summarize: The *real balance* or *wealth effect* of monetary change follows from the fact that the consumption and investment decisions of economic units are influenced by the *size of their real wealth (net worth) position*. Changes in money balances and in the price level ordinarily affect total private wealth. Providing wealth-owners have a preferred wealth-expenditure relationship, the wealth effect will produce a change in the *volume* of total spending for current output (an upward or downward shift in the *IS* relation of Figure 8-1).

The *portfolio balance effect* of monetary change follows from the fact that in an uncertain world the consumption and investment decisions of economic units are influenced by the *composition of their total balance-sheet position*. Changes in money balances and in the price level always affect the composition of wealth portfolios. Providing that wealthowners have some preferred portfolio relationships (the *PP* relation in Figure 8-1), the portfolio balance effect produces a divergence between actual and desired asset stocks, and so a change in the *composition* of total spending for current output between consumption and investment goods. This occurs both directly, without any change in interest rates, as wealthowners adjust the amount of tangible assets demanded in response to portfolio imbalance (the disequilibrium position F in Figure 8-1), and indirectly, as wealth-owners readjust the amount of tangible assets demanded in response to changes in financial asset prices and yields which more rapidly reestablish partial portfolio balance in financial asset markets (the disequilibrium position G in Figure 8-1).

The *distribution effect* of monetary change follows from the fact that the magnitude and symmetry of the *wealth* and *portfolio balance effects* may be expected to differ among economic units. Changes in money balances and in the price level ordinarily affect the distribution of total wealth and the composition of balance-sheet positions among economic units.

Monetary Change in a Growing Economy

The previous analysis of a once-and-for-all change in the nominal quantity of money in a stationary economy cannot be used to demonstrate the effects of a change in the rate of change of the money stock. It is therefore necessary to reexamine monetary disturbance within the context of a growing economy. The simplest case to consider analytically is that of balanced growth, defined as that growth configuration at which all factor inputs and output grow at the same constant rate (g), factor productivity remains unchanged, and the ratios between all real variables remain constant.

In a growing economy net investment and saving are positive. Full employment equilibrium in factor and product markets requires that for price level stability aggregate demand for current output grow at the balanced growth rate g. Surplus spending by the household sector is then exactly offset by deficit spending by the business and government sectors. Price stability in financial asset markets requires that demand for financial assets and the stocks of nominal financial assets outstanding both grow at the balanced growth rate g. Saving by surplus spending units is allocated in a constant proportion to the accumulation of financial assets issued by deficit spending units. It follows that *persistent* sectoral deficits and surpluses are a necessary condition for price level and interest rate stability in the moving equilibrium of balanced growth.

It should be emphasized at once that the concept of balanced growth, while analytically convenient, it is but one of an indefinitely large number of conceivable equilibrium growth paths. With rising real per capita incomes and changes in social or demographic factors the desired ratio of certain types of wealth and financial assets to income ordinarily will increase secularly (an income elasticity of demand greater than unity), so that long-run equilibrium may be consistent with stocks of financial assets growing much more rapidly than income. For example in the post-war American economy rates of growth of most financial assets and liabilities have been approximately double that of *GNP*.

For an economy in balanced growth what are the implications of a once-and-for-all change in the rate of increase of the nominal money stock? Failure of the money stock to grow at the balanced growth rate g generates excess demand for or supply of other assets throughout the transition period, as a result of the portfolio balance effect. Unlike the stationary state, a growing economy is characterized by *continuous* wealthowner adjustment of existing asset stocks to some higher desired level. As long as the rate of price adjustment to excess demand for money balances is not instantaneous, a constant rate of nominal money increase different from the balanced growth rate may be shown to affect incremental demand for other assets, and so the rate of real capital accumulation. The economy is thus pushed into a *perpetual* disequilibrium configuration, and remains held at some phase in its adjustment path. This is not surprising once it is remembered that excess demand for or supply of money balances must persist in order to generate recurring pressure for further price change, if a constant rate of deflation or inflation is to continue.

This situation may be shown in Figure 8-1. From an initial position of balanced growth moving equilibrium E assume that there is a once-and-for-all increase in the rate of growth of nominal money issue to some constant rate $(g + x)$ above the balance growth rate g. As the growth of real income and wealth continues at the balanced growth rate g, the price level initially remaining unchanged, the share of real money balances in wealth portfolios cumulatively rises, shifting the AA curve rightward.

Portfolio Balance is disturbed by the increased proportion of money balances in wealth portfolios. Temporary equilibrium in organized financial markets is restored relatively rapidly by a rise in the price of existing securities and a fall in their yield. The rise in the share of money balances in wealth portfolios, plus the fall in the cost of debt issue, simultaneously throws potential debtors with lower aversion to risk and/or higher opportunity curves from wealthowner-ship into a position of portfolio imbalance. The result is to increase incremental demand to add to tangible asset stocks. The rise in investment expenditure shifts the composition of aggregate demand and generates a rise in the price level. Even without the existence of any excess supply of portfolio money balances, the flotation of securities by debtor units transfers idle portfolio money balances of creditors into active transaction money balances of debtors, which are dispatched into the income stream as an increase in investment expenditures. Excess demand for current output is reinforced by any wealth and distributional effects in response to the initial increase in the real value of money balances. The resulting rise in the price level operates to reduce the share of money balances in wealth portfolios, causing interest rates to rise.

Balanced growth equilibrium is eventually restored at some point (e.g., K in Figure 8-1) at which configuration money balances again increase at the balanced growth rate, and the composition of wealth portfolios remains constant. The rate of growth of real money balances g in the new moving equilibrium is accounted for by an increase in the stock of nominal money balances at the rate $g + x$ and a constant rate of price inflation of x per cent.

The system cannot return to the initial configuration E because excess demand for current output must persist in order to generate a continuous rate of inflation. The magnitude of excess demand for current output required in this new moving equilibrium position K, and the accompanying reduction in the rate of interest on securities, will depend on the degree of price flexibility of the system, and the rate of price inflation required. The greater the rate of increase in nominal money $g + x$, the more rapid is the rate of price inflation x required to adjust nominal to desired real stocks of money balances. As a result the greater is the persistent excess demand for current output, and the greater the nonneutral consequences of the portfolio balance effect in lowering interest rates and twisting the composition of aggregate demand and output toward investment goods.

A symmetrical converse analysis is applicable to a once-and-for-all reduction in the rate of nominal money issue to some constant rate $(g - x)$ below the balanced growth rate g. This operates to increase incremental demand for nominal money balances, and reduce incremental demand to add to other asset stocks. Portfolio balance is reestablished with a lower proportion of money balances and a higher level of interest rates. Assuming perfect resource mobility, so that full employment is maintained continuously, the reduction in investment expenditure shifts the composition of aggregate demand for current output and generates a fall in the price level. In the new moving equilibrium position (e.g., L in Figure 8-1), the increase in real money balances at the balanced growth rate g is restored by a constant rate of price deflation of x per cent, and accompanied by a permanently higher level of interest rates.

The previous analysis has proceeded under the implicit assumption of static expectations. Under the very weak assumption that past price movements are incorporated into expectations of future price movements (an elasticity of expectations > 0), a constant rate of inflation or deflation will alter the expected rate of return on all financial assets fixed in money terms, and so the differential return between financial and tangible assets. Anticipated inflation reduces the real return on money balances and fixed-income securities, and increases the relative attraction of holding equities and tangible assets, while deflation has the opposite effect. This important result can be shown to occur because *the nominal yield on fixed-interest securities will not adjust sufficiently to offset even a perfectly foreseen rate of inflation*, so long as the yield on money balances is institutionally fixed and money and bonds are to some extent substitutes in wealth portfolios.

This may be demonstrated by a reexamination of Figure 8-1. Anticipated inflation or deflation shifts the *SI* relationship upward or downward by an amount exactly equal to the *expected* rate of price change, but leaves the *PP* relationship between money and securities defined in fixed money terms unchanged. In the case of anticipated inflation, the point of intersection *E* will occur with a higher nominal return on nonmonetary securities. But any increase in the nominal yield on securities raises the real return on securities relative to the real return on money balances. The resulting increase in relative portfolio demand for securities at the expense of money balances in the new position of portfolio equilibrium operates to prevent the price of securities from falling (yield rising) by an amount sufficient to leave the real return on securities unchanged.

Conversely, with anticipated deflation as the nominal yield on bonds falls the real return differential on bonds over money balances declines. In this case the resulting reduction in the desired proportion of securities demanded in wealth portfolios prevents the price of securities from rising (yield falling) by an amount sufficient to leave the real return on securities invariant.

The extent to which the real return on securities will vary inversely with the anticipated rate of inflation or deflation can be seen to depend on the prevailing slope of the *PP* relationship. If portfolio preferences were completely inelastic, so that the *PP* relationship is vertical, the neoclassical conclusion of complete interest rate adjustment follows. There is then no relative increase in demand for securities, and the real return on securities remains unaffected by anticipated future price changes. In this case only the real return expected and realized on money balances will rise or fall. At the other extreme, when the *PP* relationship is horizontal, the nominal return on bonds remains completely unchanged by the rate of expected inflation or deflation. This represents the Keynesian "liquidity trap" case of perfectly elastic portfolio preferences. The entire portfolio adjustment must then fall on real capital formation and the marginal productivity of capital.

Only if the yield on money balances is not institutionally fixed, but includes an explicit and *variable* income return, can the relative returns on financial assets, tangible assets, and consumption goods, and so the preferred portfolio composition and the composition of demand, remain invariant to an expected rate of change in the future level of money prices.

The above analysis has shown that a monetary policy of inflation in a growing economy operates to increase the demand to accumulate capital assets, both by creating persistent excess demand for tangible assets through the portfolio balance effect, and by increasing the return differential between capital goods and fixed-income financial assets and debt. At the same time inflation represents a tax on holders of money balances. As a result the expected average return on total wealth portfolios will fall, tending to reduce planned saving as a proportion of total income. To the extent price level instability reduces the mean expected return on tangible assets, and/or increases the uncertainty with which this return is expected, the productivity of capital, the utility from wealthownership, and the ratio of wealth, saving and investment to income will tend to fall. These considerations form of course the central core of the case against inflation as a means of stimulating economic growth.

An *acceleration* in the rate of nominal money issue will *per se* always generate disequilibrium portfolio demand for other assets, and so tend to raise investment expenditures. But the recognition of the effects of expectations imposes severe limits on the ability of a government to use this path successfully to force the rate of economic growth, other than as a one-shot effect. An accelerating rate of inflation, by increasing the climate of uncertainty, is likely to reduce the expected utility from wealthownership, and eventually to prove explosive and cause the payments system to degenerate.

The relaxation of neoclassical assumptions with regard to price flexibility, mobility of resources, and full employment again increases the real importance of the behavior of the nominal money stock. Failure of the nominal money stock to grow at the balanced growth rate will then cause, in addition to the twist in the composition of aggregate demand away from investment goods, a reduction in the absolute level of aggregate output. Unemployment of productive factors will appear, and will be particularly concentrated in the capital goods sector. The amount of unemployment will depend on the degree of downward wage and price inflexibility, and the rate of deflation required.

Conversely, the shift in the composition of aggregate demand toward investment goods as a result of a rate of growth of the nominal money stock in excess of the balanced growth rate will, in the presence of resource immobility, result in a smaller shift in the composition of aggregate output toward investment goods. Inelastic supply schedules in the capital goods industries will result instead in a relative rise in tangible asset prices, and a backlog of unfilled orders.

Types of Monetary Assets— Inside, Outside, and Commodity Money

The previous discussion has purposely refrained from consideration of the specific transactions that bring about a change in the nominal stock of monetary assets. It is now necessary to recognize the fact that different types of monetary assets exist, that these different assets originate in different ways, and that the real effects of a given degree of nominal expansion or contraction of alternative types of monetary assets differ.

Assets generally accepted as a means of payment are either claims against the government, or claims against private financial institutions. Monetary assets that have their origin in the act of government purchases of goods and services or transfer payments have been termed *outside money*, since they represent a net claim of the private sector against the government and so "outside" the private sector.[2] As a result of the existence of outside money changes in the price level affect a wealth transfer between the private and public sector. An asymmetry is introduced since the wealth effect is conventionally held to influence the behavior of private but not public economic units.

Monetary assets that are claims against private financial institutions have been termed *inside money*, since they represent assets and liabilities "inside" the private sector. Monetary claims against private financial institutions originate only in the act of purchase of securities, since financial institutions are not permitted to purchase goods and services except as incidental to their financial function. Monetary assets that are claims against the government issued in payment for government purchases of securities held by the private sector are also *inside money*, since claims of the private sector against the government are then exactly counterbalanced by claims of the government against the private sector, and so "inside" the private sector. Changes in the real value of inside money due to movements in the level of prices do not involve a net wealth transfer between private and public sectors, but only within the private sector between debtor and creditor groups. No net wealth effect is held to occur in the case of inside money since, in the assumed absence of distributional effects, the behavior of private debtors and creditors is offsetting.

An important consequence for a growing economy is the fact that different monetary assets are created in different ways, the previously mentioned *Cantillon Effect*. A change in a stock must by definition always be accompanied by a change in a flow. Consequently, the effects discussed in the first two sections of this chapter, that follow from a change in the stock of nominal monetary assets, must be sharply distinguished conceptually from the effects that follow from the flow transactions that *accompany* the change in monetary stocks.

A change in the nominal stock of *outside money* comes about by a change in government budgetary expenditures and receipts for goods and services, transfer payments, or taxes. In the period during which outside monetary change occurs general equilibrium is disturbed by a change in government expenditures and private disposable income. This change in aggregate demand and its composition occurs *quite*

2. The terminology is that of J. Gurley and E. Shaw, *Money in a Theory of Finance*, (Washington, 1960), ch. 3.

independently of, and supplementary to, any wealth, distribution, and portfolio balance effects caused by the disturbance in the stock of nominal balances. While such a change is by definition transitory in the case of a once-and-for-all change in the nominal stock of money in a stationary economy, in a growing economy in which the nominal stock of money also grows outside monetary assets are injected into the economy by a *recurring* flow of government expenditures or transfers. That portion of saving by private economic units allocated to the accumulation of nominal outside money balances will then result in equivalent capital formation only if outside money is injected by an act of public investment expenditure.

The above discussion illustrates the critical importance in a growing economy of the manner in which the government chooses to spend the proceeds from monetary issue, as well as the rate of nominal money issue itself, both for the allocation of resources between the private and public sector and between consumption and investment goods. Acceleration of the rate of outside nominal money issue increases (and deceleration reduces) the real share of resources flowing to the government within any given tax structure. But since continual acceleration of the rate of nominal money issue leads to a continually increasing rate of inflation, governments cannot continue to increase their real share without limit by ever-accelerating the rate of nominal money issue. This is because as previously shown anticipated inflation reduces the return expected from holding monetary assets, while leaving the return on tangible assets unaffected, so that the proportion of total assets and total saving that private units choose to hold in money balances declines. It can be shown, under the restrictive assumption that real output remains unaffected by the rate of price change, that the rate of deficit spending and inflation at which the allocation of resources to the public sector is maximized occurs at that rate of inflation where the demand for outside money balances has unitary elasticity with respect to the expected rate of inflation.[3]

Government deficits or surpluses that accompany the act of nominal money issue or withdrawal need not arise from government purchase or sale of current output nor government provision of transfer payments. The government may choose rather to purchase

3. Martin Bailey, "The Welfare Cost of Inflationary Finance", *Journal of Political Economy*, Vol. 64, (April, 1956).

or sell nonmonetary financial assets. If nominal monetary issue originates in the act of government purchase of securities, for example through open-market operations by the central bank (inside money), private saving allocated to the accumulation of money balances are transformed into incremental demand for securities to finance private deficit-spending and so real capital formation. Since inside money balances are exchanged for securities already in private wealth portfolios, the composition of financial portfolios, and so the price of securities, is necessarily changed by a greater proportion than in the case of outside money issue for any given change in the stock of nominal monetary assets.

The government through the central bank acts as a financial intermediary by acquiring primary securities in open-market operations and issuing in exchange its own debt, currency, a secondary security. The effects of the issue of inside money representing a claim against private financial institutions, for example bank demand deposits, is similar to the issue of government inside money, except that different types of securities and debt are ordinarily purchased, so that the composition of portfolio and incremental demand for securities, and consequently the relative structure of security prices and yields, will be altered.

All modern economies are characterized by a mixture of inside and outside monetary assets, the particular ratio depending primarily on the reserve requirements imposed on the banking system and the transactions by which central bank liabilities originate. The rate at which the total nominal money stock must increase for price level stability depends on the rate of balanced growth. If government borrowing and the tax structure may be regarded as exogenously determined, for example by political constraints, the higher the ratio of inside to outside money in a growing economy the lower will be the level of interest rates on securities, but the lower will be the level of government expenditures on goods and services. Conversely if government borrowing and expenditures are postulated as given, then higher ratios of inside to outside money will be associated with lower levels of interest rates but higher tax rates. Only if total government spending for nonfinancial goods and services, transfers, and total taxes are all exogenously determined will differences in behavior between an inside and outside money economy disappear. Under such conditions any rise in the ratio of inside money through open-market purchases will necessitate an offsetting increase in government bond issue exactly equal to the increased open-market purchases, so that interest rates will remain unaffected.

To the extent that government borrowing is exogenously constrained, increasing the proportion of inside money will reduce interest rates, but must necessitate either an increase in taxes or a reduction in government expenditures for current output or transfer payments. An increase in the proportion of inside money is effectuated by increased government loans, that is purchases of debt securities, and it is this which causes interest rates to fall.

It follows that the *level* of reserve requirements required of the commercial banking system may be expected to have real economic significance *per se*, quite apart from the question of the rate at which total nominal monetary assets are permitted to expand. By lowering reserve requirements and increasing the proportion of inside money not accompanied by additional government borrowing, the government exchanges money for bonds in wealth portfolios. By substituting an asset of lower risk and higher liquidity, the total risk and uncertainty that must be borne by private wealthowners is reduced, and a greater proportion of current saving is made available to finance private deficit-spending.

Outside fiat money issued in an act of government deficit-spending for public goods or transfer payments is not the only type of outside payments media generally in use, and historically it has not been the most important. Outside money may directly take the form of commodities, or paper money may be required to be backed by a certain weight of precious metals, as in a gold standard system, or commodities, as in a commodity-reserve currency. Commodity money as is well known ties the incremental supply of money to the supply of the particular money commodities, which in the case of gold will only fortuitously match incremental demand for nominal money balances at constant prices. In such a system that part of current saving allocated to the accumulation of money balances is destined to result *neither* in capital formation nor in current consumption. Instead resources must be devoted to producing the money commodity, from which no services as a commodity are received. In addition interest rates are higher because saving allocated to accumulate money balances is not transformed into demand for securities. Since fiat money can serve equally well to provide the exchange-convenience and capital-certainty properties of a payments media, the reserve stock of such money commodities, the cost of their production and storage, and the resulting higher level of interest rates all cause a misallocation and waste of resources having a positive opportunity cost. In any modern social framework, where legislation can confer general acceptability on fiat money, commodity money can only be regarded as an economic anachronism. It represents an open confession of failure on the part of the political decision-making process to agree on the rate at which the managed nominal money stock ought to be increased.

RECOMMENDED READING

An excellent analysis of the general forces determining the demand for money is Milton Friedman's, "The Quantity Theory of Money, a Restatement," in Milton Friedman, ed., *Studies in the Quantity Theory of Money* (Chicago, 1956). Friedman's explanation of the mechanism by which monetary disturbances are transmitted is outlined in M. Friedman and Anna Schwartz, "Money and Business Cycles," *The Review of Economics and Statistics*, Vol. XLV, No. 1, Pt. 2, Supplement (February 1963). James Tobin has suggestively explored the same question in, "Money, Capital, and Other Stores of Value," *American Economic Review*, Vol. 51 (May 1961).

There have been a large number of attempts to estimate the demand function for money balances. For an excellent recent summary see David M. Jones, *The Demand for Money: A Review of the Literature*, Staff Economic Studies, Federal Reserve System, 1966. An important empirical attempt to relate movements in interest rates to portfolio composition is J. G. Gurley's, *Liquidity and Financial Institutions in the Postwar Economy* Study Paper 14, Joint Economic Committee, 86th Congress, Washington, 1960. For a related approach, see the two articles by H. A. Latané, "Cash Balances and the Interest Rate—A Pragmatic Approach," *Review of Economics and Statistics*, Vol. 36 (November 1954), and "Income Velocity and the Interest Rate—A Pragmatic Approach," *Review of Economics and Statistics*, Vol. 42 (November 1960).

Frank de Leeuw has developed and estimated a general model of the financial behavior of the United States economy using portfolio adjustment principles, "A Model of Financial Behavior," in *The Brookings Quarterly Econometric Model of the United States*, edited by J. Duesenberry, G. Fromm, L. Klein, and E. Kuh (Chicago, 1965).

9

Monetary Control
and Financial Policy

To sell for money would then be as easy as to buy for money.

—John Gray, 1848

Introduction

The previous chapter completed the analysis of the disequilibrium adjustment process consequent upon monetary change. The present chapter is devoted to a discussion of the alternative techniques by which governments deliberately provoke such disequilibrium in pursuit of their stabilization objectives.

Monetary control refers to the systematic action adopted by governments to regulate the volume and terms of monetary intermediation. Such regulation is conventionally carried out by means of two analytically distinct classes of control techniques. The first section discusses the most important control category—manipulation of the nominal stock of legal money. Changes in the stock of government non interest-bearing claims represent a general and indirect

241

control instrument. Such changes can only occur as a result of government transactions on income or capital account. All private wealthowners are affected, though by no means equally, by changes in the total quantity of cash balances available, and all retain complete freedom to follow their own self-interest in adjusting their behavior.

The second general monetary control category considered is the direct regulation of the lending and borrowing activities of monetary intermediaries. By explicit interference with commercial bank operations, which take the form of requirements and prohibitions having force of law, governments are able to alter commercial bank behavior and so the volume and/or terms of monetary intermediation.

These two types of monetary control techniques are shown to affect in different ways the cost schedules of providing bank credit, as described in the theory of the firm model of bank operations of Chapter 6, and so bank lending, borrowing, and profit rates. Their differential effects are developed in the present chapter by a geometric presentation of the volume of monetary intermediation in terms of balance-sheet variables.

It is possible to distinguish a third general class of financial control techniques, comprising the direct regulation of nonmonetary intermediary behavior, and a fourth class concerned with direct regulation of nonfinancial spending units. The number of possible direct financial controls is virtually unlimited, and beyond the scope of the present discussion.

The last section outlines the general significance of alternative financial policies for real economic behavior. Monetary, debt, and fiscal policy are presented and distinguished as complementary means to particular ends. It is shown that only if these policies are appropriately coordinated can governments hope to attain efficiently their desired set of stabilization objectives. Nevertheless, due to the pervasiveness of allocation and distribution effects of public stabilization programs, an optimum control mix can never be uniquely specified. It remains the responsibility of the legislative and executive branches of government to select the tradeoff between stabilization, allocation, and distribution objectives.

Control of the Nominal Stock of Legal Money

Changes in the stock of legal money can occur only as a result of deficits or surpluses in the cash budget of the government sector.[1] Increases in the stock of legal tender represent interest-free borrowing by the government to finance current expenditures in excess of current cash inflows. Reductions in total legal money outstanding represent repayment of interest-free debt, made possible by a surplus of current cash inflows over current expenditures. Different economic goods are taken in exchange for government expenditures, for example, productive factors, currently produced output, previously existing tangible goods, new and previously existing financial assets, or no *quid pro quo* may be involved, in which case government expenditures represent a transfer payment (positive or negative) to the private sector.

Governmental cash deficits or surpluses are conventionally distinguished according to the type of agency and transaction for which they were incurred. In modern economies, treasury or finance departments and central banks commonly share a dual responsibility for the determination of the nominal stock of legal money. Day-to-day management customarily resides with the latter, while the government in power bears ultimate responsibility. The degree of independence that central banks possess in regulating the legal money base of an economy varies widely between different countries, and frequent examples occur of the two agencies pursuing uncoordinated operations with conflicting effects.

Treasury Operations—Imbalance on Government Income Account Government cash deficits or surpluses on income account occur whenever government income receipts, primarily from taxation, fall below or exceed government current expenditures for goods and services or transfer payments. Responsibility for imbalance in the government's cash budget lies with the treasury or finance department within the government, and the techniques by which the budgetary process may be used to influence private economic behavior form the content of fiscal policy. Imbalance in the government's cash budget always causes an identical proximate change in total financial assets

1. In the following discussion the central bank is always regarded as a part of the government sector.

of the private sector, and in total private net worth if public goods are valued at cost by private economic units. The change in total private assets is reflected in increased or reduced holdings of government debt held by private economic units.

Imbalance on income account results in changes in the stock of legal money only to the extent that budgetary deficits or surpluses are financed by currency issue or reduction. The treasury may itself directly issue or acquire its own non interest-bearing debt. Alternatively, the treasury may vary its direct borrowing (issue of interest-bearing debt) from the central bank, and in return increase or reduce the amount of central bank debt.

Central Bank Operations—Imbalance on Government Financial Account. The central bank, customarily a semi-independent department of the government, is explicitly responsible for regulating the supply of legal tender to the private sector. All liabilities of this agency, whether notes or deposits, are acceptable as legal tender. Consequently the type of government transaction most closely identified with changes in the stock of legal money is purchase or sale of existing financial assets by the central bank, generally interest-bearing treasury debt. Such changes in the stock of legal tender may occur quite independently of treasury budgetary inbalance on current account.

Central bank operations conventionally include the purchase and sale of outstanding government debt, gold, and foreign exchange. In most countries it is purchases or sales of marketable interest-bearing government debt in organized security markets that are primarily relied upon to regulate total commercial bank reserves. Such transactions alter the composition of government debt outstanding in private portfolios between legal money and interest-bearing securities. They do not affect total government debt, nor total financial assets and net worth of the private sector, except insofar as the market valuation of interest-bearing securities is affected by central bank operations.

RESPONSE OF COMMERCIAL BANKS

The total stock of legal money M is held either in currency balances outside the banking system C, or in bank cash reserves R:

$$M \equiv C + R \tag{1}$$

Portfolio preferences of private spending units determine the relative amounts of total currency balances and deposits demanded, given the yield on legal money r_M and bank deposits r_D. For any particular differential $r_D - r_M$, the nonbank public has some preferred ratio of currency to deposits $K = C/D$, and banks have some preferred ratio of cash reserves to deposits $L = R/D$. The stock of legal money then determines the amount of deposits supplied in equilibrium by the banking system. Substituting in Equation 1:

$$D = \left(\frac{1}{K + L}\right) M \qquad (2)$$

So long as public and bank portfolio preferences between legal money and deposits are known and stable, treasury and central bank operations are able to establish total bank reserves at any desired level. In practice changes in public and bank preferences due to seasonal and random factors force central banks to undertake continual offsetting or "defensive" open-market sales and purchases in order to maintain bank reserves at the desired level.

The determination of the amount of total bank deposits outstanding under such conditions may be shown geometrically.[2] If bank capital accounts are for the moment disregarded, total bank deposits D are identical to bank earning assets E plus bank cash reserves R:

$$D \equiv E + R \qquad (3)$$

In Figure 9-1, for a given stock of legal money, the banking system's total deposits and reserves are measured on the vertical axis, and total earning assets on the horizontal axis.

The curve DD represents the relationship between bank lending and borrowing operations for a *given* stock of legal money. It has a positive y intercept, that indicates the quantity of deposits demanded OD when banks hold 100 per cent cash reserves. As banks increase their earning asset holdings, total deposits increase, but by a smaller amount, due to the leakage of bank cash into general circulation as spending units maintain their preferred proportion K of currency

2. The diagrammatic presentation has been adopted with kind permission from an unpublished manuscript of James Tobin.

balances to deposits. As a result of this internal currency drain the slope of DD is less than unity $(1 - K)$.[3] Unless a change occurs in asset preferences of spending units, or in asset return differentials as the volume of bank intermediation increases, DD will be a straight line.

In an uncertain world future deposit totals must be viewed as an expected probability distribution for any given level of earning assets.

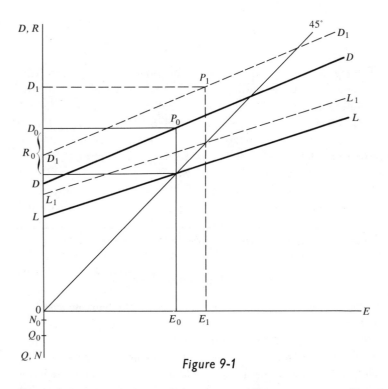

Figure 9-1

Points on DD must then be interpreted as a measure of central tendency. The vertical distance between DD and a $45°$ line through the origin measures the expected amount of *actual* cash reserves $R \equiv D - E$ available to the banking system as banks increase their purchases of earning assets.

3. If $K = C/D$ has a value of approximately 0.25 as in recent American experience, DD would have a slope of 0.75.

The curve LL represents the preferred ratio of cash reserves to deposits $(L = R/D)$ that banks maintained to ensure the continual convertibility of their deposits into legal money. The slope of LL is equal to $(1 - K)(1 - L)$. This liquidity requirement represents the banking system's desired proportion of primary reserves to total deposits. The vertical distance between DD and LL represents *desired* cash reserves at each level of earning assets and deposits. In addition, banks hold noncash reserve assets of high liquidity for portfolio purposes, which are here defined as included in earning assets E. The composition of total bank reserves between cash and noncash assets, and so the position of the LL relation, is determined by legal requirements, asset exchange costs, and relative asset yield differentials, as described in Chapter 6.

The total volume of bank intermediation in equilibrium is uniquely determined at P_0. Only at this output, where the LL curve intersects the 45^0 line, does the level of *actual* reserves equal *desired* reserves.

Given the stock of legal money M_0, equilibrium is established with an amount of deposits D_0, earning assets E_0, and cash reserves R_0. At any other level of monetary intermediation banks would be in a position of portfolio imbalance, and would purchase or sell earning assets to adjust their actual cash reserves towards their desired stock of cash reserve assets.

This geometric presentation of the determination of the level of bank intermediation has the advantage of introducing explicitly the behavioral supply and demand relationship hidden behind the conventional algebraic presentation of the bank credit multiplier. It must be remembered that changes in relative asset prices and yields, which are affected among other reasons by the volume of monetary intermediation, alter bank and nonbank asset preferences, and so the slope of the LL and DD relationships.

The analysis may also be applied to the case of an individual bank. The deposit retention curve DD is then much flatter than for the system as a whole, with a slope approaching zero for a small unit bank. For an individual bank DD is convex from above, since the rate of cash leakage to other banks increases as the area of loan operations is expanded.

The causal process by which changes in the stock of legal money affect the level of bank intermediation and spill over into other markets may be briefly described. Excess supply of legal money creates, through the portfolio balance, wealth and income effects, excess demand for other goods, but in particular for bank deposits, the closest currency substitute. A change in the amount of currency that spending units desire to deposit with commercial banks shifts the amount of primary reserves available to the banking system at every level of earning assets. The earning asset deposit retention relationship DD in Figure 9-1 shifts upward or downward, (e.g., to D_1D_1) by an amount equal to, or by the ratio $D/(D + C)$ of, the change in legal money, depending on whether bank or public legal money balances are initially altered. Bank portfolio balance is eventually restored at a level of earning assets E_1 and deposits D_1, where actual and desired primary reserves are again equal.

This result can be represented in the model of bank operations of Chapter 6 by a *horizontal* shift in the average and marginal cost of funds schedules to individual banks. If the demand schedule for bank loans remains unchanged, banks respond to this shift primarily by adjusting the amount of marketable bonds in their investment portfolios.

It is sometimes overlooked that the effects of a change in nominal deposits that occur as a result of a change in bank bond holdings, differ from those of an identical change in deposits resulting from a change in bank loans. The particular change in bank assets that gives rise to the change in bank deposits determines the manner in which the change in deposit balances is initially distributed among different spending units. It also determines the corresponding changes in the magnitude, composition and distribution of nonmonetary assets and liabilities held by nonfinancial units.

A change in the stock of legal money as a result of government open-market operations induces banks to eliminate excess demand or supply of reserves primarily by the purchase or sale of existing marketable bonds, except in situations where there is a previously unmet excess demand for bank loans. The initial result is an exchange of deposits for bonds in private wealthowner portfolios. There is no concurrent change in total assets, nor in the distribution of total asset ownership, apart from any gains or losses generated by the transaction, in private wealthowner portfolios.

In contrast a change in nominal deposits consequent upon an

increase or reduction in bank loans, which except for the case of an unsatisfied fringe of credit-worthy borrowers is much less likely to be initiated by government manipulation, results in a concurrent change in total assets and liabilities of private units. In addition it is accompanied by a change in the distribution of total asset ownership towards or away from debtor spending units, whose portfolio preferences differ from those of creditors. If, as is ordinarily the case, deficit units desire to hold a smaller proportion of deposits and a larger proportion of tangible assets than surplus units, the subsequent proportional change in aggregate demand for current output, and in the price level, will exceed the proportionate change in nominal deposits. Otherwise expressed, the change in the distribution of total asset ownership between wealthowners of diverse portfolio tastes causes a leftward shift in the economy's portfolio balance relationship PP, and so in the new general equilibrium configuration of financial asset prices. It is consequently essential to consider the concurrent changes in bank and public balance sheets in any examination of the effects of a change in bank deposits on aggregate demand.

Changes in bank lending to spending units is accompanied *pari passu* by changes in convenience lending of depositors in the aggregate to the banking system, as defined by the earning assets-deposit retention relationship DD. This occurs even though no individual depositor remains a lender for longer than his convenience dictates, and makes no sacrifice of liquidity or current expenditures as a result of the loan. The magnitude of the response in the level of bank intermediation to changes in the nominal stock of legal money depends on the slope of the deposit retention relationship, and on bank liquidity preferences. The lower the public's preferred marginal ratio of currency to deposits K (the steeper the DD and LL curves), and the lower the banks marginal liquidity requirements L (the steeper the LL curve), the greater will be the resulting change in bank earning assets and deposits in response to any given change in the stock of legal money.

Bank capital Q may be introduced without difficulty into the previous analytical framework. From the identity:

$$R + E \equiv D + Q \tag{4}$$

in Figure 9-1 the amount of bank capital Q_0 may be measured from the origin downward, and a 45° line drawn to pass through Q_0. The distance between DD and the new 45° line again represents the amount of cash reserves available to the banking system as its purchases of earning assets increase. An increase in bank capital results in a downward shift in the 45° line, and an identical rightward shift in the DD relationship, since a given amount of deposits is now consistent with a larger quantity of earning assets.

Central Bank Lending. The exercise by central banks of their function as lender of last resort to the banking system enables commercial banks to vary their cash reserves at their own initiative, without a corresponding change in currency deposited with them by the public. The recognition of commercial bank borrowing from the central bank N necessitates a distinction between net $R - N$ and gross R reserves of the banking system. The quantity of such borrowing N_0 may also be represented in Figure 9-1 by an equivalent downward shift in the 45° line and rightward shift in DD (from the balance-sheet identity: $R + E \equiv N + D$).

An increase in commercial bank gross reserves R enables the banking system to increase its earning assets and deposits. As Figure 9-1 suggests, an increase in commercial bank gross reserves through rediscounting (a downward shift in the 45° line, accompanied by an equal rightward shift in the DD relation), results in a greater increase in bank earning assets, but a smaller deposit expansion, than would occur as a result of an identical increase in bank reserves provided by treasury expenditure or central bank open-market bond purchases (an upward shift in the deposit retention relationship DD). Use of the rediscount privilege, by permitting a reduction in the ratio of net reserves to deposits, lowers the cost of earning asset funds schedules to individual banks.

The fact that rediscounting and repayment of rediscounts occur at the initiative of commercial banks rather than the central bank complicates the precise regulation of bank deposits and earning assets by the monetary authorities. Open-market operations then have their proximate impact on the quantity of bank borrowing N, so that their impact on gross reserves, the critical variable for deposit regulation, is weakened. The rediscount privilege, insofar as it enables banks to reduce their net reserve ratio, operates to offset legal requirements that force banks to maintain minimum gross reserves. Because rediscounting introduces additional slippage into central bank control of the volume of monetary intermediation, the rediscount privilege in many countries is not a simple right. In the United States during periods of monetary restraint the Federal Reserve Banks ration the amount of funds granted at the rediscount window.

Once central bank lending is recognized it becomes a particularly heroic assumption to regard the desired liquidity relationship LL of the banking system as invariant to central bank open-market operations. In the United States the difference between gross reserves R and required reserves RR is conventionally defined as excess reserves $R - RR$, while the difference between excess reserves $R - RR$ and commercial bank borrowing N is termed net free reserves $(R - RR) - N$. This represents the excess of net reserves over required reserves $(R - N) - RR$, and may be positive or negative. Required reserves are the proximate target variable of the second category of monetary control techniques. The bulk of central bank open-market transactions—so-called defensive operations—is undertaken to offset seasonal and random variations in gross primary reserves—gold purchases, sales, shifts in treasury deposit balances, bank float, and shifts in the public's currency-deposit ratio—so as to maintain gross reserves R at some desired level.

The conventional assumption that nondefensive open-market operations induce a change in required reserves RR identical to the change in gross reserves R, and so a multiple expansion in deposits by the bank multiplier relationship, requires that banks normally maintain net free reserves at some constant value, except during transitory periods of adjustment. Such an assumption is invalid since, as already shown, both the composition of bank reserve portfolios, and the desired relationship between total reserves and earning assets, are partly determined by the differential returns available on alternative asset categories. In particular the rediscount rate charged by the central bank, the rate on Treasury Bills and other money market assets, and the return and lending opportunities on bank investment and loan portfolios, all effect the level of net free reserves.

To the extent open-market purchases lower the rate on money market assets, net free reserves may be expected to rise systematically and permanently as the central bank increases the supply of primary reserves. Conversely, open-market sales will produce a systematic fall in the desired net free reserve position as banks adjust their net reserve ratio to a new yield structure of financial assets. The ratio of net free reserves to secondary reserves desired by commercial banks, and to a lesser extent total reserves to earning assets, will vary significantly as money market rates change relative to the rediscount rate. As a result the short-run relationship between changes in gross primary reserves ΔR supplied by the monetary authorities, and changes in the volume of commercial bank total assets and deposits ΔD, becomes substantially *lower* than that indicated by the deposit multiplier calculated from average values.

Changes in the rate charged for rediscounting enable the central bank to exercise some influence on the amount of commercial bank borrowing by inducing banks to alter their net reserve ratios, and hence the level of their earning assets and deposits. Raising the rediscount rate brings gross and net reserves towards equality, while lowering the rediscount rate encourages banks to increase their borrowing. The rediscount rate charged by the central bank is conceptually analogous to a negative rate on marginal holdings of reserve balances by commercial banks, while intramarginal reserve balances bear a zero yield. The comparison is not completely accurate, since as stated rediscounting is not generally regarded as an automatic right, but only to meet "legitimate" needs for credit, so that nonprice rationing is important.

There is in principle nothing to prevent central banks from paying (or charging) a nonzero rate on total or marginal reserve balances. Payment of a positive rate by the central bank would induce commercial banks to increase their reserve positions, while in the face of a negative rate (charge) commercial banks would adjust their portfolios so as to reduce their reserve balances. Such a mechanism would enable the central bank to induce commercial banks to adjust their liquidity ratios LL in desired directions, weakening, from the viewpoint of deposit control, the necessity for coercive legal reserve requirements.

Direct Regulation of Commercial Bank Behavior

REQUIRED RESERVE RATIOS

Regulation of the total volume of bank intermediation by changing the nominal stock of legal money is compatible with the absence of any direct control of bank cash ratios. As long as the general acceptability of deposits for direct transfer requires their convertibility into legal money on demand, individual banks will voluntarily maintain some minimum liquidity position of cash reserves to deposits against the contingency of net deposit withdrawal. Since bank cash ratios represent a position of portfolio balance between liquidity and profitability, the particular ratio maintained will shift in response to changing yields on financial assets, in particular to the rate differential between earning assets and reserves. Shifts in bank preferred liquidity positions increase the uncertainty associated with indirect monetary control techniques. A given change in bank cash reserves is compatible with a range of values for total bank deposits and earning assets, depending on the cash ratios adopted by banks in the new equilibrium position. The effects of such variations on the volume of bank intermediation may again be demonstrated in Figure 9-1 by a shift of the level and slope of the *LL* relationship upward or downward, while the *DD* curve remains constant.

Although banks historically have adhered to a "conventional" ratio of cash to deposits in their everyday operations, sufficient variability has occurred in critical periods to increase significantly the volume of central bank open-market operations required to produce a desired change in the volume of bank intermediation. In consequence central banks have widely requested and received authority to establish a minimum ratio of cash to deposits, below which no commercial bank may operate. The result has been to increase the temporal stability of the *LL* relationship, by constraining downward shifts in bank preferences for cash reserves. Required reserve ratios may be regarded as a legislated increase in the demand for legal money. They represent a direct restraint that prevents the banking system from eliminating what would be a position of portfolio imbalance.

Secondary reserve requirements imposed by the central bank do not operate to regulate the total volume of bank assets and liabilities in the manner of cash reserve requirements unless the central bank effectively controls the stock of securities eligible for secondary reserves. If the supply of such securities is not controlled by the central bank, secondary or security reserve requirements operate not on the total volume of bank intermediation, but rather on the composition of bank asset portfolios. The allocation of bank credit between loans and investments, and among spending units, may then be regulated, and an expansion of bank loans through the liquidation of bank investment portfolios prevented. Such requirements by the monetary authorities represent in effect a legislated increase in bank demand for government borrowing, but at the expense of bank profits and an unsatisfied fringe of private borrowers.

CHANGES IN RESERVE REQUIREMENTS

Changes in the required reserve ratio shift the position and slope of the *LL* relationship, but leave the *DD* relationship unchanged. This permits central banks to regulate the quantity of total bank deposits without altering the nominal stock of legal money. The consequences of reserve requirement variation can be illustrated for the individual banking firm (in the model developed in Chapter 6) by a *vertical* displacement in the average and marginal cost of funds schedule. This is in contrast to the horizontal shift that occurs with manipulation of the nominal stock of legal money.

An increase in required reserve ratios reduces the ratio of bank earning assets to total deposits, causing an upward shift in the cost of earning asset funds schedules to individual banks, and a reduction in bank investments. Total demand for legal money is in effect raised by a legislated increase in bank demand for primary reserves, leaving the cash position of non-bank economic units unaffected. The full-employment level of private aggregate demand is then consistent with a larger nominal money stock. In consequence the proportion of its budgetary expenditure that the treasury can finance through interest-free currency issue, or direct central bank borrowing, consistent with any given level of aggregate private demand, is increased. Conversely, a reduction in reserve requirements transfers earning assets from the central bank to the banking system, lowers bank cost of funds schedules, and raises the cost of financing to the treasury.

The impact effect of reserve-requirement variation creates windfall gains or losses for bank shareholders, which in the longer run may be redistributed towards depositors and borrowers. The fact that windfall gains may prove temporary for bank shareholders does not, of course, make them undesirable. If through the force of competitive pressures windfall gains from reductions of reserve requirements are gradually distributed to bank depositors in the form of a higher return on deposits (assuming bank capital ratios remain unaffected), this will increase the size of the banking system relative to nonbank intermediaries. The consequent larger incremental supply of bank credit reduces the return on primary securities, so that private deficit spending units also gain, at the expense of the government and taxpayers.

Changes in required-reserve ratios effectuate a change in the ratio of *inside* to *outside* money, defining "money" broadly to include legal money plus bank deposits, providing legal money is not entirely of the inside money category. The level of reserve requirements selected consequently exerts a separate and important influence on primary security prices and so the level of interest rates, as well as government interest expense, for any given stock or incremental supply of nominal money.

This conclusion is in sharp contrast to conventional monetary analysis, which regards the particular reserve ratio established as a fulcrum for monetary control as a matter of indifference—apart from the fact that the lower the ratio the greater the "multiple of expansion" from central bank operations, so that a more nimble manipulation of the stock of legal money by the central bank is required to avoid disstabilizing overcompensation. If a rapid growth in the rate of private capital formation is regarded as a primary policy goal, the present argument suggests a strong presumption that the "optimum" level of required reserves is the lowest operationally workable, in order that the inside money component of the money stock may be maximized. The other extreme, 100 per cent reserves, would maximize government outside money issue, and so minimize the level of tax rates required to finance any given level of government expenditures at stable prices. This would occur at the cost of a higher level of interest rates, and lower current deficits and holdings of tangible assets by private economic units.

It has been argued that a significant asymmetry exists between the effects of central bank open-market operations and changes in required reserve ratios, which militates against the use of the latter as an instrument of countercyclical control. Higher reserve requirements in a boom, by causing an upward shift in the cost of providing bank credit, reduce bank net profits as compared to an equivalent restriction in bank intermediation brought about by central bank open-market sales. To the extent that the marginal utility of bank income is raised, banks' desired portfolio balance position between liquidity and profitability is adjusted downward, so that banks are induced to shift further into loans by selling off their secondary reserve holdings of investments. This shift is accentuated wherever higher reserve requirements meet a greater proportion of bank liquidity needs. Such a response is undesirable at a time when the central bank is attempting to restrict aggregate demand. Conversely, a reduction in reserve requirements in a recession, to the extent that it reduces the marginal utility of bank income relative to an equivalent expansion of bank reserves by open-market purchases, does not provide the banking system with as great an incentive to make additional loans, and so is again an inferior technique of control. An admitted important advantage of reserve requirement variations over open-market operations is that they affect *all* banks *immediately*.

If the above asymmetry were quantitatively significant, the countercyclical effectiveness of monetary control could be increased, not as suggested by refraining from reserve requirement variations in favor of open-market operations, but by an appropriate *simultaneous* use of *both* techniques. In a boom the optimum control mix would comprise open-market sales more than sufficient to offset simultaneous reductions in required reserve ratios. This would raise bank profits and reduce the marginal utility of an additional dollar of income return, thus providing the banks with minimum inducement to expand loans at the expense of their investment portfolios. Conversely, in a slump the optimum control mix would be to combine open-market purchases with less than offsetting simultaneous increases in reserve requirements. By reducing bank profits this would raise the marginal utility of income relative to risk, thus inducing a maximum response of increased lending on the part of commercial banks. Such a policy would however increase the procyclical variability of commercial bank profits.

REGULATION OF BANK DEPOSIT AND LENDING RATES

A final technique of deposit control consists of regulation of the maximum rate that commercial banks may pay for deposits r_D. Increases in this rate increase assetholders' demand for deposits relative to currency balances, and so produce an upward shift in the DD relationship, an increase in bank reserves, and an expansion of bank deposits and total assets. As previously developed, a permitted increase in the deposit rate paid, by enabling commercial banks to increase the volume of bank intermediation compatible with price level stability, is likely to result in a fall in the entire yield structure on primary securities.

Unless compensated for such an increase would ordinarily prove expansionary. Providing the banking system's preferred ratio of cash reserves to deposits (L) is less than the public's preferred ratio of currency to deposits (K), an increase in the demand for bank deposits consequent upon a rise in the deposit rate would reduce total demand for legal money. If the stock of legal money was not reduced by the monetary authorities, the excess supply of money balances would generate excess demand for other assets and a rise in asset and commodity prices. For the converse case in which L exceeds K, an increase in the demand for bank deposits would increase total demand for legal money. Unless compensated for by increases in the nominal money stock, excess demand for money balances would provoke excess supply of other assets and a fall in asset prices, as wealthowners adjust their actual stocks of assets held towards portfolio balance.

It is not difficult to demonstrate that ceilings on bank deposit rates must reduce the countercyclical effectiveness of monetary control, although the magnitude of this effect does not appear to be substantial. Such restrictions impair the ability of one type of financial intermediary, commercial banks, to sell their secondary securities, worsening the competitive position of the banking system and the allocation of credit in competitive capital markets. A fixed ceiling on bank deposit rates inhibits expansion of the volume of monetary intermediation to a greater degree during periods of monetary restraint, when market interest rates are high. This effectively reduces the amount of bank credit available in such periods. But at the same time it encourages assetholders to switch toward the now relatively more attractive secondary securities of nonmonetary intermediaries, thus generating an increase in the volume of nonbank intermediation. The same degree of restraint on the volume of monetary intermediation can always be achieved by control of the stock of legal money, while removal of the ceiling on bank deposit rates would reduce the tendency towards an offsetting expansion of nonbank intermediation as monetary control is made more restrictive. Such a policy is preferable on allocation grounds to the alternative of extending required reserve or interest rate control over nonbank intermediaries.

A similar conclusion applies to government determination of the maximum rate that commercial banks are permitted to charge borrowers for bank credit. When such ceilings are effective, they reduce the volume of commercial bank intermediation and interfere with the allocation of credit among private borrowers. Elimination of ceilings on bank lending rates that do not apply to other intermediaries would enable banks to compete for various types of loans from which they are now excluded.

A limited case can perhaps be made for selective lending rate regulation to prevent bank exploitation of their monopolistic position in those markets where borrowers have no effective alternative sources of funds.[4] As oligopolistic sellers of a homogeneous product bankers widely engage in explicit or implicit price fixing. Yet as purveyors of a service they are in many countries, e.g., Canada and the United Kingdom, exempt from antimonopoly regulation. On economic efficiency grounds a preferable policy would be the encouragement by the regulatory authorities of more effective competition in loan and deposit markets, both among banks and between banks and other intermediary groups. One important step in this direction would be the easing of regulations with regard to barriers to entry and branch banking.

Alternative Instruments of Financial Policy

Chapter 5 developed the theory of the determination of financial asset prices and yields for a closed economy, in which government financial operations were ignored. It is now necessary to recognize that the behavior of the public sector critically affects the supply and demand for financial assets, and so the *temporary* and *full temporal equilibrium* matrix of financial asset prices and returns.

The possibility and purpose of financial control follows essentially from the observation that, by changing the stock of debt forms in private wealth portfolios, governments can create portfolio imbalance,

4. The "10 per cent banks" in the United States, those small rural unit banks that historically have charged the legal maximum on loans, are an excellent example.

and so a divergence between the temporary equilibrium level and structure of financial asset prices and their full temporal equilibrium values. Knowledge of how private economic units respond permits governments to impel private spending and saving decisions in desired directions.

Chapter 8 analyzed the disequilibrium adjustment process by which excess supply or demand for nominal monetary assets provokes a situation of general portfolio imbalance, and spills over to create excess demand or supply in markets for current output and a change in the composition of aggregate demand. Most generally, government manipulation of the volume and terms of financial assets and financial intermediation may be viewed as an attempt to create controlled disequilibria, in order to contrive some desired adjustment response in the behavior of private economic units. The larger purpose is to stabilize the level and composition of aggregate demand and supply in some relation to one another so as to achieve some set of general policy goals, for example, full employment of labor, price stability, rapid growth, and stable exchange rate.

Such objectives, if not mutually incompatible, can in general be attained only by an appropriate mix of a number of nonidentical regulatory instruments that exceeds the number of objectives. The particular control mix adopted by a government in pursuit of its stabilization goals necessarily has important allocational and distributional significance. It is the recognition of these diverse effects of financial policies that provides the compelling rationale for the coordination of stabilization techniques under a single authority for effective social decision-making.

The most important financial operations of governments and their chief effects may be briefly summarized.

MONETARY POLICY

Central banks, by changing the composition of outstanding government debt between legal money and interest-bearing securities, compel a change in the ratio of currency and bank deposits to financial and tangible assets held in private wealth portfolios. In this manner the monetary authorities are able to alter directly the price of bills, bonds, and the Bank Rate that commercial banks must pay to increase their cash reserves. Temporary-equilibrium portfolio balance is re-established only with a higher or lower complex of most financial asset prices and lending terms.

Institutional suppliers of loanable funds accept these key market rates as a datum in setting their own administered rates. Consequently at any particular time the real opportunity cost of finance that private debtors must pay is proximately determined, within a broad range, by central bank control of the nominal stock of legal money. Changes in the terms on which surplus-spending units are induced to add to their stocks of financial assets, and to yield up disposal over current output to deficit-spending real wealth administrators, in turn affect the demand for real capital, the level and composition of private consumption and investment expenditures for current output, and the level of prices and unemployment.[5]

As previously developed the various transactions that affect a change in the stock of legal money and bank deposits do not have identical consequences. Deposit expansion or contraction is not analogous to minting or counterfitting, since it is associated with a change in the liability or asset position of other economic units. The consequences of central bank open-market operations are not identical to those following an equal change in the stock of legal money as a result of government budgetary imbalance on income account. The

5. The results of a recent simulation of the U.S. economy on the 176 simultaneous-equation condensed version of the Brookings econometric model suggest that prices behave in a manner not widely anticipated by the Federal Reserve Board. The effect of an increase in the discount rate of 0.5 per cent is to create a *rise* in the GNP implicit price deflator of 0.4 per cent after two years, which only then begins to fall slowly. This seemingly paradoxical result comes about because inertial factors of the employment process cause the speed of adjustment of employment to a reduction in aggregate demand to be less than the rate of change of output. Thus, when output falls or increases at a relatively slower rate, unit labor costs rise, generating upward price pressures. This suggests a tendency towards overadjustment of monetary restraint whenever the price level is held to be an important target of monetary policy.

The simulation also indicates a much greater proportionate reduction, resulting even in a greater absolute reduction, in total real investment than in total real consumption. This suggests the important impact of monetary change on the composition of aggregate output, and provides one measure of the empirical magnitude of the portfolio balance effect. See Gary Fromm, "Recent Monetary Policy: An Econometric View," *National Banking Review*, Vol. 3, No. 3 (March, 1966).

latter is accompanied by changes in total private assets and net worth, and so has a greater effect on the level of aggregate demand for current output. Changes in the stock of legal money due to open-market operations on the other hand cause a greater movement in financial asset prices, since private holdings of interest-bearing government debt exactly offset changes in the stock of currency outstanding. These different consequences may be explained in terms of the previously developed distinction between *inside* and *outside* monetary assets.

By changing the ratio of outside to inside money, that is the extent to which incremental supply of monetary debt originates in government purchases of current output rather than in government and intermediary purchases of primary securities, the monetary authorities are able to affect even the full temporal equilibrium level and structure of financial asset prices. Given the level of real public expenditure, raising the proportion of outside money implies a lower level of tax rates and a higher level of returns on financial assets. The net effect will depend on which taxes are reduced. Divergences between temporary and full-temporal equilibrium asset prices produced by the monetary authorities alter the allocation of current output between consumption and investment goods, the rate of growth of real wealth and real income, and the final full temporal equilibrium configuration.

Regulation of the quantity of legal money has in all countries proven to be a more flexible control technique than direct regulation of commercial bank intermediation. Changes in bank reserve requirements and in bank lending and borrowing rates could, in principle, be made by small degrees so as to eliminate any shock effect on commercial bank portfolios and on bank lenders and borrowers. But the central explanation for the widespread reluctance of central banks to use direct controls for countercyclical purposes probably lies in the fact that they prevent private economic units from behaving freely in their own self-interest.

If stabilization techniques are to be used flexibly and effectively, it is desirable that they interfere as little as possible with freedom to dispose of property, and that their distributional effects be of secondary magnitude, or, at the very least, disguised from public view. Otherwise their unidirectional exercise will be supported or resisted by special interest groups on distributional considerations. Changes in the level of reserve requirements, for example, are unavoidably a device for allocating real profits between the central bank and the private banking system.

DEBT POLICY

Debt policy, though conventionally the responsibility of treasuries rather than central banks, is in its operation formally analogous to monetary policy. Debt policy like monetary policy operates by changing the composition of outstanding government debt, but primarily between short- and long-term bonds rather than between legal money and short-term bonds. Portfolio balance is reestablished only with a different structure and level of financial asset prices and returns, particularly between short- and long-term obligations, and spill-over effects on private consumption and investment expenditure for current output again occur due to portfolio, wealth, availability, and interest rate effects.

The monetary policy of "bills only" represents the voluntary confinement of central bank open-market operations to the sale and purchase of short-term obligations; Treasury Bills, notes, certificates maturing in less than one year. The announced philosophy behind this policy was the desire to interfere as little as possible with the market-determined maturity structure of interest rates and asset prices. But the effective result was to produce very large cyclical swings in short-term interest rates, while long-term rates moved by a much smaller amount, with a consequent wide cyclical variation in the yield structure. If the government chooses to exercise financial control, it can no more through a "bills only" monetary policy than through a "debt lengthening" debt policy evade responsibility for influencing the level and structure of interest rates.

The temporary equilibrium interest rate differential between bills and bonds, as discussed in Chapter 5, provides an indication of the extent to which the liquidity preferences of assetholders are being met. A rate differential between bills and bonds high relative to normal long-term experience (full temporal equilibrium) indicates that wealth portfolios are starved for liquid assets, while an abnormally low bill rate relative to bonds indicates that liquidity requirements are more than usually satisfied. Central governments are typically unique among debtor units in that they are not limited by financial conventions in the extent to which long term or even permanent requirements may be financed with short-term debt instruments.

Given the basic asymmetry between short- and long-term debt and asset preferences of private debtor and creditor units, government short-term debt issue plays a crucial role in accommodating the liquidity requirements of portfolio managers, and so in lowering the general level and structure of financial asset returns. If debt policy explicitly tailors the composition of primary governments securities to fit the diverse portfolio requirements of different economic units, the average reward that must be paid to nonadministering ultimate wealthowners can be substantially reduced, in a manner exactly analogous to the operation of financial innovation.

FISCAL POLICY

Whereas monetary and debt operations operate directly on temporary equilibrium asset prices and returns and, apart from variations in the ratio of inside to outside monetary debt, affect full temporal equilibrium incremental supply and demand relationships only indirectly, fiscal policy operates directly on both the temporary and full-temporal equilibrium structure of asset prices. Changes in the aggregate stock of government debt outstanding and in total private net worth and its distribution among economic units directly affect the temporary equilibrium matrix of financial asset prices and yields. In addition by varying the level and composition of government expenditure for goods and services, taxes and transfer payments, and by nonbudgetary legislation, fiscal operations directly affect the volume and allocation of private expenditure and output, and so the structure of financial asset prices in full temporal equilibrium.

Fiscal measures that alter the relationship between involuntary saving and investment change the incremental demand for and supply of financial assets generated in full employment. For example, a higher level of government deficit-spending for public consumption goods reduces total involuntary saving, and increases incremental supply of primary securities relative to incremental demand for financial assets. The price of financial assets satisfying full temporal and temporary equilibrium is consequently lowered, and the higher cost of external finance discourages deficit spending by private economic units for investment and consumption purposes.

A related effect of the mix of fiscal operations is to alter the structure of financial asset prices and yields. Depending on the elasticity of portfolio preferences, a relative increase in government incremental supply of bonds reduces the price of bonds vis-à-vis corporate equities. Those corporate business units that rely on bond rather than equity financing find the cost of external finance relatively and possibly even absolutely increased. As a result private and public debt-financed expenditure will become more expensive relative to private equity-financed capital formation, and the average reward paid to nonadministering wealthowners is likely to increase. One solution would be for the government to issue purchasing-power securities, for example index bonds, which are closer substitutes for corporate equities in wealth portfolios. It would also be possible for the government to issue equities, based for example on future government tax receipts or future levels of national income, whenever such instruments reduce the average cost of capital to the treasury.

CONCLUSIONS

The particular mix and degree of government stabilization control exerted over any period is the result of a compromise of pointer-readings, as diverse authorities operating within a thicket of institutional and political constraints attempt to offset inflationary or deflationary movements in private expenditure. While it is formally correct to regard market prices and yields of financial assets at any particular time and place as governed at the margin by their opportunity cost, the latter necessarily depends critically both on the government control mix finally selected and on the vigour with which stabilization objectives are pursued.

When financial policy is not coordinated, each separate authority must regard financial asset yields as beyond its own final control. Temporary equilibrium financial asset prices, while determined proximately by the monetary authorities, are indirectly dependent on the extent to which the concurrent operations of fiscal and debt authorities are expansionary or restrictive in effect, and the extent to which they impinge on portfolio and incremental demand and supply of financial assets.

The particular stabilization control techniques emphasized by a government desirous of retaining political power necessarily reflect a variety of policy considerations, one of the most significant being anticipated effects on the distribution of income, wealth, and power between various economic and social groups. Financial asset prices and yields necessarily affect the distribution of property income between profits to real wealth administrators and rentier income to owners of financial claims. In the longer run the return to financial assetownership is likely to affect the division of aggregate income between labor and property shares.[6]

The payment of interest on accumulated debt represents in an important sense the past's dead hand upon the present. A change in the level of financial asset returns changes the terms of trade between past and future achievements, as well as producing a transfer of income and wealth between debtor and creditor groups. A rise in interest rates as is well known *reduces* the present value of future income and production. It is less widely recognized that a rise in interest rates at the same time *increases* the present value of past savings. The impact of the redistribution effect between debtor and creditor groups may be particularly acute for the income and capital position of those financial intermediaries whose asset and liability income streams are not similarly distributed through time.

Out of concern for such redistributional consequences most governments have been unwilling to countenance large swings in financial asset prices and yields, even if this implies a considerable compromise of stabilization objectives. "The problem of incidence has no unique application to stabilization by taxation, but applies to other forms of stabilization policy as well. Differences in incidence must be taken into account when choosing between various approaches to stabilization, and they must be compensated for in the overall budget plan by appropriate adjustments."[7]

6. In the United States in the decade after the "rediscovery" of monetary policy in 1950, short-term interest rate approximately tripled, and long-term rates rose by more than 80 per cent. Total personal income rose by 76 per cent, while personal interest income rose by 154 per cent. Total monetary interest paid increased from $16.0 billion in 1950 to $45.0 billion in 1960, an increase from 6.6 to 10.8 per cent of total national income. Since wages and salaries rose from 64 to 70 per cent of national income, the rise in interest payments appears to have occurred at the relative expense of other property income.

7. Richard Musgrave, *The Theory of Public Finance* (New York, 1959) p. 615.

The pursuit of a plurality of stabilization objectives necessitates the exercise of at least an equal number of control techniques, but in practice an "optimum" control mix can never be *uniquely* specified by stabilization ends alone. This is because all stabilization policies have allocational and distributional consequences in addition to an impact on stabilization targets. A democratically-elected government must somehow attempt to take these consequences into account and specify, whether explicitly or implicitly, the tradeoff between these different objectives. The development and application of benefit-cost analysis to all government programs is gradually but very considerably improving the quality of information available to public decision-makers concerning the complex of effects of government policies.

Rather than describe government policy normatively as the will of some *deus ex machina* attempting to maximize an ineffable social welfare function, government policy in a two-party democracy may more fruitfully be explained as an attempt to maximize votes and so the period of tenure in political office. Such a formulation forces a consideration by social scientists of the distributional incidence of alternative policies on the welfare of sub-groups possessing political power within the economy. "If, as I believe, the ends of men are many, and not all of them in principle compatible with one another, then the possibility of conflict—and of tragedy—can never wholly be eliminated from human life, either personal or social. The necessity of choosing between absolute claims is then an inescapable character-istic of human condition."[8]

8. Isaiah Berlin, *Two Concepts of Liberty* (Oxford, 1958), p. 54.

RECOMMENDED READING

There is an enormous theoretical and descriptive literature on monetary control and policy. M. Friedman and Anna Schwartz, *A Monetary History of the United States 1867-1960* (National Bureau of Economic Research, New York, 1963), is one monumental reference study of the development and effectiveness of monetary control in America.

For a formulation of the wealth adjustment process using portfoilo analysis to explain the transmission of monetary control, see K. Brunner and A. Meltzer, "The Place of Financial Intermediaries in the Transmission of Monetary Policy," *American Economic Review*, Vol. LIII, No. 2 (May 1963).

A suggestive discussion of government and central bank financial operations may be found in J. A. Galbraith, *The Economics of Banking Operations* (Montreal, 1963), Chapters 6 and 7.

A number of descriptive and empirical studies of monetary control were commissioned by the Commission on Money and Credit. Especially valuable are *Impacts of Monetary Policy, Stabilization Policies, Monetary Management*, and *Fiscal and Debt Management Policies* (Englewood Cliffs, New Jersey, 1964).

In an important paper Arthur Okun attempted to measure the effect of certain hypothetical monetary, debt, and fiscal policy decisions on the level and structure of interest rates using recent historical data. Debt policy was found to have little impact on either the bond or bill rate, and open-market operations to have a much more pronounced impact on the bill rate than on the bond rate. "Monetary Policy, Debt Management, and Interest Rates: A Quantitative Appraisal," *Stabilization Policies* (*op. cit.*). Okun's conclusions have been reexamined over a longer time period, and the stability of the coefficients confirmed, by John Arena, "Monetary Policy and Debt Management Revisited." *The National Banking Review*, Vol. 3, No. 1 (September, 1965).

10

The Special Case

of Equity Instruments

The current rate of interest depends, not on the strength of the desire to hold wealth, but on the strengths of the desires to hold it in liquid and illiquid forms respectively, coupled with the amount of the supply of wealth in the one form relatively to the the supply of it in another."

—*J. M. Keynes*
The General Theory of Employment, Interest, and Money, 1936

Introduction

This final chapter provides an application of the theory of financial behavior under uncertainty to the special and difficult case of corporate equities. If the portfolio approach to financial phenomena presented in this book possesses explanatory value beyond that of an organizing analytical framework, it must upon application lead to the understanding and, ideally, to the correct specification and measurement, of observed empirical relationships between real economic phenomena and behavior in particular financial markets. In financial theory as elsewhere the final proof of the pudding is in the eating.

Insofar as the previous chapters have been addressed to forces affecting the level of financial asset prices and returns, the analysis has proceeded for the most part in terms of movements in a single composite price and return on financial assets. Diverse movements in relative asset yields have been specifically considered only with reference to the term structure of interest rates. Although financial assets are extravagantly diverse with respect to risk, maturity, marketability, and a host of other asset characteristics, the recognition of such heterogeneity does not seriously invalidate the above procedure. With two important exceptions an extremely large proportion (ordinarily more than 90 per cent) of the movement in individual financial asset prices and returns is associated with movements in the general level of financial asset prices and returns. The first exception is the relative variation between short and long term rates, discussed in Chapter 5. The second exception is corporate equities, whose behavior has been relatively neglected by economists, and for which the very concept of rate of return presents operational difficulties.

The first section describes the characteristics of the market for corporate equities in the post-war American economy. New equity issues accounted for a small and declining proportion of corporate total sources of funds, while the market price and total value of corporate stock outstanding rose dramatically. The average annual return on equity ownership, including capital gains, was slightly above 12 per cent, even though the earnings- and dividend-price ratios fell significantly. Some of the most widely-accepted explanations for an inelastic supply of new issues of equities are briefly reviewed.

The second section then considers the significance of business reliance on retained earnings and an inelastic supply of new equity offerings for the real contours of a growing economy. A simple portfolio model is developed to explain the behavior of the real value of the stock of equities outstanding in a moving equilibrium of balanced growth. Assetholders are shown to allocate their saving in such a way as to maintain some desired composition of financial asset portfolios. Given the community's saving preferences, the growth of total financial assets is related to the growth of total income, the stock of tangible assets, and the rate at which future income is discounted. Under such conditions the rise in individual share prices is shown to be related inversely to the rate at which corporations raise additional external equity capital. Equities are shown to be unlike other financial assets in that continuously rising share prices need not reduce the expected return from equity ownership, nor the cost of equity finance. The implications of the prevalent financial behavior of business firms as described in the first section for the allocation growth, stabilization, and distribution of real output and income in real world economies are then explored.

The chapter closes with a brief discussion of the relationship of the conclusions reached to some familiar concepts in modern macro-economic theory.

Some Characteristics of Corporate Equities

Corporate equities, like other financial assets, may be viewed as having two distinct effects on economic behavior, corresponding to flow and stock relationships.

Intermediation Effects concern the allocation of current saving among users and uses. Incorporation permits business units to finance the accumulation of tangible and financial assets in excess of current income by attracting the saving of large numbers of surplus spending units. The latter are simultaneously enable to accumulate income-earning financial assets representing a *pro rata* share in the management, ownership, and earnings of business units, but with none of the risk, administrative inconvenience, or illiquidity of direct tangible asset ownership. *Intermediation Effects* raise the full-employment ratio of saving and investment to current income, given the underlying "real" factors of thrift, risk aversion, and productivity.

Asset Transmutation Effects concern the transformation and trans-fer of ownership and control. Corporate equities are characterized by much greater income certainty, marketability, liquidity, divisibility, and homogeneity than the tangible assets they indirectly represent. Wealthowners consequently may diversify and transfer their port-folios more efficiently, yet still protect their savings against upward movements in the price level and participate in future productivity gains. *Asset Transmutation Effects* raise the opportunity curves from wealth ownership and so the equilibrium ratio of wealth to income, given the underlying "real" factors of thrift, risk aversion, and productivity.

The market for corporate equities in the post-war American economy did not play a large role in the first function, the allocation of current saving among users and uses. New stock issues accounted for a small and declining proportion relative to the issuance of other capital market instruments, the volume of corporate financing, and the value of corporate stock outstanding. From 1945 to 1965 net issues of stock by non-financial corporations as reported by the SEC totaled only $33 billion. This represented less than 2 per cent of total net financing in the economy, and a decline over the period from 6 to less than 3 per cent of nonfinancial corporate total sources of funds. Equity issue accounted for an insignificant proportion of total sources of corporate funds (currently less than 1 per cent) in manufacturing, mining, and trade, but a significant share, declining from one-quarter to one-sixth of total sources, in public utilities and communication. Corporate reliance on internal equity finance, through retained earnings and depreciation allowances, has enabled them to circumvent the capital markets as a source of funds.

With regard to the second function, the facilitation and transfer of ownership and control in existing assets, the value of outstanding stock rose dramatically, both absolutely and as a proportion of investor portfolios, and trading in existing issues increased proportionately. The market value of primary corporate equities outstanding rose from $120 billion in 1945 to $740 billion in 1965, increasing the share of corporate stocks in household total financial assets from one quarter to nearly one half. Corporate stocks were the only capital market instrument whose yields showed a decline over this period. However this decline in yields accounted for only a small proportion (less than one-quarter) of the rise in stock prices. Standard and Poor's earnings-price ratio on common stocks fell from 6.4 to 5.9 per cent in the twenty years from 1945 to 1965, and the dividend-price ratio fell from 4.1 to 3.0 per cent. Over the same period the common stock price index increased more than six times, compared to a doubling of the consumer price index. Since corporate stock ownership is very highly concentrated, with the wealthiest one per cent of all adults accounting for approximately three quarters of total stockholdings, this relative rise in stock prices and equity values operated to increase the inequality in the distribution of wealthownership. Measured either by value outstanding or by volume of trading, corporate stock constituted by far the largest sector of the American capital market.

Several difficulties arise in the specification and measurement of the appropriate return on and cost of equity instruments from the market information available on share prices. While as stated average dividend- and earnings-price ratios have fallen over the post-war period, the average experienced returns on equities (dividend yield plus annual capital gains) have been very much higher, and have exhibited no parallel tendency to fall. Calculated on the basis of a five-year moving-average of annual changes in stock prices, the average return on equities rose from 12 per cent in 1945 to over 20 per dent in the mid-fifties, and then fell back toward 12 per cent in the sixties. When calculated on an unsmoothed annual basis the fluctuations in average equity return are of course much wider, while variability correspondingly diminishes as the time period over which average capital gains or losses are calculated is extended. The first difficulty therefore lies in determining the empirical relationship between the widely gyrating market-recorded annual rates of return, including capital gains, and those rates of return anticipated by wealthowners on which they base their portfolio and spending decisions.

If it were possible to specify exactly the income of a share of stock for all future years, the market rate of return on corporate equities could be determined from their market value in the same manner as the yield is derived for fixed-income bonds. But future receipts from a stock are not concrete promises to pay as in the case of bonds. They are rather an estimated set of possible future incomes, each best described by a statistical distribution with some expected mean and variance. The rate at which these future income receipts are discounted is a function of the variance of the subjective probability distribution of expected returns, both of which ordinarily will increase as the income stream extends into the misty future.

The appropriate *ex post* measure of the return on equities is unambiguously total past income, that is dividends plus capital gains or losses, divided by market value. But dividends plus recent capital gains or losses on a stock are not necessarily the best measure of *ex ante* return. This is because capital gains or losses embody the *capitalized* value of any change in expected income, and so are ordinarily larger than the change in expected income itself, which is the relevant quantity for the measurement of future return. Presumably for this reason book earnings, or dividends plus retained earnings, are more frequently used by investors than dividends plus capital gains in approximating future expected income for portfolio selection. Given the accounting flexibility in determining book income, book earnings are subject to considerable accounting error as a basis of measuring the expected income from ownership of particular equities. Because expected income cannot be measured directly, and the rate at which expected future receipts are discounted will rise as they extend into the future, it is extremely difficult to devise operational measures of the equity market rate of discount.

A third problem concerns the relationship between the rates of return expected by stockholders, and the estimated cost of equity capital from the viewpoint of corporate managers. As shown in Chapter 3, the cost of capital represents the implicit rate at which capital markets discount a corporation's future earnings in pricing its outstanding securities. The cost of equity capital is dependent upon the earnings-price ratio of the corporation's stock, adjusted upward by some factor related to the expected future rate of growth of earnings. Should stockholders expect the market to value future earnings even more highly in the future, this will raise current share price-earning ratios, without depressing the future return anticipated from share ownership. At the same time the rise in share price-earnings ratios consequent upon such expectations decreases the cost of equity capital to an issuing corporation. As in the case of bonds, expected future capital gains or losses due to an anticipated fall or rise in future market rates of discount drive a wedge between the current return to financial assetholders and the current cost to assetissuers.

The failure of corporations to issue additional equity shares in response to the experienced rise in share prices and fall in the relative cost of equity capital in the post-war period is in part attributable to a concurrent decline in corporate total external financing *requirements*. This decline in turn can be related to a fall in marginal tangible capital-output ratios, accompanied by a rise in the ratio of depreciation to gross capital formation. Interview studies reporting the strong and widely-held preferences of corporate treasurers for internal over external equity finance have powerful empirical support. The fall in stock issues as a proportion of long-term *external* financing was associated with a roughly proportionate rise in *internal* equity financing. The result has been to maintain total equity financing, internal plus external, at a relatively constant proportion (70-73 per cent) of total sources. This is consistent with stable preferred debt and equity balance-sheet ratios. It is primarily retained earnings that have accounted for the substantial absolute increase in corporate equity accounts over the post-war period.

As described in Chapter 3, there are persuasive theoretical grounds to suspect that the incremental supply (new issues) of corporate equities may be extremely price-inelastic. Corporate management is properly concerned with the market performance of its shares, and must subject all proposed investment and financing projects to the test that they not lower the price of the corporation's stock. Retention of earnings has several advantages over sale of common stock from the viewpoint of long-run effect on per-share value. Most importantly, differential personal income tax rates, which tax only *realized* capital gains income, and at one half the rate applied to dividend income, shift the optimal finance mix towards a lower payout ratio and a greater reliance on retained earnings. This is particularly the case for upper income stockholders. In addition treatment of interest but not dividends as a deductible expense for corporate tax purposes shifts the optimal external finance mix away from equity towards debt financing.

In consequence of imperfect information and diverse expectations under uncertainty, the issue of new stock ordinarily has to be under-priced to induce existing stockowners to increase their holdings and to persuade new stockholders to join the corporation. In addition to such market underpricing, corporations realize substantially less than the price paid by investors for new issues, due to the selling and underwriting expenses of flotation. These expenses, because of a large fixed cost component, are disproportionately high for small issues.

In an uncertain world short-run behavior of future earnings, dividends, and price per share is more easily discerned and more confidently anticipated by investors, and so is heavily reflected in current share prices. Since in the short run new equity issue or its prospect is likely to lower earnings-per-share, corporation managers may require a higher expected return on investment projects to justify new external equity financing. Even if this results in a less rapid long-run rate of growth of total profits, and a lower corporate long-run value, such behavior may be quite consistent with rational utility maximization, since risk at least from the point of view of management is reduced. In addition external equity financing is commonly regarded with some distaste because of its effects in diluting the interest of existing owners.

The above factors combine to suggest the existence of considerable *discontinuities* in corporate cost of capital schedules, with a particularly sharp upward displacement at the point where retained funds and debt financing are exhausted. Most corporations other than utilities appear to issue new equity instruments only when no other financial alternatives are available, and yet overriding market reasons exist for an expansion of capital expenditures.

Some Consequences of An Inelastic Supply of Equities

What are the forces that determine the price and return of an inelastic stock of corporate equities in a growing economy, and what is their significance for economic behavior?

In order to examine this question with some precision, consider a simplified model of an economy in which only three homogeneous primary financial assets exist—money, bonds, and equities. All reproducible capital goods K are assumed owned by business units, and all business bonds and equities are owned by household units. The marginal efficiency of investment is the return on tangible capital r, so that total property income equals rK. For presentational convenience only primary financial assets will be considered, in order that the effects of financial intermediaries may be neglected.

Money M will be defined as the non interest-bearing debt of the government (fiat money) bearing an implicit convenience and certainty yield of r_M. Money originates only in an act of government deficit expenditure. Taxes are assumed to be zero, and the government neither purchases nor issues bonds nor equities.

Bonds B will be defined as fixed-income claims against business units paying $1 per year in perpetuity, and r_B is the rate at which future interest income is discounted in the bond market. The market price of bonds is therefore $1/r_B$, and the market value of the stock of bonds outstanding is B/r_B.

Corporate equities represent a property right to participate in all per-share cash dividends D declared to stockholders. Stock dividends and splits are excluded by assumption. The price of shares S is established in the stock market where equities are traded. The *yield* on equities r_E is equal to the dividend-price ratio D/S. If the number of shares outstanding is E, the market value of the stock of equities is ES, and total dividend payments are DE. The *return* on equities must be defined to include anticipated future annual capital gains or losses ΔS, expressed as a per cent of market value $\Delta S/S$, in addition to the dividend yield r_E.

The cost of debt capital to business corporations is r_B. The cost of equity capital to corporations will be regarded as a first approximation as simply equal to the earnings-price ratio on corporate stock $(rK - B)/ES$. (As shown in Chapter 3 for a growing corporation this must be adjusted upward by some factor related to the growth rate of future earnings.) This is equal to the dividend/price ratio r_E only in the polar case when all net earnings are paid out as dividends, but the two move proportionately providing payout ratios remain constant. The question of the effects of leverage, taxes, default risk, and exchange costs on the cost of corporate capital are not central to the present argument, and for simplicity will henceforth be ignored. The average cost of corporate capital q under such assumptions is then simply the weighted average cost of debt and equity capital

$$q = r_B \left(\frac{B/r_B}{ES + B/r_B} \right) + \left(\frac{rK - B}{ES} \right) \left(\frac{ES}{ES + B/r_B} \right)$$

this reduces simply to the ratio of gross corporate profits before interest payments to the total current market value of corporate obligations:

$$q = \left(\frac{rK}{ES + B/r_B} \right)$$

The demand for financial assets and debt in an uncertain world is regarded as based upon general portfolio principles. Assetholder behavior is consistent with the maximization of a bounded (i.e., risk-avoiding) utility function from wealthownership, which considers both expected return and risk (variance) of expected return. Households are assumed to maintain a preferred portfolio composition between money, bonds and equities. Business corporations similarly attempt to maintain a preferred balance-sheet composition between money, tangible assets, debt, internal and external equity finance. All assets are regarded as gross substitutes, so that *ceteris paribus* a rise in the expected return on one asset will increase its relative equilibrium share demanded in wealth portfolios. The particular speed of adjustment to eliminate portfolio imbalance in different markets is not specified, but it is assumed that wealthowners ordinarily adjust their financial and tangible asset holdings at a differential rate towards a desired portfolio composition.

Consider first a position of stationary general equilibrium in which real income, prices, and nominal stocks of tangible and financial assets are constant. In stationary equilibrium both household and business net saving is zero. In such a world an autonomous increase in household saving propensities, or a shift in household asset preferences, will in the short run tend to raise the price of bonds $(1/r_B)$ and equities S. This will continue until, at some lower expected rate of return on these assets, households will be just content to hold the existing stocks of money, bonds, and equities. Given an unchanged return on tangible assets r, the resulting lower cost of debt and equity finance would lower the cost of capital q, push corporations into a position of portfolio imbalance, and create excess demand for tangible assets. Firms respond by issuing bonds and equities in order to finance increased accumulation of tangible assets and money balances. In this manner, over some longer run depending on the speed of adjustment of debtors to disequilibrim, increased household saving will provide the finance for, and be exactly offset by, increased deficit investment-spending by business units. The increase in household saving propensities would create first a rise and then a fall in financial asset prices, and first a fall and then a recovery in aggregate demand for current output. The net effect and the length of the transition period depend critically upon the responsiveness of debtor units to the temporary fall in the cost of external finance.

Receipts from new share issues, plus receipts from the issue of nominal bonds, govern the amount of external funds available to finance additional business capital accumulation. In the case of both bonds and equities, if business firms do not respond by raising additional external capital, the rise in bond and equity prices, and the resulting fall in their yield, must be relied on to adjust the real value of existing stocks of financial assets to satisfy increased portfolio demand of financial asset-holders, and to adjust aggregate demand to aggregate supply of current output.

Consider the extreme case in which business units fail to issue any new equity shares in response to a fall in the cost of external equity finance. Under such circumstances an autonomous increase in household saving preferences to accumulate equities cannot be transformed into increased business demand for tangible capital assets. It results rather in a permanent rise in equity prices, and a permanent fall in the yield and cost of equities r_E. Throughout the transition period capital gains are received by corporate shareholders. In the new stationary equilibrium position future corporate profits are capitalized at a higher value, and the return on equities has fallen relative to other assets.

Consider now the previously described economy in a position of balanced growth, defined as that configuration in which all real variables increase at a constant relative rate g so that the ratios between all real variables remain constant. Price level stability requires that aggregate demand for current output grow at the same rate as aggregate output. In the model this necessitates that increases in the stock of nominal money, originating in government deficit spending, precisely equal incremental demand for money balances. This in turn is identical to the excess of planned private saving (by households and business units) over planned private investment (by business units), so that government deficit spending must exactly offset private surplus spending on current account.

Bond price (interest rate) stability requires that planned real accumulation of bonds by households equals planned issue of nominal bonds by corporations. Equity yield and return stability requires that planned real accumulation of shares by households equals planned internal and external equity finance by corporations. More generally, stability of financial asset returns requires that for *each* financial asset portfolio demand equal the existing stock, and planned incremental demand by surplus units equal planned incremental supply by deficit units. Persistent deficits by both the business and government sector equal to total household surpluses are thus a necessary condition for current output and financial asset price stability in the moving equilibrium of balanced growth. In addition for relative financial asset price stability the portfolio tastes of surplus spending units must precisely meet the portfolio preferences of deficit spending units.[1]

If nominal money fails to grow at the balanced growth rate, endemic excess demand for money balances can be satisfied only by continuous deflation or inflation. This in turn changes the expected return on bonds and money balances. Assume that nominal money is supplied at the appropriate rate, so that the complications of price level change may be disregarded. Business units must borrow to increase the nominal stock of bonds outstanding at the balanced growth rate. If this condition is not satisfied the debt burden of firms and the interest cost of borrowing will not remain constant. Finally, corporations must raise *total* new equity capital, including both internal and external equity finance, at the balanced growth rate in order that the return and cost of equities remain constant. But business new *external* equity issues need not equal total planned household equity accumulation, and the price of equities need not remain constant, in order to maintain a stable expected return from equity ownership.

The equilibrium condition for equity return stability merits special consideration, since the usual condition of equality of planned accumulation by surplus spenders and planned new issue by deficit spenders does not appear to be satisfied. Business units in balanced growth maintain a constant leverage ratio of debt to total assets, and business capital formation and net worth grows at the balanced growth rate. If all earnings were paid out as dividends, so that business internal equity finance were zero, corporations would by assumption raise all equity capital externally through new stock issue. Price per share would remain constant throughout the growth process, the yield and return on equities would be identical, and as in the case of bonds planned household equity accumulation out of current saving would equal current new share issue to finance business deficits.

Reliance on retained earnings for equity finance enables business units to circumvent the capital markets by reducing their planned deficits. Their reduced dependence on external sources of funds presumably lowers business risk. The retention of earnings by business

1. These relationships and their implications are developed more rigorously and in greater detail in J. Gurley and E. Shaw, *Money in a Theory of Finance.* Chapter 4.

units will increase future dividends per share, and so individual share values, unless accompanied *pari passu* by stock dividends or splits to increase the number of nominal shares outstanding at the balanced growth rate. But failure to issue equities and positive business saving in balanced growth is quite consistent with a constant return on corporate equities.

Positive business saving may be regarded for analytical purposes as "involuntary" saving by those household stockholders who are the ultimate owners of business enterprises. Total household saving in a world where businesses retain part of their net earnings consists of "voluntary" saving, undertaken directly by households, and "involuntary" saving, undertaken indirectly on behalf of their household owners by business units. In balanced growth retained business earnings result in *identical* increases in the income of ultimate household wealthowners, in the form of capital gains on existing stockholdings. The process is equivalent, if all exchange costs were zero, to business units first paying out all their earnings as dividend income to their household owners, and then borrowing back, in exchange for new share issue, that portion of earnings that they retain. But as will be shown the economic effects of internal and external equity finance are not identical. Changes in the corporate retention ratio change both the proportion of household income received in the form of dividends and capital gains, and the relation between the yield and the return on corporate equities.

These relationships are illustrated diagrammatically in Figure 10.1 below. Households allocate their total saving S_H (as shown in Figure 10-1a) between accumulation of money balances ΔM_H, bonds $\Delta(B/r_B)$, and equities ΔES. Corporations accumulate money balances ΔM_B and tangible assets ΔK as shown in Figure 10-1b, and finance this accumulation out of receipts from the issue of bonds $\Delta(B/r_B)$ and equities ΔES, and from retained earnings S_B. Household total equity accumulation equals new issues of equities by corporations (external, or "voluntary" equity finance: ΔES_V), plus the increase in the value of equities resulting from business saving (internal or "involuntary" equity finance: ΔES_I). Finally, in Figure 10-1(c), total private saving, household plus business, equals private capital formation ΔK plus government deficit spending G.

Household "involuntary" saving, which in balanced growth is

exactly equal to business retained earnings, is shown as the shaded area in Figure 10-1(a). Such income is attributed only to business units in conventional national income accounting. It follows that in a growing economy national disposable income exceeds aggregate output at constant prices, by an amount depending on the volume of business saving. Retained earnings thus provide an accretion of purchasing power to *both* the business and the household sector.

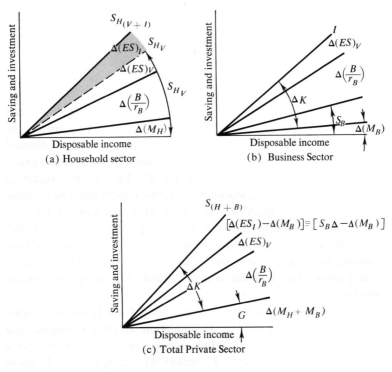

Figure 10-1

In the balanced growth model developed above, total equity financing and the stock of equities outstanding grow at the balanced growth rate *g*, but the proportion accounted for by internal and external equity finance was unspecified. It is possible to conceive of a whole family of balanced growth paths, each with a different *mix* of internal and external equity finance. In all such configurations the return on all financial assets, including equities, and all prices, except the price of equities, remain constant. A rise in the proportion of internal equity finance through greater business reliance on retained earnings increases the amount of involuntary saving undertaken by household units, reduces the dividend yield on equities, and raises the rate of growth of share prices.

Consider the polar case in which zero external equity financing is undertaken by corporations during the growth process, investment, consumption, income, and all "real" factors remaining unchanged. Corporations then retain a larger proportion of their earnings to finance capital formation at the balanced growth rate. Dividend income is therefore lower. The number of shares outstanding E_0 remains constant, since stock splits and stock dividends have been excluded by assumption. Nominal money issue and nominal debt financing are assumed to continue to grow at the balanced growth rate g. Corporate debt ratios, and household financial-asset portfolio preferences, are assumed to remain unchanged. In such a situation household demand to accumulate equities is satisfied by a continuous rise in equity prices at the balanced growth rate $(\Delta S/S = g)$. This creates recurring capital gains for existing stockholders ΔSE_0 exactly equal to business saving, i.e., "involuntary" saving by the ultimate owners of business enterprises. In equilibrium the dividend-price ratio is lower, but dividends per share, total dividends, and the market value of outstanding equities all rise at the balanced growth rate. The return on equity ownership, and the cost of capital to corporations, remain constant.

Such a situation is illustrated in Figure 10-2. Households again allocate their saving to the accumulation of money, bonds, and equities (as shown in 10-2a), but now the *entire* increase in equity values represents "involuntary" household saving through business retained earnings. Corporations accumulate tangible assets and money balances, but (as shown in Figure 10-2b) accumulation of assets in excess of retained earnings is financed solely through the issue of bonds. Household voluntary saving out of disposable income is lower, although total household saving $S_H(V + I)$ is held for comparison unchanged. In conventional national income accounting the household sector now appears to have a smaller current surplus, and the business sector to have a smaller current deficit. For the private sector as a whole (Figure 10-2c) total saving remains unchanged, business saving simply replacing that part of household voluntary saving previously allocated to the accumulation of equities.[2]

So long as the rate at which the market discounts future earnings remains unchanged throughout the growth process, business saving through retained earnings exactly equals capital gains on equities

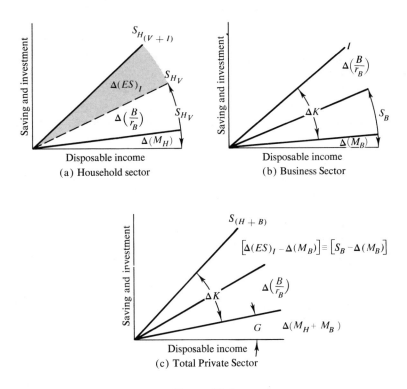

Figure 10-2

2. In the United States corporate internal equity finance in the postwar period accounted for most of the increase in business net worth, and most of the increase in equity values. Corporate undistributed profits are nearly as large as total personal saving, and in boom years stockholder involuntary saving has equaled and even exceeded total voluntary saving. In 1965 undistributed corporate profits were $25.6 billion, while personal saving was $24.9 billion. Figure 10-2 is thus a closer representation of postwar American experience than Figure 10-1.

received by household stockholders. The return anticipated on corporate equities in such a configuration is equal to the now lower dividend yield, plus the expected rate of growth of dividends per share, which is also equal to the rate of growth of capital gains $[(D/S) + (\Delta S/S)]$.

Whether the rate of return and the cost of equity capital is invariant to the ratio of internal to external equity finance depends on the rate at which investors discount an uncertain *growing* earning and dividend stream per share, including future capital gains, compared to the rate at which they discount on equally uncertain but *less rapidly growing or constant* earning and dividend stream per share associated with a greater reliance on external equity financing.

As developed in Chapter 3 there is some circumstantial evidence that capital markets discount more-rapidly growing earning streams at a higher rate. This is in part due to the expectation that very high rates of growth of *individual firms* cannot be sustained indefinitely.[3] In the model, since real capital formation and business earnings have been *assumed* invariant to the retention ratio and the mix between internal and external equity finance, the total present value of business corporations would remain unaffected, providing the degree of uncertainty, tax rates, and asset exchange costs on future income streams are ignored. To the extent household investors discount income which is more distant in the future at a higher rate, or are not indifferent between future dividend and capital gain income, the cost and return on equities will not be identical in the two situations.

A fall in household dividend income caused by a rise in corporate earnings-retention ratios will, *if* the rate of discount remains unchanged, be thus exactly offset by a rise in household capital gain

---

3. To review the argument of Chapter 3, the rate (q_0) at which the market discounts an uncertain but constant expected future stream of dividends of corporation A is simply the dividend-price ratio $(D/S)_A = q_0$. For a corporation B of similar risk, whose earnings and dividends are expected to grow at a constant rate (g_B), the dividend-price ratio will be lower by some function, e.g., $b(g_B)$, of the expected growth rate (1) $(D/S)_B = q_0 - b(g_B)$. Inverting, (2) $(S/D)_B = 1/[q_0 - b(g_B)]$. Since share prices of rapidly growing companies, where g_B may be expected to exceed q_0, do not approach infinity, the function $b(g)$ must increase by a smaller absolute amount than (g). Otherwise expressed, the market rate of discount must rise with the expected rate of growth of the future income stream.

income. But as seen in Chapter 3, in determining consumption decisions, capital gain income is ordinarily *not* regarded by households as equivalent to current earned income. As a result household "voluntary" saving is unlikely to fall by an amount sufficient to offset exactly the increase in "involuntary" household saving associated with an increase in business saving. Total private saving in Figure 10-2 is thus likely to be *higher* than in the balanced growth path of Figure 10-1.

More generally, the extent to which corporations rely on internal equity financing in growing economies affects the proportion in which new equity issues and increases in equity prices account for the rise in the total value of the stock of equities outstanding. This in turn affects the ratio of capital gains to total household income, the level of total (voluntary plus involuntary) private saving, and the composition of current output between consumption and investment goods.

In a world in which corporations face a sharp upward discontinuity in their cost of capital schedules for external equity finance, an increase in household saving propensities to accumulate corporate equities will not provide corporations with increased funds to finance tangible asset accumulation. An increase in planned voluntary saving allocated to corporate stock will result instead in higher equity prices, a fall in dividend yields, and increased capital gains income and net wealth to other household shareowners. Total capital gains income over the transition period to a new equilibrium will *exceed* total business savings. Changes in the price and yield of financial assets are of course the common short-run mechanism by which actual asset stocks are adopted to desired levels to eliminate portfolio unbalance.

One further complication must be noted. The higher the expected return on equities, the greater will be the equilibrium proportion of equities demanded in household wealth porfolios, and so the larger will be the equilibrium ratio of the stock of equity values to income and wealth, and of capital gains on equities to household earned income, throughout the growth path. The rise in the level of equity prices has been shown to be inversely related to the rate of corporate external equity financing, with an upper limit equal to the growth rate of business income when corporations issue no new equity securities. Given the level of corporate real investment, a fall in the risk (variance of expected return) associated with equity ownership, a rise in the rate of growth of the economy, an increase in the share of business income in total income, *and a fall in the rate of corporate external equity financing*, will all raise the rate of increase of equity prices, the composition and ordinarily the level of expected return from share-ownership between dividend and capital gain income, and so the equilibrium ratio of total equities and total capital gains to household income and wealth.

Once an equilibrium growth path is attained, per-share dividends and equity prices grow at the same constant relative rate, and the ratio of total equities to income and wealth remain constant. But real world economies move in unbalanced growth. A shift in any of the above relationships will alter the rate of change in equity prices, and so the expected return on equities, and the equilibrium ratios of equity values to income and wealth, throughout the transition period. Moreover, the process of convergence to a new equilibrium configuration need not be monotonic, and will overshoot if elasticities of expectation are sufficiently high.

In a growing economy the current return on equities, and hence the rate at which the market discounts future business income, may be prevented from falling by the expected future rise in per-share dividends and share prices that accompany business internal equity finance. This is because with a growing future income stream, the rate at which it is discounted must exceed the expected rate of growth in order for its present value to be finite.[4] Consequently the return received from equity ownership may act as a floor to sustain the reservation return that lenders are willing to accept on other financial assets, and so the marginal efficiency of investment demanded on tangible assets.

In moving equilibrium household voluntary saving allocated to equity accumulation must equal new external equity financing by business units, as shown in Figure 10-1. But even in the extreme case in which new corporate external finance is zero, the planned allocation

4. The present value of an infinite-lived current income stream Y_0, growing at a constant g per cent per year and discounted at a constant q per cent is: $PV = 1/(q-g) \, Y_0$. In balanced growth the return on a constant stock of equities (zero external equity finance) equals the dividend-price ratio D/S plus the growth rate g. The return on equities cannot therefore fall below the rate of growth of national income, but must in general exceed it.

of some proportion of household voluntary savings to the accumulation of corporate stock need not create a persistent deflationary gap. There is an automatic adjustment mechanism at work. The rise in the market value of the existing stock of equities, which reduces the equilibrium return on equities and permits the satisfaction of household portfolio demand for equities, simultaneously increases household disposable income, in the form of capital gains on existing stockholdings, by an identical amount. As a result throughout the adjustment period aggregate disposable income, including capital gains, exceeds the aggregate supply of current output of real goods and services at current prices.

The argument may be pushed further. In economies characterized by a tendency toward a secular insufficiency of aggregate demand, that is an excess of planned household surpluses over planned business deficits in full employment, an inelastic supply of corporate equities is not fortuitous. By raising consumption of the household sector rather than financing business capital formation, it acts in effect as an endogenous governor on the system to prevent an even greater tendency towards structural imbalance and excess capacity.[5]

The more rapidly an economy, and hence future corporate profits, are expected to grow, the higher will be the present value of claims to these future income streams, and the higher will be the ratio of total household wealth and capital gains to current income and output. For this reason aggregate private demand may be expected to be higher, relative to full employment aggregate supply, the more rapid an economy's rate of growth. Growing economies are thus likely to be relatively wealthy and buoyant economies due to the capitalization of their relatively greater expected future income streams.

While an inelastic supply of new equity issues need not create deflationary pressure, it does have several implications for the *composition* of aggregate demand between consumption and investment expenditures. First, an increase in planned voluntary saving to accumulate equities by some household units will finance greater consumption spending out of capital gains income by other stockholding units in the household sector, rather than greater capital investment expenditure by deficit-spending business units. Secondly, given the

5. In the United States the household sector has been a net seller of corporate equities from 1959 to the present (1966).

retention ratio, the rise in dividends and share prices in a growing economy is governed by the rate of growth of corporate earnings, which in turn is related to the rate of growth of GNP. Since as has been shown there is some evidence that the rate at which a future income stream is discounted may be expected to vary directly with its expected rate of growth, the higher the rate of growth of the economy, the greater is likely to be the rate at which future income is discounted. A higher rate of economic growth consequently may raise the floor reservation price of lenders on all types of financial assets, since the return on equities will not exceed the return on other financial assets by more than some premium sufficient to offset differential services and risk.

This suggests that the general level of interest rates and the cost of external finance may be expected to be related positively to the rate of growth of income and output. Consequently in more rapidly growing economies a higher expected return on real investment may be required if such investment is to be undertaken. To the extent that the savings ratio and the marginal efficiency of tangible capital are independent of the growth rate, this tends to establish both a ceiling and a floor to the rate of capital formation. This relationship will not hold if equity prices are prevented from rising by an incremental supply of new equity issues equal to the growth in business net worth. Moreover as seen in Chapter 3 both planned saving and planned investment are positively related to the rate of growth of income.

The effect of a growth-induced increase in future income and so in portfolio demand for long-lived tangible assets in inelastic supply is similar to the case of equities. Increased expected rent payments, and consequent increased demand for land in fixed supply, results in a persistent rise in the price of land, and so in the real value of the existing stock of land, until portfolio demand is satisfied.[6] It has been recognized at least since Adam Smith that site rent represents "unearned" income, which increases with the growth of income and popu-

6. Goldsmith has estimated that though the value of land fell from 35 to 18 per cent of total national wealth in the United States between 1900 and 1958, the value of land in current prices increased from $31 to $311 billion, representing net capital gains to landowners over the period of $280 billion Raymond Goldsmith, *The National Wealth of the United States in the Postwar Period*, (New Jersey, 1962), Table A-5.

lation and is captured by landowners without a corresponding productive service being provided in exchange. Quantitatively more important than increased land rent payments as an economy grows are the socially created increments to land values, which capitalize expected future rents and adjust the actual to the desired capital stock of land. Current voluntary saving may be allocated to land accumulation, and the real value of land may rise continuously, without a fall in its expected rate of return. As in the case of equities, the expected return on land may be expected to be positively related to the rate of growth of national income.

It is important for questions of social policy to distinguish the different causes of capital gains income. Since the price of an asset represents the capitalized value of its expected future services, capital gains can occur as a result of a fall in the rate at which future income is discounted and/or a rise in the expected future income stream itself. The latter may come about as the result of changes in the level of prices, or in the quantity of the future services yielded.

A fall in the rate at which future income streams are discounted, to the extent it increases wealth values, raises the real claim over current output that is received as a sort of tribute in the form of capital gains by all owners of long-term claims to future income streams. At the same time it reduces the present income from past achievements held in liquid form as claims to current output.

Now consider the case in which the rate at which future income is discounted remains unchanged. It is at this point that the similarity between capital gains to stockholders and capital gains to landowners ceases. Capital gains to stockholders are then identical to the present value of retained earnings by business corporations. Such capital gains represent that part of stockowner current income which has been saved and invested "involuntarily" by their corporate administrators. As such, like other labor and property income from current output, they represent payment for a socially productive contribution that increases total real output. Capital gains on land generated through the growth process with a constant discount rate cannot be regarded as a reward for a socially productive service. Unlike capital gains on equities, they are not in return for any lending of current income (saving) which results in an increase in the aggregate future supply of real goods and services available to the economy.

Concluding Comments

It is perhaps appropriate in closing to try to relate briefly the above observations to the corpus of modern macro-economic theory. Since Keynes a prominent place has been given to the role of liquidity preference or hoarding in saving behavior. Yet a change in preference to accumulate money balances in fixed supply has an obvious formal similarity with a change in preferences to accumulate financial or tangible asset stocks in inelastic supply. The initial impact effect in both cases is to reduce aggregate demand for currently produced output as income is diverted to asset accumulation.

In the case of a change in liquidity preference, if the nominal money stock remains constant the general commodity price level must be forced up or down until the real value of the actual stock of nominal money balances is adjusted to the desired level. In the case of nonmonetary assets, financial or tangible, the effect of a change in preference is to raise or lower the price of the asset in question until the real value of the existing stock reaches the desired level. In the latter case there is no necessary change in other prices, since the adjustment process is centered in one market. As a result it occurs more rapidly than in the case of money, and with much less disruption of current output. But in each case the increase in disposable income and wealth through capital gains induces some assetholders, through income, wealth, and portfolio effects, to increase their purchases of current output, in particular reproducible capital assets, thus offsetting the reduction in aggregate demand for current output.

Only if an asset is characterized by perfectly elastic incremental supply in the short run will changes in demand to accumulate existing stocks of that asset leave aggregate demand for current output invariant. The purchase of existing assets by some spending units will then result in exactly equivalent spending by assetissuers or producers. The degree of supply responsiveness to a change in portfolio demand may be measured indirectly by the observed variation in asset prices. The existence of a widely held concept of a "normal" price of an asset serves to prevent persistent upward or downward price movements, since divergence from the "norm" sets up expectations which offer increasing resistance to further divergence.

It was Keynes' contribution to point out that this does not apply in all powerfully to money, as the classicists frequently had implied. Because the concept of a "normal" price of money in terms of commodities is weak or nonexistent, its anticipated "own" rate of return need not decline as the price of money increases. The concept of a "normal" relative price is most highly developed for bonds, and much less so for equities and land. In the case of both the latter it frequently occurs that changes in current price induce short-run self-sustaining expectations of future price movements, which lengthen the adjustment period and prevent expected returns from falling.

Keynes did not distinguish between "investments," "capital," "securities," or "investment goods", but tended to use the terms interchangeably, and so did not develop the independent significance of equities. He did emphasize that the failure of the own rate of return on land as well as on money to fall could limit real investment, not by lack of saving, but by lack of willingness to lend to deficit-spending units at a return that makes investment in productive tangible assets attractive.[7] But because he did not consider the implications of a growing economy, Keynes failed to analyze or explain why a rise in the market price of a physical or nonmonetary financial asset in inelastic supply, such as land or equities, need not lower its expected own-return towards zero. Finally, because he did not appreciate the significance of portfolio behavior and financial intermediation, Keynes was led to emphasize money alone, to the neglect of all the other financial assets which are instrumental in placing the purchasing power of surplus-spending units at the disposal of deficit spenders, and in so doing shape the real functioning of an economy.

7. "That the world after several millenia of steady individual saving is so poor as it is in accumulated capital-assets, is to be explained, in my opinion, neither by the improvident propensities of mankind, nor even by the destruction of wars, but by the high liquidity premiums formerly attaching to the ownership of land." *The General Theory of Employment, Interest, and Prices,* *op. cit.*, p. 242.

RECOMMENDED READING

The market for corporate equities has been strangely neglected by American economists, at least as an academic concern. One brief though important recent exception is W. J. Baumol, *The Stock Market and Economic Efficiency* (New York, 1965). Another is S. Robbins, *The Securities Markets*, The Free Press, 1965.

A comprehensive summary of trends in capital financing may be found in Simon Kuzets, *Capital in the American Economy*, Princeton University Press, 1961. Also to be recommended is Raymond Goldsmith, *Studies in the National Balance Sheet of the United States*, Vols. I & II, Princeton University Press, 1963.

A persuasive explanation which relates the fall in external equity financing in the post-war period to tax considerations, combined with stable corporate debt-asset preferences, may be found in A. W. Sametz, "Trends in the Volume and Composition of Equity Finance," *Journal of Finance*, Vol. XIX, No. 3 (September 1964).

Index